the
**About.com** guide to

# OWNING
# A DOG

From Sit and Stay to Positive Play—
A Complete Canine Manual

**Krista Mifflin**

Adams Media
Avon, Massachusetts

About.com is a powerful network of more than 500 Guides—smart, passionate, accomplished people who are experts in their fields. About.com Guides live and work in more than twenty countries and celebrate their interests in thousands of topics. They have written books, appeared on national television programs, and won many awards in their fields. Guides are selected for their ability to provide the most interesting information for users, and for their passion for their subject and the Web. The selection process is rigorous—only 2 percent of those who apply actually become Guides. The following are some of the most important criteria by which they are chosen:

- High level of knowledge/passion for their topic
- Appropriate credentials
- Keen understanding of the Web experience
- Commitment to creating informative, actionable features

Each month more than 48 million people visit About.com. Whether you need home-repair and decorating ideas, recipes, movie trailers, or car-buying tips, About.com Guides can offer practical advice and solutions for everyday life. Wherever you land on About.com, you'll always find content that is relevant to your interests. If you're looking for "how to" advice on refinishing your deck, About.com will also show you the Tools You Need to get the job done. No matter where you are on About.com, or how you got here, you'll always find exactly what you're looking for!

# About Your Guide

Growing up in the Okanagan Valley of British Columbia, Krista Mifflin developed an early interest in learning everything she could about animals. It wasn't unusual to see an Audubon Field Guide protruding from her pocket or, to her mother's dismay, a "friend" that had followed her home that day.

When Krista moved to Ontario, she turned her passion to dogs and devoured every bit of information she could find on them. She has been the Dogs Guide for About.com for more than four years, bringing you dog care and training information. Dogs are now a huge part of her life and will always be a part of her family. She will continue to learn and explore the dog world with a dog or two by her side.

## *Acknowledgments*

For my son, Eric, whose enthusiasm has kept me going on many dreary mornings; my oldest, Jordynne, who is wise beyond her years and without whom I could not have finished this book; and the baby, Leala, who makes me laugh no matter how grumpy I am after a late night of writing. For David, who never once laughed at my dreams but pushed me in their direction; and my parents who had faith in me.

Thank you to all the members of the Dog Park forum on my About.com Dogs site. You are my inspiration for new topics and fun things to write about and you keep me coming back every day to see what is new in your lives. And Dale, for being the best host I could ever have asked for.

Thanks to my furry foot-warmers, the boys, past and present: Oscar, Loki, Kari, Ozzy, and Raider—their cold noses kept poking me awake every time they thought I needed it.

## ABOUT.COM

CEO & President
*Scott Meyer*

COO
*Andrew Pancer*

SVP Content
*Michael Daecher*

Marketing Communications
Manager
*Lisa Langsdorf*

Director, About Operations
*Chris Murphy*

Senior Web Designer
*Jason Napolitano*

## ADAMS MEDIA

### Editorial

Publishing Director
*Gary M. Krebs*

Managing Editor
*Laura M. Daly*

Acquisitions Editor
*Brielle Kay*

### Marketing

Director of Marketing
*Karen Cooper*

Assistant Art Director
*Frank Rivera*

### Production

Director of Manufacturing
*Susan Beale*

Associate Director of Production
*Michelle Roy Kelly*

Senior Book Designer
*Colleen Cunningham*

Published by Adams Media, an F+W Publications Company
57 Littlefield Street
Avon, MA 02322
*www.adamsmedia.com*

ISBN 10: 1-59869-279-8
ISBN 13: 978-1-59869-279-2

Printed in China.

J I H G F E D C B A

Library of Congress Cataloging-in-Publication Data
Mifflin, Krista.
The about.com guide to owning a dog / Krista Mifflin.
p. cm. — (An about.com series book)
ISBN-13: 978-1-59869-279-2 (pbk.)
ISBN-10: 1-59869-279-8 (pbk.)
1. Dogs. I. Title.
SF427.M535 2007
636.7'083—dc222007001118

This publication is designed to provide accurate and authoritative information with regard to the subject matter covered. It is sold with the understanding that the publisher is not engaged in rendering legal, accounting, or other professional advice. If legal advice or other expert assistance is required, the services of a competent professional person should be sought.

—From a *Declaration of Principles* jointly adopted by a Committee of the American Bar Association and a Committee of Publishers and Associations

Many of the designations used by manufacturers and sellers to distinguish their product are claimed as trademarks. Where those designations appear in this book and Adams Media was aware of a trademark claim, the designations have been printed with initial capital letters.

*This book is available at quantity discounts for bulk purchases. For information, please call 1-800-289-0963.*

# How to Use This Book

Each About.com book is written by an About.com Guide—an expert with experiential knowledge of his or her subject. While the book can stand on its own as a helpful resource, it can also be coupled with the corresponding About.com site for even more tips, tools, and advice. Each book will not only refer you back to About.com, but will also direct you to other useful Internet locations and print resources.

All About.com books include a special section at the end of each chapter called Get Linked. Here you'll find a few links back to the About.com site for even more great information on the topics discussed in that chapter. Depending on the topic, you could find links to such resources as photos, sheet music, quizzes, recipes, or product reviews.

About.com books also include four types of sidebars:

- **Ask Your Guide:** Detailed information in a question-and-answer format
- **Tools You Need:** Advice about researching, purchasing, and using a variety of tools for your projects
- **Elsewhere on the Web:** References to other useful Internet locations
- **What's Hot:** All you need to know about the hottest trends and tips out there

Each About.com book will take you on a personal tour of a certain topic, give you reliable advice, and leave you with the knowledge you need to achieve your goals.

# CONTENTS

# CONTENTS

# Introduction from Your Guide

*Deciding to share your life with a dog is a big commitment—one I hope you haven't entered into lightly.* You'll be wholly responsible for this creature, providing all of its care including food, shelter, health maintenance, and medical care. Your dog could live for eighteen years, and at no point in his life will he become independent of your care. That can seem like a pretty daunting task when it's laid out in full like that, but it can be even more rewarding than it is challenging.

There will be frustrating times ahead, days when you may question your sanity in adding this furry dynamo to your family, but I promise you'll come to cherish your dog's personality and vibrancy and wonder what you would have done without him. Your dog will become your best friend, your favorite pillow, and your faithful ear when you are having a bad day. Nobody will listen to your troubles like your dog will, and nobody will ever be quite so excited to see you after you've returned from a five-minute excursion without him.

Dogs are "feel good" animals. No other creature will look up at you with such complete awe, and give out so much unconditional love that they could pull people out of depression or give the agoraphobic the courage to venture forth into the public. Adding a dog to your life guarantees you that somebody will always be happy to see you and be there for you to lean on.

From choosing the type of dog that will fit into your lifestyle the best all the way to starting over after your first dog has gone to the Rainbow Bridge, this book, along with my About Dogs Web site (http://dogs.about.com) will help you on your journey to become a responsible dog owner. With its blend of information, both in the book and the resources I've chosen on the Internet, you will have everything you need and want to know about owning dogs.

The unique sidebars will give you tidbits of information and tell you about items I've found particularly useful with my dogs, and you'll find things to do with your dog in every chapter. I think you'll find this is a great book to keep on your bookshelf to refer to as you and your dog move along in your relationship and you become less of a novice dog owner. If you put the time into your dog in the beginning, you won't be a novice for long, and you will find that you are ready to handle new and exciting challenges with your dog after you've weathered the puppy years.

Ninety percent of dog ownership after the puppy months (all eighteen of them) is supposed to be fun. Even the parts that resemble the dreaded four-letter word (w-o-r-k) aren't hard when you are happy with your dog and pleased with the training you have given him. The only part I'd happily skip is the poop patrol. And really, that's a very small price to pay considering all that we get in return.

I'm happy that I can help guide you through your dog experience and help you become the dog owner that your dog deserves. Sit back, relax, and let me introduce you to the dog world.

## Chapter 1

# What Are You Looking for in a Dog?

### Your Decision to Get a Dog

Realizing that millions of people can't all be wrong, you have now decided to join their ranks as part of the dog-owning public. Well, perhaps you've just now decided it's time to get a dog because you have more time or space, or maybe your life situation has completely changed and a dog would be a good fit. Or maybe your kids have been bugging you about a dog just like Timmy's down the street. Whatever your reasons may be, welcome to our world!

After making the decision to include a dog in your family, your first order of business is assessing your lifestyle. Assess yourself realistically, not ideally. Ideally I would like to power-jog for an hour twice a day, plus enjoy afternoon and evening walks, but it just isn't going to happen any time soon. Therefore, a young Border collie isn't in my time budget for this decade (but hopefully one

▶ If you don't know what kind of dog will best fit your personality and home life and want to try a few dogs on for size, so to speak, ask your local shelter and breed rescues near you about foster programs. Foster programs allow you to give a homeless dog much needed socialization and a home environment for the dog to flourish in. Some foster situations can last for months, others just a few days. If you meet the criteria for a foster home, you'll get to know different types of dogs and provide a much needed service for the rescue community.

will fit in the next). By making a realistic time and energy schedule, you won't shortchange any breed of dog you do acquire. Other very important factors to consider are: Who or what else occupies your day? Who will your new dog be sharing you with? Use the information in the following sections to evaluate your life and match yourself up with what will ultimately become your new best friend and life partner.

**Whose dog will this dog be?**   Parents, this is your warning: Any dog you get for the kids will be your responsibility. Kids will beg and promise to do all the work, but that usually only lasts for the first month, or worse, the first time they have to clean up dog poop in the yard. My recommendation is to look for a dog that fits you, the parent, because this dog will be your dog. If you aren't willing to be the dog owner, then please drop the idea of a dog altogether. You'll save everybody from numerous hassles and heartache in the future.

This will be your dog. You are the one reading this book. You will be the one making the trips to the veterinarian, feeding her (or delegating feeding duties), cleaning up after her, and training this dog to be a good canine citizen. Get the dog that you want, not the dog the kids, spouse, or roommate wants.

**How much dog experience do you have?**   This is a very important point that a lot of new dog owners don't think of. There are many breeds that should not be considered by novice dog owners. Large livestock guardians, powerful working breeds, and some of the more driven sporting breeds are best left to those with a lot of dog experience in their past, as early training mistakes with some breeds can have long-lasting effects on a dog's temperament.

Judge your own dog experience realistically. And be forewarned that even mixed breeds can be challenging, especially mixes that include one (or more) of the more difficult breeds. My first dog was a mixed-breed Alaskan malamute and German shepherd with a little bit of Labrador retriever thrown in for good measure. Looking back now, it's easy to see that he was really too much for me as a new dog owner. I made a lot of mistakes with him, and it was not the relationship it should have been.

**What is it that you expect from a dog?** Your determining factor should be what you want from a dog in your home. Do you want a working partner for a specific job, a hunting partner, a companion to your children, or something else? There is a dog out there for everyone, and often more than one dog breed or mix of breeds will fit your needs and wants perfectly.

**I couldn't possibly live with a dog that does that.** This will be your final pruning criteria. If there is something about a dog that you just can't deal with, how it looks or sounds, now is the time to get it out in the open. You should have a workable list of breeds or types of mixes that seem to fit you the best. If you know that you absolutely cannot stand a drooling dog, then all dogs with looser lips, such as Saint Bernards, boxers, and coonhounds, should be crossed off your list.

## Different Breeds for Different Folks

So, you know you want a dog. That's a good start. But there are so many different breeds, types, sizes, and other details to consider. If you think these things don't matter and you'll be happy with whatever dog you see first, think again. Seemingly insignificant aspects like the thickness of a dog's hair or the strength of

**ASK YOUR GUIDE**

*Aside from playing with my friend's dog, I don't have any dog experience. What kind of dog should I be looking for?*

▶ Every new dog owner is bound to make some mistakes during dog training at first. With this in mind, there are some breeds that tolerate mistakes better than others, and allow slip-ups to be corrected a lot easier than others. Labrador retrievers, collies, and golden retrievers are all dogs whose intelligence, desire to please, and affability help them to be more forgiving of early training mistakes.

his bark can have a huge effect upon your relationship with your new pet. It's worth it to do your research before you take the plunge.

**Yes, size does matter.**   Some people don't care what the size of a dog is, as long as it is a dog. Others may have size restrictions in place due to a landlord, space in the home, or just personal preference. What's your preference? I am definitely a big-dog person. I do like small lapdogs that curl up on my lap or pillow, but I really prefer to snuggle up to a large moose dog that keeps my entire bed warm during the cold winters. Slinging my arm around the dog and leaning on him when we are at rest is just one of my pleasures that I couldn't do with a small dog. Neither is better than the other, just different, and it's up to you to decide which you would prefer.

Dog "types" come in all sizes. Large breeds can be as docile as couch potatoes or as energetic as a room full of seven-year-old boys. Small breeds are just as diverse, although their capacity for speed and endurance may not be as much as an Alaskan malamute. You do have to take in a dog's overall size when figuring out what his main activities are going to be. A Pomeranian wouldn't be very good at keeping up with a speed jogger for an hour, but it would be in heaven with an hour-long hike on a trail. Likewise, a Great Dane would delight in joining you on the jogging route, but it might not be such a great canoeing buddy. You'll need to choose your dog according to what you do with your time.

What if you really want a Great Dane but don't have a big house? Even if your apartment is small, a Great Dane might be a good fit for you. Sure, they do take up a lot of floor or sofa space, but for all their size, they are a very laid-back housedog. An adult Great Dane is not a high-energy dog. It needs only moderate

▶ In deciding which breed would work out best for you, a good dog breed encyclopedia that covers all of the dog breeds from around the world (more than 400 of them!) will be your most valuable asset. Make sure it has all the information you will need: a dog's country of origin, what it was originally bred for, how big they are as adult dogs, both height and weight, their general temperament, variations within the breed itself, and basic grooming needs. Look for one that has at least a full page for each dog breed.

exercise, two fair-length walks and a good running session, through-out the day. In actuality, any size of dog, any breed, will do just fine in an apartment as long as it has the space to lie down, because exercise should happen outside anyway. As long as you provide the proper amount of outdoor activity for your dog's needs, she will live happily ever after, no matter what size her home is.

**How active are you?** This will be your determining factor in the breed type you choose. Types of dogs, or groups, are organized by the major national and international kennel clubs according to the activity needs of the dog. For example, herding types tend to need an exceptional amount of rigorous exercise. Like the legendary Border collie and his vibe of perpetual motion, most herding breeds need hours of run time and a "thinking" activity every day or they become bored and destructive. Many toy breeds, however, are perfectly content with a couple of sedate and relatively short walks each day and some off-leash play time.

In between those extremes are the working breeds. These dogs need a couple of hours of strenuous exercise and a job if you have one available, but after work they just want to lay down and be foot warmers. These dogs are big, stocky dogs, built to be powerful, and those muscles need to be worked out daily. The Saint Bernard is an exceptional dog, one who will happily slog through snow and mud pulling a sleigh or breaking trail by your side for hours on end. His muscular build and size make him a fantastic working companion during the day, and a beautiful fur rug impersonator in the evening.

Terrier breeds are best known for their tenacity and prey drive. Mainly bred for hunting rodents, most terriers are small, lean, and extremely fast. Terriers are very charismatic dogs that

▶ When you are choosing a dog breed, or even a mixed breed, it's a good idea to keep a list of breeds that seem to fit what you are looking for. As you continue with your search, you can scratch off dogs that seem to no longer fit, or have undesirable traits. Be sure and mark beside each breed what it is that keeps it on the list or eliminated it.

have a whole lot of personality, even in the smallest breed. Terriers do require a firm hand, and the larger, more powerful breeds like American Staffordshire, and American pit bull terriers are best suited to an experienced dog home. A bored terrier will dig up yards and destroy items in the home, so be sure and keep your terrier occupied throughout the day. Short but numerous, rigorous play sessions and walks will keep that terrier energy contained properly.

Dogs from the hound group, sighthounds and scenthounds, are the most fascinating dogs in my opinion. Sighthounds (also known as gazehounds) can run like the wind and are notoriously unreliable off leash. They watch and focus on a fast-moving "prey" and will be off after it before you know it. No amount of training can overcome these instincts. A sighthound running after a lure can travel for miles before stopping. But they are also quite happy with a couple of short runs each day, expending energy in bursts and spending the rest of the day as foot warmers and fur rug impersonators.

The sporting dogs, such as retrievers, Weimaraners, setters, standard poodles, and many more breeds, are a sportsman's dream. These dogs can flush game, retrieve birds, and point out prey. Hardy dogs that come in a vast array of sizes and colors, sporting breeds are the ideal active family pet. These dogs are independent thinkers, and they need to be thoroughly exercised when not out in the field. While intense and prey-driven outside, these dogs tend to have an instinctive knowledge of when to play or work and when the more laid-back aspect of their personality is required. Discuss your household with any potential breeder or rescue contact, however, as some dogs may have such a high drive that they would be a poor (possibly even dangerous) match in a home with other, smaller pets.

**You need to consider the rest of your family.** If your family includes small children, there are several breeds that work better than most, and several that should be removed from your possible list. Dogs with really high prey drive may also target small, running children as prey. Herding dogs may try to herd your children into a tight little group. While this isn't necessarily a bad thing, some herding breeds will do this by nipping at your children, which is a problem.

I also don't recommend the really tiny toy breeds for families with children under the age of seven years old. Tiny, fragile little limbs of dogs like Chihuahuas, Yorkshire terriers, and papillons are a bad combination with small children. Bones can break very easily, and "too much love" is indeed possible when children aren't aware of their own strength yet. A toddler's enthusiastic cuddle can mean an emergency run to the veterinarian's office and a $1,000 vet bill.

Not all smaller breeds are as fragile though. The sturdier Maltese and pug are very well-adjusted breeds overall, and their easygoing personalities meld right into a family life. The miniature poodle and Cavalier King Charles spaniel are more active and outgoing breeds of the toy group, ideal for the average family. Older children will enjoy the energy these dogs put out, and their basic grooming needs aren't as high maintenance as one would think. Regular trimmings for a miniature poodle kept in a "puppy cut" (shorter all over, no elaborate detailing) and regular brushing for a spaniel is all that is needed.

Getting away from the toy group, the nonsporting group includes a number of smaller breeds that fit very well into an active family life but aren't big enough to take over a sofa. The bichon frisé, Boston terrier, and keeshond are all great family dogs that are full of personality, don't have the fragility of toy dogs, and won't break the bank with food bills. Grooming is more involved with some of these dogs, but it won't become a hassle if it's done regularly.

**ELSEWHERE ON THE WEB**

▶ The American Kennel Club Web site is a great resource for reading up on breed groups and individual breed standards. It also has a large library of dog information in general, from choosing the dog that fits you to showing and sporting events. It also lists the parent club for each of its recognized breeds. Visit www.akc.org and start your quest for more dog knowledge.

**Are hypoallergenic dog breeds really good for people with allergies?**

▶ To be hypoallergenic is to have a decreased tendency to cause allergies. Hypo means less, not none. Hypoallergenic dog breeds will still produce allergens, but because of their coat type they will typically produce less dander and allergens than other breeds. People with severe allergies and asthma will still be affected by a hypoallergenic dog.

Other adults you share your home with will also need to be consulted. It's one thing to tell yourself that since you will be doing all the work it should be your decision alone. The reality is another thing altogether. Your spouse, roommate, or even adult children will share the home with your new dog, and in order to fully welcome a dog into the family all the adults need to be on board with the decision. It's no fun at all to share your house with your perfect dog but have your spouse despise the dog for whatever reason. The friction this will cause is significant, and it's a serious problem that isn't easy to overcome without a lot of pain on one side or the other.

You will also want to avoid dog breeds with a high prey drive if you keep a lot of small animals in your home. Bringing home a saluki (a tall Middle Eastern gazehound) wouldn't be a smart idea if you have a rabbit-breeding hobby. Cats and birds might be in danger from some terrier breeds or gundogs. Even other dogs might present a problem if your chosen breed has a tendency to be dog aggressive. If you are adopting an adult dog from a shelter or a rescue, this is one piece of information that the shelter workers can tell you before you go any further in the adoption process. Most puppies can be taught to live harmoniously with almost any animal that is currently present in your home.

**How much time do you want to spend grooming your dog?** There are a lot of factors to consider when choosing your new dog, and required grooming is a big one. Every dog breed or mix needs some kind of grooming, though some require a much more involved process than others.

Dogs that look fluffy and cute on television often take quite some time to appear that way, and long-haired breeds may take more time and effort than you are willing to give. Silky terriers, afghan hounds, and Maltese dogs need a lot of brushing to keep their coats looking good if they aren't kept in a short cut. You might find that effort is something you are okay with, but the cost of professional grooming might be off-putting. Even fur that is only a couple of inches long can quickly develop mats that will pull and tear the skin underneath when a dog has a very thick coat. Medium-length coats need brushing too, though not as often. Border collies and Siberian huskies start to look ragged if they aren't brushed at least twice a week, and matting is a danger for them as well.

Short-haired dogs, such as boxers and pugs require minimal grooming, just what every dog needs: a good coat massage to loosen any of their hidden dead hairs, baths when they need it, and regular toenail clipping will keep these types of dogs in fine shape.

**Considering a breed's looks isn't just vanity, it's good sense.** If you find one breed of dog or another to be so ugly that you simply can't stand to look at his pointy ears and pointy, witch-like nose, then it just makes sense to eliminate all breeds with pointy ears and noses from your list. Love to gaze longingly into the depths of wrinkles, trying to locate your dog's eyes? Maybe a Chinese shar pei or a bulldog type would be your perfect pet. Beauty is in the eye of the beholder, and you will be beholding your dog for the next ten to fifteen years, so be sure that he is beautiful to you.

## Purebred or Mixed Breed?

Now that you have a general idea of what type of dog you want, it's time to answer a tough question. Do you want a mixed-breed or a purebred dog? Mixed-breed dogs are widely available for comparatively low cost (beware of so-called "designer" crossbreeds!),

WHAT'S HOT

▶ My Dog Park forum (http://about.com/dogs/forum) is a great place to ask questions or to share a story about your favorite furry friend. One of our favorite games is "Guess the Mix!" You can post a picture of your new Wonder Dog and members will have fun trying to guess the breeds that make up your new companion. Interaction on the forum does require registration, but you can register easily and, best of all, it's free!

ASK YOUR GUIDE

**Why can't I rescue a puppy from the pet store? Won't I be saving it from misery?**

▶ It's a sad sight, I know. I've argued with myself over this before, too. But buying even just one dog from a pet store tells pet-store owners and puppy millers that it works to make them money. They don't care about your reasons for buying the pup; they just care that it netted them a tidy profit.

and almost every town has an animal shelter of some sort. An endless guessing game when parentage is uncertain, mixed-breed dogs could look like any combination of breeds. A couple of years ago, one of my Dog Park members coined the term "Wonder Dog," as in "Gee, I wonder what's in him? But it doesn't matter; he's wonderful!" Mixed breeds have been referred to as "Wonder Dogs" on my Web site ever since.

A mixed-breed puppy will take the dominant traits from both parents. This includes intelligence, temperament, physical appearance, and the propensity for breed-related health issues. If a pup's sire is a breed of dog prone to hip dysplasia, and his dam is a breed prone to von Willebrand's disease, the puppy could end up with both of these serious health issues. Hybrid vigor is a myth when it is applied to dogs and the artificial means of keeping them alive when natural selection would have eliminated them in the wild. However, the reverse is also true; your mixed-breed puppy may have inherited his dam's healthy joints and bones but not her poor vision.

In this same way, it is impossible to tell whether a crossbred puppy from a golden retriever and a poodle will be a dog who sheds (double coat) or not (single coat). It matters not which breed is which parent. One-third of his siblings may have a double coat and the other two-thirds a single coat. It's also not something that becomes noticeable until your puppy has reached the age where he'll start to shed (or not), around nine to twelve months.

A mixed-breed dog is absolutely unique. No other dog will ever look exactly like him, or act like him, so if you want a truly unique dog, a Wonder Dog is the way to go. Don't waste valuable snuggle time trying to figure out what mix of breeds your dog may be if it isn't known already, just be assured that he will be lovable, trainable, and your greatest companion.

If you want a puppy that has a predictable future look and temperament, then a purebred dog is the right choice for you. A well-bred purebred will give you a predictable adult dog. Individual personalities are always something to count on, but your dog will look a certain way and follow a standard temperament. And I do caution you about individual personalities. Kari the moose dog is a Beauceron, a breed known for independent thinking (check), stamina (check), herding instinct (check), grace (ummm … ), and fearlessness (oh dear). He looks like everything he should be and is as healthy as a dog could be, but he has a very nervous temperament. It takes a lot to get him to feel comfortable in strange surroundings. Buying a purebred puppy from a breeder who breeds responsibly is almost a guarantee of temperament, but nature does like to throw curveballs every now and then.

## Buying from a Dog Breeder

Buying a puppy from a reputable dog breeder has a lot of advantages. How much you pay will depend on what you are looking for in a dog, whether a show or working prospect or a companion dog. Toy breeds and rare breeds are generally more expensive than well-known larger breeds. Your very first clue that a breeder is not worth the name is if she hasn't bothered to certify her dogs' hips with the Orthopedic Foundation for Animals (OFA) or have their eyes certified by the Canine Eye Registration Foundation (CERF).

Your purebred puppy, whether a pet or a show prospect, should include the following:

- A pedigree of three generations or more
- Titled champions within the first two generations listed (parents or grandparents)

▶ Patience is something you need to keep with you when you're searching for your perfect pooch. Understand that you can't really choose in a day, and that the ideal dogs come to those who wait. Avoid the impulse buy! Pet stores and unethical breeders count on people's impulsiveness to line their pockets. They won't try to talk you out of a sale—they only want your money. Buying a dog from somebody like that could leave you with a lot of heartache in the near future.

- OFA-certified hips and elbows with a Good or Excellent on both parents
- Eyes have been CERFed free of genetic abnormalities
- A guarantee that your dog is free from inheritable diseases and conditions, with replacement (not exchange) or refund terms should something happen
- Right of first refusal should you need to relinquish the dog
- Care and grooming information
- A good, even temperament, usually well matched to the family/home he is being placed into (keeping in mind that individual dogs may vary)
- A healthy, well-socialized puppy who should adjust easily
- A mentor if you are planning to show, work, or breed your new dog

Also, a good dog breeder will be willing to help you with your new puppy. Every breed has its idiosyncrasies, and everybody needs help sometimes. The price of a purebred puppy should include all of these things. If it does not, you should be looking elsewhere. If you really want a healthy, happy, purebred dog, the price is worth it.

Breed clubs and associations for your chosen breed will have a list of recommended breeders that operate within their code of ethics. You can also join any online communities that focus on your chosen breed. There are hundreds of e-mail groups and discussion forums regarding dog breeds. Most of the time members will be willing to share their experiences with certain breeders and will be able to give you names and contact information of good breeders in the area you live in or that breed for the qualities you are looking for.

Good breeders ask a million and often personal questions! Be prepared to answer questions about the people who live with you, what hours you work, what kind of visitors you get, what your yard layout is like, what you are willing to spend, and more. A good breeder who cares will want to ensure that her puppy is going to the best home. Be prepared for nosiness and welcome it! If you call a breeder and she does not ask you questions, find another.

When you are calling breeders about your chosen dog breed, keep a checklist handy during your initial phone interview. Use a new one for every breeder. Use this sample checklist to help you develop your own, or photocopy it and use it as is:

Breed:
Kennel Name:
Breeder's Names:
Location:
Price of Dog:

*The good points:*
- ○ Breeder is upfront and open about answering questions regarding her kennel, how the dogs are kept, and where the puppies are raised.
- ○ She welcomes you into her kennel and lets you look around.
- ○ Breeder has had the parents tested for hereditary diseases and guarantees the puppy to be free of said diseases. Some hereditary problems are virtually impossible to guarantee against, and you will have to decide if you want to take the risk of your puppy coming up with a problem known to be prevalent in the breed. The very least the breeder should have done is grade the hips via PennHIP or OFA, and CER-Fed the eyes.
- ○ Puppies stay with the litter until eight weeks of age or longer.
- ○ She has the parents' pedigree back at least three generations.

▶ Every Web site for breed clubs and associations (these are groups of breed enthusiasts) will have a directory of "code of ethics" breeders. These are breeders that have agreed to abide by the clubs standards and codes of conducts regarding ethical breeding practices. This won't be a guarantee of an ethical breeder, but it will give you a great jumping point to locating the right breeder for you. To see what a club's code of ethics looks like, check out the Bulldog Club of America's code (www.thebca.org/code.html).

○ The puppy's parents are proven dogs with achievements of note.

○ She has a contract half a mile long that vaguely resembles an FBI investigative report.

○ She has a spay/neuter clause unless the puppy is sold under a show contract.

○ She will take back the dog if the buyer cannot keep him for any circumstances.

○ Her puppies have been vaccinated, and had a thorough health check performed.

○ Breeder can answer any question you may have about their breed of dog's history, origins, lifespan, hereditary illness the breed is prone to, temperament of their dogs in particular, weaknesses in their dogs, etc.

○ She has the names of people who have her puppies and is willing to give references.

○ How does she make you feel?

Remember also that you will be convincing an ethical breeder that you are worthy of one of her dogs. If a breeder gives you a hard time and asks questions about your home life, relationships, children, and neighbors, it's only because she wants the very best home for her puppies. Not just anyone will do.

Other things you need to watch for and ask about:

● Is the puppy guaranteed for life, or just a year or even a few months, against inherited diseases and genetic defects? Good breeders offer guarantees for life.

● What about returning your puppy? A good breeder will take back any dog or puppy from their breeding lines even if they didn't actually breed the dog.

- Do they work with breed rescue? Often breeders that care are closely involved in their breed rescue.
- Have their hips been guaranteed? Are their OFA (www. offa.org) records available?
- Have the dog's eyes been CERFed (Canine Eye Registration Foundation)?

Even if you have received recommendations and references, it is still possible to run afoul of a breeder unworthy of the term ethical. Go with your gut, and if you feel uncomfortable, don't be afraid to take your money elsewhere. Keep an eye out for these red flags:

- He won't let you see the puppy's parents (the father may not always be on site; this is normal).
- He won't let you tour his breeding facility.
- He can't produce registration papers for the parents.
- His puppies aren't registered, or registerable.
- Neither parent dog is pedigreed.
- His puppies aren't guaranteed.
- None of his dogs have been checked for genetic diseases.
- He doesn't care about the future of your dog (that came from him).
- He breeds a lot of unrecognized "designer" breeds.
- No veterinary health checks of the puppies from birth.
- No mandatory spaying/neutering of pet-quality animals.
- His puppies haven't been vaccinated.
- He doesn't know the breed's background and history.
- His dogs don't look healthy.
- He always has puppies for sale, sometimes two or three litters at a time.

▸ The Petfinder Web site (www.petfinder.com) is a vast database of animals up for adoption all over North America. You can search by breed of dog, by location, or even select certain criteria that you are looking for (large dog, black, senior dog, and male), and it will pull up a list of results that are tailored to your wants. There are thousands of pets listed. Visit Petfinder today and see if they have the dog you are looking for.

- He can't/won't produce veterinary records for at least the mother on hand.
- He won't give references from owners of pups from previous litters.
- The puppies are ready to go before they should be (under eight weeks of age).
- He sells pups for little money, too little to be taking proper care of the dogs.

By ensuring you have located a good breeder who cares more about her dogs than making a dollar, you also ensure that your dog is a fine specimen of his breed, has excellent bloodlines, and is as free of genetic complaints and hereditary diseases as the modern world can make him. It is worth the extra time and money, as you'll see in the future, too. A well-bred dog will be healthier and happier than a poorly bred dog.

## Adopting from a Rescue or Shelter

Humane societies, SPCAs (Society for the Prevention of Cruelty to Animals), city pounds, animal shelters, and designated breed rescues are my favorite places to find dogs. Millions of dogs throughout the world are waiting in a shelter or rescue for somebody like you to come along and give them a happy home for the rest of their life.

Did you know that deciding you want a purebred dog doesn't mean you are stuck buying from a breeder? Purebred dogs are often found in animal shelters, and if you can't locate the breed of your choice at your local humane society, then you'll be sure to find one in a breed rescue. Even if you want a puppy, there are almost always puppies available for adoption at shelters and breed rescues. You can find a local rescue for the breed of your choice by looking on the breed club's Web site. They will have all the rescue contacts and their locations listed.

Adopting an older dog has numerous advantages over a puppy. You already know what he'll look like and how big he'll be when he grows up, and the shelter/rescue workers will have a good idea of what his usual temperament is like. That's just the beginning, too. An adult dog won't need to taken outside at four in the morning to pee unless there are health issues involved. Most of the adult dogs in the shelter have some basic training already. If they don't, they usually pick it up very quickly. And if you work during the day, your new adult dog can be left for a lot longer than three hours.

When adopting a dog of any age, most of the time the volunteers will be able to tell you the dog's approximate age and his former living situation. Usually this includes the reasons the dog is in the shelter to begin with. It's not always a bad reason; sometimes it's as simple (relatively speaking) as "We were moving and couldn't take him" or the family could no longer spare the time and effort. Not every dog waiting in a shelter is there due to behavior problems. And the ones that are can usually be retrained or properly trained for the first time. Most behavior issues that land a dog in the shelter are caused by lack of exercise and attention.

Sometimes dogs in a rescue or shelter have been in foster homes and have been evaluated for their tolerance to children, other dogs, and other small animals. Ask if your potential dog has been evaluated. You may find that you'll need to look at a different dog if the one you are thinking of has issues with something in your family situation.

Your newly adopted shelter dog will more than likely be **neutered** or **spayed** before going home with you. If he's too young,

**ASK YOUR GUIDE**

***Do I need to bring anything with me when I go to a shelter to adopt a dog?***

▶ Yes, this is a situation where you don't want to arrive empty-handed. If the rescue requires permission from your landlord (if you rent), references, or any other pertinent household information (and they will ask), have it ready. Ask questions of your own: about the dog's reaction to the other dogs, and what type of situation he came from. If they don't tell you ahead of time, you need to ask. Not only will this show that you are willing to go to the lengths they ask, but it will also show that you are prepared for some of what having a dog entails.

the shelter will usually issue a certificate to have him neutered for a greatly reduced price, sometimes for free. He will also have been given the standard vaccinations already.

## Get Linked

*There are a number of useful tools on my Web site to help you choose the dog that best fits your family and lifestyle. Here are my favorite ones.*

**THE WONDER DOG GALLERY**

Here are hundreds of mixed-breed dogs for your viewing pleasure. You can see the diversity in size, shape, and color in mixed breeds by looking through this huge gallery.

http://about.com/dogs/mixedbreedgallery

**BREED CLUBS AND ASSOCIATIONS**

Each of the alphabetical pages (top and bottom letters) contain a listing of dog breeds that begin with the selected letter. Each dog breed listed has its own page of clubs listed.

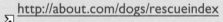
http://about.com/dogs/breedclubindex

**INDEX OF RESCUES AND SHELTERS**

This is a huge index of rescues and shelters throughout the world. The rescues and breeds listed in these pages are updated frequently. Please feel free to suggest a site for addition.

http://about.com/dogs/rescueindex

## Chapter 2

# Getting Started as a New Dog Owner

### A Dog's Basic Needs

Adding a dog to your home means you have agreed to provide all of your new dog's basic needs. Every dog on earth has four basic physical needs that must be provided in order for him to survive: food, shelter, water, and exercise. But every dog also has emotional and mental needs. A dog needs companionship, affection, and mental stimulation in order to stay healthy. Your job as a responsible dog owner is to provide these essential items.

You don't have to feed your dog the most expensive dog food available, but it does need to have passed the **Association of American Feed Control Officials (AAFCO)** standards. These standards govern the quality of dog food and the nutrients it contains. However, feeding a better quality of dog food will save you money as your dog grows. Better food is preventative maintenance

▶ During hot weather you may find that a large water cooler for dogs is the ideal thing for keeping fresh water available all the time for your dog. I may not live in an area that gets high temperatures, but we are a lot more active outside in the summer so we have two of them; one inside and one outside. You can get them in a variety of sizes.

✳ Play Time
✳ Nadz

for a variety of digestive troubles as your dog ages. He will also eat less of a food with better ingredients than of one made mostly with fillers. You can learn more about your dog's nutritional needs and how they affect his health in Chapter 4.

Your dog must always have fresh, clean water available to drink. During warm weather you may be refilling his water bowl three or four times daily. If he spends any amount of time outdoors, it helps to have two or more buckets of water placed in shady areas that you refresh throughout the day. Drinking out of the toilet or the kids' wading pool and eating snow are not acceptable, even though dogs will do it anyway.

Your dog has strict exercise needs that must be met in order for him to maintain good health. In almost every dog, a lack of exercise leads to destructive behavior. In fact, most of the biggest problem behaviors in dogs can be directly linked to a lack of appropriate exercise. It's a shame that such a simple thing to take care of often proves to be the most commonly neglected. I understand that getting up at six in the morning so you can take your beagle out for a jog isn't any fun at all, but it's something you should have thought about before you chose a beagle.

Your dog needs to play and use his brain. Thinking games, like Hide and Seek, will keep his mind and reflexes sharp. These games will also teach him new ways of doing things and new ways of thinking about different situations. Play with him often.

Your dog needs you to protect him. Taking a dog into your home means that you promise to let nothing happen to him. You won't let people abuse him, nor will you abuse him yourself. You will keep him contained, and safely leashed at all times. You will not allow him to run free and get hit by a car or catch diseases or parasites.

Most important of all, your dog needs you. He needs to be by your side, at your feet, and in your home. Dogs are, above all, pack animals, and they need to be with their pack. You are your dog's pack. Don't take it away from him. A lonely dog will bark, try to escape, dig, and exhibit other undesirable behaviors. Most important of all, a lonely dog will not stay a healthy dog for very long.

## Things You Can't Live Without

Warm up your credit card—it's about to get a good workout! I think every dog owner should have a number of essential items. From simple time-savers (even if it's just a few seconds!) to items I can no longer live without, they have all made my hectic life a whole lot easier. We'll get into the details of training tools and other items later on, but the following sections will get you off to a good start as a new dog owner.

**A crate and food and water bowls are the first items on your list.** For a crate, you can choose between a plastic airline-approved crate or a stainless steel collapsible wire kennel. Make sure it's the right size for your dog: big enough for him to stand up in, turn around, and lie down comfortably.

The benefits of crate training done properly are numerous. Dogs have a very strong den instinct. Most will not eliminate in their den, and being in there gives them a more secure feeling. Your dog will grow up a little more confident if he knows that he has that safe place to go to when the world becomes too much for him to handle. (Read more on crate training for housetraining in Chapter 7.)

Tip-proof food and water bowls are an absolute must if you have a dog that likes to pick up his full dishes and wander through

ASK YOUR GUIDE

*I think the crate I bought is too big—my puppy still pees in it. Do I need to buy another one?*

▶ You can still use this crate, but you will need to make its internal space a little smaller. You can do this by putting a box in the crate that will fill up the back half (or however much you will need). The remaining space should be just big enough for your puppy to lie down, stand up, and turn around comfortably.

the house looking for you so he can dine in your presence. Tip-proof is also the way to go if you have kids in the house; they're even more likely to kick the bowls around than the dog!

**A collar and leash are essential.**   A flat buckle collar, either nylon or leather, is first on the list. There are a variety of training collars available, which you'll read about later on in the book.

As for a training collar, a Gentle Leader head halter is a great choice. A halter with a loop around your dog's nose, and one behind his ears, the Gentle Leader will do just what its name implies: it will lead your dog gently wherever you want him to go. Don't confuse this halter with the Halti, which has a similar design.

A six-foot nylon leash with a looped handle is another necessity. The width you need depends on your dog's size. For really big dogs, they come in double thickness with a heavy-duty clip on the end. I do not recommend using a retractable leash at all. Some dog owners like them because they allow their dog to roam ahead a little bit while still following the leash laws. I really, really dislike the things though. The locking mechanism on the handle of the leash is too fragile to withstand even a medium-sized dog's lunge, and most dog owners' reflexes aren't quick enough to lock it in time anyway. Retractable leads allow dogs to annoy other people, and the majority of dog owners who use these leads allow their dogs to annoy other people as well.

A tethering leash is another item you might want to look into. This is a six-foot nylon leash, but instead of the usual loop at the end there is a locking clip. You can keep it closed for a hand loop, or open it to clip around a pole to tie your dog outside of a store for a few minutes. Or use it during puppy training for tethering your dog to your waist. Tazlab ([www.tazlab.com](www.tazlab.com)) has a very nice one that comes in a variety of pretty colors.

**A seatbelt system or pet barrier is a must if you drive with your dog.** Your dog should be restrained at all times when in a vehicle. Even a very small dog can turn into a deadly projectile in a crash. Check out http://about.com/dogs/carrestraints for some great restraining systems that will keep you and your dog safe in the car. You can buy a barrier or seatbelt system at any of the big chain pet stores.

**Don't forget about fun stuff!** Toys may not seem like dog necessities, but they are very important for your dog's comfort and development. Get some squeaky toys or balls that are dog safe. Most dogs love to play, even by themselves, and a toy like a BusterCube (a ball that dispenses tiny treats as it rolls) is ideal for a dog to occupy himself.

A Chuckit! is a great product for all owners of hyper dogs, or for those who don't like picking up slimy, slobbery tennis balls but love to play fetch with their pups. The Chuckit! is an arm that picks up the slobbered-on balls with ease and flings them a whole lot farther than you could with your bare hand.

Another fun item that you may already own if you have kids is a hard plastic children's splash pool. Throw balls in it when it's full of water and watch your ball-crazy dog try to pick them up again. It's cheap entertainment for the whole family, and it's a great way for the dog to cool off when it's hot outside.

## The First Twenty-Four Hours

Your first day and night with your new dog can be both exciting and nerve-racking. You've probably heard countless horror stories about new puppies crying all night long or chewing everything in sight. Adult dogs can also cause problems, especially if they're large and untrained when you bring them home. This is all true, but your first night with your new dog doesn't have to turn into a nightmare.

Before you even bring your dog home for the first time, consider the following advice. If you take these steps, you should be able to spend that first night in relative peace.

## TOOLS YOU NEED

▶ Hard plastic baby gates are ideal for keeping puppies secure in a specific area of the home. Don't use the wooden accordion-style gates, though. It's too easy for a puppy to fit his head through the holes, and what could happen after that is a horrible thing to consider. Make sure the holes aren't big enough for paws either; some puppies are very agile climbers even at a young age, and a gate he can climb won't contain him long.

- Puppyproof the house before you bring him home. Electrical cords, cleaners, and houseplants all need to be secured so a curious puppy can't eat them. And they do eat cords. Gate off any sections of the house you don't want the puppy to have access to. You'll want to begin as you mean to go on when it comes to keeping puppies out of rooms.
- Introduce your new dog to the rest of your family members. This means all of them, Johnny's hamster included. Your dog needs to understand that all creatures that live in the home are supposed to be there.
- Keep the excitement to a minimum. Your dog is going to feel a bit stressed out, and it's really best if you keep visitors out of your home for a few days at first. Let him get used to the people who live there first before adding more excitement.

**Crate him for the night in a location near you.** He'll feel more at ease if he can hear and smell a familiar person. I have always done the "bad" thing and let my puppies sleep with me on the bed. I found it made it much easier for me to get up in the middle of the night and take them out if they had to go, and I wasn't kept awake by him whining all night either. It's no longer looked at as a bad idea, thankfully, so if you feel comfortable with this idea, then I highly recommend it. Mind you, it is much easier on everybody if you are a light sleeper who will wake up if your puppy starts to whine.

If you find she is whining a lot in her crate, take her out of the crate and immediately to her bathroom area to see if she needs to urinate. If she does, praise her (but not too loudly), and if she hasn't gone, return her to her crate with no fanfare after waiting about ten minutes. Don't let her think that it's play time, snuggle time, or eating time. It's bedtime, and she will learn that whining only gets a quick trip to the bathroom and nothing more in the middle of the night.

After you've made sure that she doesn't need to go to the bathroom by taking her outside for a quick pee, you can try covering the crate (if it's a mesh crate) with a blanket to give it more of a "den" feeling, and you can give her something of yours, like a recently worn shirt, to sleep with. It will help her settle if she's able to surround herself with a familiar scent.

**Don't expect too much of your dog during the first day and night.** He may have accidents in the house; he may chew things and bark or howl. Don't get angry; just remind yourself that your dog doesn't know any different yet, and that these behaviors will change as your dog learns your rules. It's possible that he came from a place where eliminating on the floor was accepted, or he may have been a stray. If he's a puppy, much of these things may be attributed to his age, and as he grows he will have better control of things.

## The "Do Not" List

Right off the bat you need to start getting used to some basic dog owner's ground rules. You will often be walking your dog in public areas, taking him to the park to play, and going various other places with your canine companion by your side. But despite your dog's wishes, the entire world is not his playground. You will often run into people who are scared of dogs, those who are allergic to them, and those who simply don't like dogs coming near them. Though you may be sure your pup is perfectly well behaved, others might not agree. Consider the following no-nos for dogs and their owners.

**Do not allow your dog to urinate on other people's property.** When your dog has extended his leash and is sniffing around the neighbor's yard, do not let him water their prize begonias. You may think "It's just pee!" but the burns in my lawn, and yours, should tell you differently. Dog urine is chock full of elements that will burn anything they land on, damaging even the hardiest of greenery. See Chapter 7 for information on how to prevent your dog from eliminating in inappropriate places and how to train your dog to eliminate on command. It's not as hard as you think.

**Do not bring your dog into a place of business unless it is posted as a dog-friendly location.** For every dog lover out there who thinks it's great that dogs are in the store, there are ten people who strongly disagree. Not displaying a No Pets Allowed sign does not entitle people to bring their animals into a business office or store. It is, in fact, the other way around. If it is not explicitly posted that dogs are welcome, then you should assume they are not. The size of your dog matters not one bit.

It's not just people who dislike dogs that would (and do!) object. Even dog lovers like me object to dogs in places of business. Whether the objection is from fear, allergies, or just dislike of dogs in general, your job as a responsible dog owner is to respect their boundaries and not inflict your dog on other people without their prior consent.

Aside from the general comfort level of the people around you, bringing your dog into places he shouldn't be is also a health risk. Animals of any kind should never be in places where food is prepared or served and people are eating. I know how fast and how far fur can travel if my dog decides to shake himself off, and as a dog owner I'm willing to risk the odd dog hair in my food. However, I am not entitled to inflict that on other people, and they do have the right to eat dust- and fur-free food.

Dog allergies are nothing to sneeze at either. They aren't just sniffles and watery eyes. Dog allergies can cause severe respiratory distress and an extremely painful skin reaction, even from ten feet away. People with severe allergies and asthma may actually be hospitalized from an encounter with your dog. A friend of my mother's landed in the emergency room after a woman with a small dog in her purse brought it in to the bank and stood behind her.

## Do not allow your dog to roam the neighborhood freely.

Loose and roaming dogs are menaces. They cause traffic accidents, scare children, bite people, and terrorize other people's pets. They also facilitate the spread of disease. Parasites and sickness can be picked up from the feces of wild animals and spread throughout the dog's territory. While a properly vaccinated dog has some immunity from infectious diseases, there is still a possibility of contracting a fatal disease. Free-roaming dogs are at the highest risk, mainly from other dogs, but also from resident wildlife. Dogs who roam at will are also rarely up-to-date on vaccinations.

**ELSEWHERE ON THE WEB**

▶ Most public beaches no longer allow dogs at all since enough irresponsible owners either failed to pick up after the dogs or didn't control them. It's an understandable reaction. So if you do find a dog-friendly beach, make sure you follow the posted rules carefully. Also, check out some great beach etiquette tips at www.dog friendly.com/server/travel/ info/tips/beachetiq.shtml.

**Do not allow your dog off its leash in public places.** Unless it's a posted off-leash dog park, your dog should never be loose. It doesn't matter if your dog is the world's greatest trained dog, the mere fact that he is off of a leash is enough to make people nervous. Even if your dog is a papillon and only weighs six pounds, it may still strike terror in the heart of someone with an acute fear of dogs or cause a near fatal asthma attack in somebody else with severe dog allergies.

**Do not bring your unvaccinated puppy out to be around other dogs.** Yes, this means waiting until your puppy is sixteen weeks of age before taking him out to visit a dog park or daycare. It's easy to fall into the trap of thinking that you'll be the only dog who wasn't vaccinated, and that may actually be true; but the adult dogs your dog will meet will have had the freedom to see other dogs, and they may have picked up viruses from them.

**Do not allow your dog to pick fights with other dogs.** People who stand back when their dog is being aggressive to another dog because they think it is cool are jerks. Please don't be a jerk. It's not cool to have a dog-aggressive dog. It makes other people dislike your dog, and your dog will miss out on a lot of fun if you let him or encourage him to be this way.

Also keep in mind that, these days, people are quicker to sue others over incidents of this nature. If your dog picks a fight with another dog and causes an injury, the owner may react very strongly and seek money to pay for veterinary bills. Aside from the unpleasant situation, a dog fight could cost you money.

**Do not allow your dog to lunge and jump on people.** This, more than anything, will put people off of your dog. It may even

▶ Off-leash dog parks are a wonderful recreational outlet for dogs all over the world. The opportunity to run and play with other dogs in a securely fenced environment is a valuable tool in their social development. Unfortunately, not every dog park is filled with responsible owners, and, as in most things, a few unmannerly people can ruin the whole experience for most. Make sure you're not one of those humans by following Bark Park Etiquette as described at http://about.com/dogs/dogparketiquette.

cost you some friends if your dog is the large, hairy, muddy-pawed type. Nobody will want to go and visit you and your dog if your dog has a habit of pouncing on people. And if he does it out in public, it is no less than an assault, and he could be deemed "dangerous" no matter what size he is.

**Do not leave your dog unsupervised with children.** Accidents happen very quickly, and your dog may not be tolerant of your child's jumping, yelling, and tendency to pull fur and ears. Your child could hurt your dog unintentionally, and the resulting mess could cause a lot of heartbreak.

And your children aren't the only ones who shouldn't be left alone with your dog without supervision. It's almost more important that you watch your dog around other children, as even the tiniest nip or scratch could upset a parent. Put yourself in that parent's shoes: If your child came home with an injury caused by someone else's dog, you'd probably want some answers, right? So take precautions now to avoid pain later.

**Do not allow your dog to bark nonstop.** Out of all the irritating behaviors that an untrained dog has, barking tops the list for the most annoying. Continuous barking has had neighbors calling police, humane societies, and even taking retaliatory action. In some cases this had included poisoning the offending dog.

Aside from the possibility of disturbing others, it's also important to take action in the case of incessant barking for other reasons. Like any excessive behavior, constant barking is likely a sign that something's not quite right. Perhaps your dog feels neglected and is trying to get your attention. Or maybe he needs more guidance and training to understand the rules of the house and feel more secure. If you can't get to the bottom of the issue on your own, consult a veterinarian or dog trainer.

**ASK YOUR GUIDE**

*My neighbor is afraid of dogs. How do I get him to like mine?*

▶ You can't force somebody to like your dog, especially when you are dealing with a fear of dogs. All you can do is train your dog to be the best canine neighbor he can be. Over time your neighbor may come to accept his presence, even if he doesn't like him for the dog he is.

## Your Dog and Other People

One thing you must keep in mind all the time is that not everyone likes dogs. Even if your neighborhood seems to be very dog friendly, be assured that nuisance dogs won't be tolerated well. Not that it matters, as your dog should never be allowed to be a nuisance anyway.

A nice, high fence will be the nicest thing you can do for your neighbors when you add a dog to your family. Your neighbors have a right to enjoy their peace and privacy without your dog interfering in any way. It sounds like an impossible goal at first, and for the first year it probably is. But if you talk to your neighbors and explain that you will be training your dog, things will go much smoother when they know you are making an effort.

Ask your neighbors if they hear anything from your dog while you are out. You may not be aware of it, but your dog may be raising the roof with howls and barking the whole time you are gone. We like to think that we'll catch them by coming up to the house quietly, but I was never able to catch Oscar. I'm pretty sure he could smell me coming from half a mile away, because whenever I was close enough to the house to hear him, he'd have stopped howling. I was sure he was quiet the whole time I was gone until one of my neighbors asked me very nicely to shut our windows when we leave. Had I just asked after the first few times, I would have been able to correct this behavior much sooner. Don't be afraid to ask, and by asking you will also be letting your neighbors know that you wish to be alerted to problems and that you will take steps to correct them. (See Chapter 11 for barking solutions.)

Consider your dog's every public appearance to be a show that many people watch. It's not fair, but people will remember that one time that your dog growled and barked at the baby stroller but not

**ELSEWHERE ON THE WEB**

▶ Susan Clothier, author of *Bones Would Rain from the Sky*, wrote this fantastic article about letting your dog run up and sniff people. "He just wants to say hi!" is a very thought-provoking look at dog behavior and how it sometimes doesn't fit in with human expectations and the public's right to be left in peace. Read it for yourself online at Susan's Web site (www.flyingdogpress.com/sayhi.html).

the many times that your dog has walked beautifully on its leash and let everybody pet him. The negative is always memorable. If you do the following, you should be in good shape:

- Always walk your dog on a leash. If he doesn't walk well on a leash, use a head halter to make him behave, and train him to heel (see Chapter 6 for information on teaching commands).
- Keep your dog away from other pedestrians. Nobody likes to be mauled by a passing puppy as they go about their day.
- Pick up your dog's messes. This is something you must do every single time. Not only does abandoned poop look and smell terrible, it also spreads parasites and disease. It makes parents see red when their kids step in it. It ruins vehicle interiors when people have it on the bottom of their shoes and don't notice when they get into a car. It's just awful, and if you don't pick it up you'll be responsible for tighter dog restrictions.

## Making Adjustments

Adding any new member to your family is a change that may take some getting used to, by everyone in your family. You will need to keep in mind that your family is a new situation for your dog, too, and things may be a little stressful for a while. Expect it to take your dog a lot longer than just twenty-four hours to settle in. New puppies will settle in much faster than older dogs. And if your new dog has come from a shelter or other less-than-ideal situation, it could be as long as a month or two. There may be accidents, and there may be some scuffles, as your dog learns your household's routine and your household adjusts to your new dog.

**You first need to adjust your schedule.**  A dog requires lots of attention and care—morning, afternoon, and night. If you're not currently an early riser, get ready for a wakeup call. Your dog will need to be taken out to do his business first thing every morning. Some dogs need to go for a walk in order to get things moving inside properly. Your dog may be one of them. Allow at least thirty minutes of walking time in case your dog takes a while to go. Your dog will also need to be taken out in the afternoon and at least once in the evening. If your new dog is a young puppy, you'll need to take him outside even more often than that.

During your working day, even a young adult dog needs to be taken care of. A lot of working dog owners will use their lunch hour to go home and take the pooch for a walk, but for people who work odd hours, or commute any kind of distance, this option just isn't practical. You may, however, have older kids that come home from school during lunch, a spouse, or even a neighbor you are friendly with that will take your dog out halfway through the day. If none of these apply to your situation, you should consider hiring a pet sitter. It won't cost a lot of money for a sitter to come during the day and walk your dog for an hour or so.

Whether you use a professional pet-sitting service, or a casual sitter who walks dogs as a side income, ask for references. Find out how much dog experience the sitter has and if he or she has her own transportation. Ask what she will be doing with your dog during the hour you are paying for. Ask if she will be available for emergencies, too. Once you've settled on a pet sitter, bring her to meet your dog and show her how you want things done.

Another option for working dog owners is doggy daycare. Like a children's facility, doggy daycare is a place to take your dog for care, exercise, and socialization during the day while you are gone.

Your dog needs to be fully vaccinated, healthy, and compatible with other dogs in order to be accepted at doggy daycare. Dog-aggressive dogs are not welcome in daycare facilities. Check your yellow pages or ask other pet owners for recommendations. A doggy daycare should be clean, fully staffed with one human for every five dogs (or more), contain separate kennels for downtime, and have a knowledgeable, experienced staff.

**Help your family adjust to the new addition.** Everyone in your house should be included in the decision to get a dog and his care, including children. Growing up with a dog for a companion is one of childhood's greatest pleasures. The happiness doesn't just happen on its own, though. Children need to be taught what they can and can't do, and the dog needs to learn that children are pack members and rank higher than he does, no matter how small they are.

The first thing a child should learn is how to be nice. This means learning how to pet the dog nicely, not smacking, and not pulling on fur. Babies as young as six months old can start learning to be gentle when petting the dog and taught not to pull ears. Consistency and gentle correction when your baby starts to pull on fur will pay off in the end, even though it is a slow process.

Children should never be left unsupervised with your dog, even if you think your dog is completely trustworthy. I cannot stress this enough. A dog is a thinking being, and children can be frightening and painful. If your dog thinks he may be in danger of injury from your child, he may bite.

Teach your children not to pester the dog when he's eating. I contradict myself later in Chapter 11, but that is dealing with adults, not children. Training your kids to leave the dog alone to eat is simple bite prevention; better safe than sorry. Your dog should be left in peace for more than just eating as well. Your dog deserves to have peaceful rest in his crate or another designated spot that he can use to get away.

Older children should be involved with your new dog's care and feeding. This will not only help teach responsibility, but it will also help cement your children's place in the pack above your dog. Kids as young as five can dish out dry dog food and help you groom your dog. Older children can help with cleaning up after the dog, walking her, and bathing her when she needs it.

## Get Linked

*The entire focus of the About Dogs Web site is responsible dog owner-ship. It's all about how to be the kind of dog owner your dog deserves. Here are a few key articles that will help you achieve that goal.*

**RESPONSIBLE DOG OWNERSHIP**  This is the agreement you made when you chose to become a dog owner. Following this agreement will ensure that you and your dog are welcomed wherever dogs are permitted.
 http://about.com/dogs/responsibleowner

**THE EVOLUTION FROM A DOG OWNER TO A DOG PERSON**  A story of the difference between dog people and dog owners, and defining the moment it happens.
 http://about.com/dogs/dogperson

**MY DOG IS MISSING!**  If your dog is gone now and you are looking for help, check these pages, along with the printable checklist, to help you out when your emotions are a-tangle.
 http://about.com/dogs/lostdog

## Chapter 3

# The Basics of Dog Health

## Practicing Good Hygiene

As your dog's owner, you are the person who will come to know him better than anyone else. This is a great thing, as it will help you form a special bond with him. But beyond that, your thorough knowledge of your dog means that you will be able to tell if something is wrong with him. A very large part of maintaining your dog's good health is catching and taking care of the little things that will bother him and upset his natural balance. If you know every inch of your healthy dog, including his typical behavior, you'll recognize your not-so-healthy dog a lot faster.

Familiarize yourself with all the parts of your dog. Every chance you get, take a few minutes to rub him down. Fondle his ears and peer into his mouth (but watch out for dog breath!). Feel his toe joints gently, and trace the pads on the bottom of his feet. This is a great thing to do with both puppies and adult dogs. Puppies need to get used to being touched and handled if they're going to grow into sociable adults, and adult dogs, especially those who were

**About**

rescued from shelters, need to be reassured that your touch is a safe one. If you make a habit of fondling your dog on a regular basis, he will be much more tolerant of the many undignified things you have to do to him to maintain his hygiene throughout his life. Bathing, brushing, nail clipping, and dental care will take some getting used to, but they are all ways that you can keep tabs on his overall health.

**Give your dog a thorough bath about once month.** Of course, if she's anything like my dogs, you'll probably have to give her a bath more often, and sometimes on the spur of the moment.

Here's where I envy small dog owners. You can bathe your small dog in the sink, or use a basin if he's too big (or too rambunctious) to fit in the sink. Use a bathtub if you suspect he'll try to escape. Your big dog will have to be bathed in the bathtub, or with the hose outside. If you are bathing him outside, a hard plastic kiddie pool is an ideal bathtub. Use a garden sprayer that has multiple settings on your hose. You may need to keep him on a leash to get his cooperation, though.

Rub the shampoo into his coat first, and then add enough water to work it into a good lather. Get every inch of him (but not his face!), from behind his ears to the tip of his tail, and everything underneath. Work the shampoo lather in good, and then rinse him off. It's easiest to rinse a dog if you start at the very top and let the water run down his sides. Rinse him until the water runs clear. Any soap residue that's left on his fur can irritate his skin and cause itchiness and flaking.

Wash his face with a clean, wet facecloth. Get the gunk out of the corners of his eyes first, rinse the cloth, then wash the rest of his face and the outsides of his ears. Don't go after the brown wax in his ears; he needs that to protect the delicate membranes inside.

After he's rinsed clean, towel him dry as best as you can. Do not use a hairdryer! They are too hot for your dog's skin and will burn him. If you throw a towel over him as soon as he steps out of the tub, you may catch him before he shakes himself off.

**Dogs with long hair need to be brushed daily.** They can get horrific mats all over their body if they are not brushed often enough, and trying to brush them out is akin to torture. You can cut some of the looser mats out with scissors, but unless you plan to shave your dog after, you'll end up with unsightly chunks out of his coat. If your dog will sit still for you, use a seam-ripper and cut a few of the hairs close to the mat. This will make it easier to cut hairs under the mat, closer to your dog's skin, too. If you don't trust your dog to hold still, take him to a professional groomer.

**Nail clipping can be the hardest part of grooming your dog.** Most dogs absolutely hate having their nails clipped and will actively fight the clippers. A lot of owners are somewhat reluctant to sit on their dogs to get them to hold still (with good reason), so it's rare that a nail-clipping experience goes smoothly. If you can't figure out a way to make nail clipping work at home, take your dog to the vet or a groomer to have his nails clipped. He probably won't put up any less of a fight for the professionals, but at least they know what they're doing and are experienced in handling unruly dogs.

**Your dog's teeth need to be cared for, too.** Dogs can suffer from tartar, gum disease, and tooth decay, just like humans. Using one of the special toothbrushes and paste combinations available for dogs, try to brush your dog's teeth at least once a week. There are several types of doggy toothbrushes on the market. I still use a finger brush though, simply because I'm used to it and I don't like

▶ I'm sure you can bathe a big dog in the bathtub without a shower nozzle that extends, but I know I wouldn't attempt it. Look for a nozzle with two or three different settings—a hard jet, massaging jet, and a normal spray setting—and one with at least five feet of hose to reach the back of your dog and under his belly as well.

change. Oh, and the dogs don't mind me sticking my fingers in their mouths, but they might look askance if I was to go after them with a foreign object (which is what a toothbrush would be to them). Your veterinarian may also suggest a tooth scaling under anesthetic at your yearly visit if he feels your dog needs it.

## Important Preventative Measures

In addition to staying familiar with your dog's body and behavior and keeping him well groomed, there are other preventative measures you can take to ensure his health. Of course, the random flea infestation or upset stomach will happen from time to time, but a few simple steps can help you avoid unnecessary costs and save your dog from discomfort.

**You can prevent your dog from picking up fleas and ticks.** There are several topical flea and tick solutions available for dogs. Instead of repelling, they kill the adult flea or tick once he has taken up residence on your dog. All of these topical solutions for fleas and ticks need to be given monthly:

- **Advantage:** A brand with a solid reputation, Advantage kills fleas but not ticks.
- **Biospot:** This one kills adult fleas and ticks and repels mosquitoes.
- **K9 Advantix:** We use this one because it actually kills the mosquitoes instead of just repelling them onto me. K9 Advantix kills adult fleas, ticks, and mosquitoes.
- **Frontline and Frontline Plus:** Another well-known name, the Frontline brothers kill fleas and ticks.

**Heartworm is a serious threat to your dog's life.** Carried by mosquitoes, heartworm can cause irreversible damage to your dog's vital organs, and without treatment it will kill your dog. Early signs of heartworm infection often go unnoticed for a while:

- Fatigue
- Lack of interest in exercise
- Bleeding nose
- Shortness of breath

Heartworm is completely preventable. You should have your dog tested at the beginning of spring every year to make sure he hasn't contracted heartworm since the last test. This is a simple blood test done at your veterinarian's office. If he tests negative, use a preventive medication to ensure he stays free from infection. Three common names in heartworm prevention are Sentinel, Heartgard, and Revolution. We use Sentinel Flavor Tabs. They are cookie-sized bits that apparently taste good enough for even Mr. Picky to eat them once a month. Just make sure you keep the rest of the package in a safe cupboard so a crafty hound after a snack doesn't get to them. I know that heartworm preventative medication is not cheap, but treatment for heartworm disease is a great deal more costly in time, effort, money, and the health of your dog.

Before your dog is treated for heartworm disease (based on a positive blood test), he needs to be evaluated thoroughly to ensure that he is healthy enough to withstand treatment. As the owner of a heartworm-positive dog, you must be completely committed to following your veterinarian's instructions exactly, and following through to the end, including all follow-up tests and appointments. Your dog must be treated for both the adult worms in his body, and the microfilariae (the pre-larval worms) in his bloodstream.

Treatment to kill the adult worms in your dog's heart will likely be done while your dog is hospitalized. Adult worms are killed using

▶ For everything you ever wanted to know about heartworm infection and disease, check out www.thepet center.com/gen/hw.html. This is the most detailed page on heartworm I have come across, and it offers information on the life cycle of heartworms, how they travel from mosquito to dog, what kind of damage they do to your dog, and everything in between. Just don't read it while you are eating.

an organic arsenic compound that is administered intravenously under a veterinarian's care. Once the adult worms are killed, they must be absorbed into the dog's body. This is a dangerous process that requires your dog to be inactive for weeks after the worms are killed. Activity can cause the dead worms to become dislodged and migrate throughout the body, possibly into the lungs or other parts of the body, causing blockages and, in some cases, death. In extreme cases your veterinarian may suggest surgical removal of the dead worms. Treatment to destroy the microfilariae in the blood may require short-term hospitalizations during each treatment to monitor for possible complications.

**Keeping your dog at his ideal weight will prevent health problems.** Obesity is a major cause for concern in dogs these days, especially in pampered house dogs. Many owners equate a lot of treats and little exercise with a happy home. But while it may be "happy," it certainly isn't "healthy." Obesity can affect every part of your dog's body in a short period of time. An overweight dog has added stress on his joints, bones, and muscles. In an accident, a bone fracture may be worsened by any extraneous weight the dog is carrying around. His muscles have to struggle to move the extra weight around causing strains and sprains, and his joints can deteriorate faster resulting in osteoarthritis in younger dogs. Hip dysplasia and other degenerative joint diseases can be directly linked to a weight problem. An overweight pet is also at risk for arrhythmia and heart failure.

To see if your dog is sitting nicely at a healthy weight, stand beside him and run your hand along his ribs. Can you feel the space between them as shallow indents under his skin? You should be able to count them by feel, but they shouldn't be protruding so much that you can count them by sight alone. Your dog should also have a discernible waist; it should be indented at the belly from behind his ribs to his legs. If you can't see where his ribs end from the side, then there is definitely a problem. And if you can't feel his ribs, take him in for a checkup and confirmation by your veterinarian.

The first step in your dog's new fitness plan is a full physical checkup at the veterinarian's office to find the cause behind your dog's weight gain. More often than not, substantial weight gain is caused by well-meaning owners who tend to give out more treats than is healthy, or think that a couch potato dog is a happy, content dog. While Oscar may be pleased for now, neither of you will be very happy when his health deteriorates.

Although most obesity problems can be easily traced back to the owners, sudden weight gain is also a symptom of underlying health problems. Hypothyroidism, Cushing's disease, and more can cause a formerly fit Oscar to pack on the pounds, which is why a vet examination is important to rule out other physical causes. Once anything medical has been eliminated, you can start to work on reducing that extra poundage.

It's easiest and safest to reduce your dog's intake of food over-all rather than switching him to a diet dog food. Many weight-loss formulas of dry dog food are lacking essential ingredients and won't meet a dog's nutritional needs. However, you can't simply cut his regular meals in half either. Start by spreading his dinner out throughout the day and reduce his total intake by about 15 percent. If your large-breed dog normally gets three cups of food in the evening, start a new routine: one cup in the morning, one cup in the afternoon, and half a cup or a small handful at night.

Most dogs tend to burn more calories during the day, so try reducing and replacing a nighttime intake with a morning and daytime intake, giving him a better chance to burn those calories throughout the day. Discuss with your veterinarian just how much food needs to be eaten in a single day, and reduce gradually to achieve that amount. Quality of food will make a big difference as well. A dog will eat less of a better dog food than he will of a cheaper type that's made with more fillers than meats.

Your pudgy pal isn't going to be in any shape for a vigorous workout just yet, so keep everything moving along slowly. If you start out too fast you could be facing some painful consequences that will end up with poor Oscar on the sofa with sore joints for a few days.

Start with a short daily walk. A half an hour a day for a couple of days should be just about right, since too long will leave you with a sore dog and possibly sore feet. After you've both had time to adjust to the new walking routine, pick it up just a little bit. Increase to two half-hour walks daily, one in the morning and one at night, for a week or two. Then bring it up to three times a day, morning, afternoon, and evening.

Be sure to take it slowly, letting your dog get accustomed to each new stage of his routine. Rapid weight loss can be just as damaging as rapid weight gain. He should be losing no more than 5 to 8 percent of his starting weight each month. If the pounds start to come off too quickly, take him back to the veterinarian immediately as it could be an indication of more serious health problems.

**Sometimes we need to medicate our dogs at home.** One of my dogs was ridiculously easy to medicate; he ate everything like it was liver biscotti. My other two were not so easy. I had to get creative with them.

Hiding pills wrapped up in cheese or pushed into wieners only worked for a short time. Pouring powdered medicine in their water failed as well after the first time, but pouring the powder between two slices of cheese worked. After that debacle, I invested in a pill crusher, and I highly recommend them for all your dog's pilling needs.

Another great little device is a pill popper. Sold at most veterinary clinics for under $10, this nifty little gadget will be a lifesaver. Push the pill into the end of the wand, insert the wand (pill end first) into your dog's mouth, past his last molars, then eject the pill. It's that simple. You could also do this with your fingers, but some dogs I just wouldn't trust my fingers to; they tend to gnaw.

## Choosing a Veterinarian

When choosing a regular veterinarian, the most important thing is that he makes you feel comfortable, and gives you no reason to doubt his abilities and ethics. Like every other profession, there are great veterinarians and there are bad ones. If at any time you cease to feel comfortable with your chosen vet, do not hesitate to look for a new one.

**Location is an important factor when choosing a vet.**
Most medical emergencies are time sensitive, but after having lived in rural northwestern Ontario for the last sixteen years, I understand that it's not always easy to find a vet within a 100-kilometer radius, or if there is one closer to your home, it may be a clinic that you just are not comfortable with. These things happen. We can't all live in the city, so you have to do your best to find a vet that's somewhat local to your area. It comes down to how far you have to travel and what kind of emergency services are available. In my hometown, our local human hospital was allowed to treat pets on a first-response basis, so that the trip to the animal hospital could be made later (it was two hours away). However, we also had a veterinarian that set up a week-long clinic every third month in our small town, allowing people who could not travel a chance to have their pets checked, neutered, and vaccinated. Something similar may be available to you.

**Ask your pet-owning friends what vets they use.** Are they satisfied with the services they receive? If they aren't completely happy with their veterinarian, find out why. It may be something that you are willing to tolerate (such as location or prices).

Once you have a list of choices, phone the prospective clinics and ask questions about the services they provide. Do they have emergency services available? What do they charge for just an office visit or for outine vaccinations? Do they offer grooming and boarding services, and is this something that you even want in a veterinarian's clinic? If they do offer boarding services, is the clinic staffed on a twenty-four-hour basis?

Check with your state's veterinary medical board to see if your potential vet has had any complaints lodged against him or his practice recently.

Ask all potential clinics about their emergency services. Do they have any emergency or urgent-care services? What is the phone number of the nearest facility that does offer emergency care? Keep this number handy at all times. I keep mine on the fridge.

**Book your dog an appointment within the first week of bringing him home.** This will accomplish two things: your dog will have a good checkup and receive any vaccinations he'll be eligible for (see later on in this chapter), and you can find out about any area-specific issues that you may be dealing with, such as Lyme disease and Rocky Mountain spotted fever if your area is known for ticks. You will also be able to see how your new vet interacts with your new dog. Does the vet seem nervous or afraid of your dog for any reason? Does he speak in a soothing manner and handle your dog gently?

## Routine Veterinary Care

Every dog should visit his veterinarian at least once a year, whether he needs it or not. The annual exam will be the one where problems are diagnosed early, hopefully early enough to correct, or at least slow the process in some cases. Make sure your pet gets in to see a vet at least once a year, even if she has always been healthy, because prevention is so much better than cure.

Your vet will start the exam at your dog's nose and work all the way down to her tail. While checking your dog's nose for nasal discharge, your vet is looking for more than just a common runny nose. Rhinitis is a symptom of many possible diseases. Canine distemper or respiratory infections are just two of many possible causes.

Your dog's eyes are a vital part of the exam. A dog with dull eyes is giving off warning signals that something is wrong. Whoever said that eyes are windows to the soul was absolutely correct. If your pet's soul is dull, your pet needs help. Persistent eye snot could indicate an eye infection. Some eye infections are contagious to other pets as well as humans. It is important to catch an infection and clear it up early.

A mouthful of healthy teeth should look clean and white, and your vet will let you know if your dog needs a deep cleaning or if you need to step up the dental care at home. If your dog's jaw is lumpy, that may indicate swelling from an abscessed tooth, oral tumors, or an allergic reaction to a bug bite. And if his gums aren't looking very good and lack color, your dog may be suffering from anemia.

Ears are notorious for harboring bacteria that cause foul odors, and ear infections. A clean ear is a good ear, and it is a very good idea to keep alert for ear mites, a pesky inhabitant of ears that are highly contagious to other pets in the household.

Your vet will also listen to your dog's chest, checking for any sign of congestion. Chest congestion is a serious symptom of several illnesses, even a heartworm infestation.

**TOOLS YOU NEED**

▶ Every time you go to the vet's office, bring a notebook of things about your dog that have given you cause for concern over the last couple of months. I promise that your vet won't laugh at you or think it's a stupid question, and he'll be happy to answer any questions you have. It's worth the peace of mind to voice any concerns you may have, whether about small things that your vet can reassure you are normal or major issues that need to be investigated more thoroughly.

Listening to your dog's heart is an important step in the exam. His normal heart rate is 100 to 130 beats per minute. Any abnormality is cause for concern. Early detection of heart disease can help your dog live a longer, more comfortable life.

## Vaccinating Your Dog

Every dog needs to be vaccinated, and in the case of rabies vaccinations, it is the law. Your vet will discuss your dog's individual needs at your first appointment. Depending on your dog's age and medical history, she may only need boosters (given annually or less often); but she may need the entire first series if she came from a backyard breeder, pet store, or animal shelter (although some shelters include these first vaccines in the adoption fee). Your vet will tailor his vaccination recommendations to your location and your dog's situation.

The first series of vaccines should be given to all puppies around six weeks of age. It's usually given in combination with vaccines for four diseases: parvovirus, adenovirus, parainfluenza, and distemper. If coronavirus is prevalent in your area, it may be included in this set.

Parvovirus is a killer **viral** disease that is easily transmitted by the stool of infected animals. Older dogs have generally built up immunity to it, but puppies are extremely susceptible to this disease, hence it's nickname "the puppy killer." Its most noticeable symptoms are lethargic behavior, vomiting a clear and foamy liquid, and bloody diarrhea. Parvovirus is treatable, and puppies can survive this disease with antibiotics and intravenous fluids, but the mortality rate is higher for younger puppies.

Adenovirus is a highly infectious viral disease with two types. Type 1 is infectious canine hepatitis. Type 2 is a form of kennel cough. It is passed on through exposure to infected animals or contaminated feces or toys. Inhalation of mosquitoes or fleas carrying the virus can also be a cause.

Similar to the human cold virus, canine parainfluenza is a virus that causes respiratory infections. Highly contagious, it is transmitted by sneezing or coughing, so in a kennel, or multiple dog situations, this virus can run rampant.

Canine distemper virus is a contagious, and incurable, multisystemic viral disease that affects the respiratory, gastrointestinal, and central nervous systems. The virus is shed from the infected animal through bodily fluids, especially respiratory secretions. Airborne inhalants are the primary cause of transmission.

At twelve weeks of age, your puppy's first rabies vaccine is given. Your dog is required by law to have the rabies vaccine in Canada and the United States. Rabies is a completely fatal disease that attacks the central nervous system, and it can be passed to both animals and humans alike. Rabies is most often transmitted by the bite of an infected animal, but it has been passed by other body fluids as well. The rabies vaccine can be given annually, or every two or three years depending upon your state or province's legislation and the vaccine given.

Twelve weeks is also when the combination booster is given. At this age, leptospirosis, coronavirus, and Lyme disease vaccines may be administered if needed. If you will be boarding your dog in a multiple-dog facility, consult with your veterinarian about the bordetella inoculation.

Lyme disease is transmitted by the bite of infected ticks. Joint pain, a low fever, swollen joints, lethargy, and loss of appetite are the main symptoms of Lyme disease. Because Lyme disease is not common in all areas, ask your veterinarian if he feels a vaccination for it is necessary.

## Should You Spay or Neuter Your Dog?

If you aren't planning to title your dog in shows or competitions, then yes, your dog should be spayed or neutered. It's a very quick

▶ If you don't want to have to vaccinate your dog every year, ask about titer testing. This may be available to test your dog for the required immunity to certain diseases instead of revaccinating every year. Be aware, though, that titer tests are expensive and not available at every clinic. These tests are especially useful when your dog has shown a negative reaction to the vaccines in the past.

▶ If your dog is the type to scratch at his or her stitches, ask your vet about an Elizabethan collar. Yes, it really does look like a lampshade, and people might laugh at your dog for a couple of days, but it could save your dog some serious trouble if his or her stitches get infected. They don't cost very much, and once you have one, hang on to it because you never know when you might need it again.

procedure with a fast recovery time; your dog will back to his old self again in just a couple of days. When I had Loki neutered, he never even noticed. I had a hard time keeping him somewhat quiet for a couple of days after the procedure when all he wanted to do was run, leap over things, and climb. Luckily my other dogs were content with being sofa hounds for a few days after their procedure before returning to their normal exuberance.

**Male dogs are much nicer pets once they are neutered.** While the term neutering refers to the removal of the reproductive organs on both male and female animals, it's also a term used to describe an orchidectomy, the desexing of male animals by removing the testicles. Neutering male dogs is best done before six months of age to prevent or eliminate these behaviors and health concerns:

- Testicular cancer
- Prostate cancer
- Penile tumors
- Perineal hernias
- Urge to roam in search of females
- Hormone-induced aggression

Once a dog is neutered, his urge to mark his territory will be greatly reduced as well. You will find that your dog is a much calmer, happier pet when he isn't being controlled by his hormones.

**The neutering procedure is very safe.** It is an all-day affair though (for your dog), and since he'll be under anesthetic, make sure you ask beforehand if your dog needs to fast for twelve hours prior to his appointment. The actual surgery itself is not a long procedure, but if you have an early morning appointment, you still don't get your dog back until late afternoon as your dog will require a bit of time to recover from the anesthetic.

You'll need to try to keep him quiet for the next few days, if that's possible at all, and out of the water. If you notice any testicular swelling, bring him back to your vet's right away. You probably won't see any change in your dog at all for a while. He likely won't even notice that his testicles are missing, and he probably won't slow down much either. Most dogs treat neutering like it was a walk in the park.

He'll start to settle down more over the next couple of months as his hormones settle. Don't expect a huge change right away; it will be several weeks at least before you'll notice anything. He'll just gradually stop marking his territory, won't be so inclined to run off, and other males just won't be such a big deal anymore. An easing up of his tense personality will be noticeable eventually.

**It's best for female dogs to be spayed before their first heat.** This is typically before six months of age. With her reproductive organs gone, your bitch will be in for a much smoother adulthood. Ovariohysterectomies eliminate these problems altogether:

- Breast cancer: If she is spayed before her first heat, the future risk of her developing mammary tumors is gone
- False pregnancies
- Pyometra and other uterine infections
- Ovarian and uterine tumors
- Real, accidental pregnancy and all the risks involved with that condition
- Hormone-induced aggression and roaming tendencies

**ASK YOUR GUIDE**

*Will my dog get fat and lazy if I neuter him?*

▶ As long as your dog receives the amount of exercise he needs on a daily basis and you aren't overfeeding him, he won't get fat and lazy at all. All that will be gone from your dog is the desire to mate, not his desire to run and play, so don't go and hang up the Chuckit! yet.

- Estrus: With her heat cycle eliminated entirely, your bitch will be a much more settled pet, and you won't have male dogs beating down the doors when she's in heat

**Spaying is a much more invasive procedure than an orchidectomy.** Female dogs have their entire reproductive system removed: uterus and ovaries. She'll definitely not be feeling quite the thing when you pick her up after her daytrip to the vet's for this surgery. Your vet may also suggest an Elizabethan collar for the next couple of days so that she doesn't pick at her stitches. You shouldn't have any trouble keeping her quiet for the next week to ten days.

If you spay your bitch before her first eostrus cycle (heat cycle), you likely won't notice very much of a difference in her. The eostrus cycle puts a lot of stress on the dog's body, and you'll have prevented that and everything that goes along with it, like the snarly mood swings and messiness.

**Pet overpopulation is one of the greatest reasons to have all your pets sterilized.** Pet population numbers are booming. The numbers of pets in shelters are overwhelming. Every year, four to five million healthy and adoptable dogs are euthanized in animal shelters in North America. It's hard to believe it, but some people seem to think that this doesn't affect them. They allow their unneutered dog to run free and produce puppies willy-nilly. Every dog owner that thinks her precious, unspayed poodle will be safe from roaming males is taking a big risk. Impregnation can happen before you can stop it, and the resulting puppies will just add to the ever-growing numbers of unwanted dogs. Please have your dog spayed or neutered.

## Get Linked

*You'll find a lot of useful maintenance and preventative care tips on my About.com Dogs Web site. These are my most popular ones.*

**YOUR DOG'S MENTAL HEALTH**

Keeping your dog in good mental and emotional health is as important as his physical health. Learn the signs of trouble, and how to help your dog overcome any problem he might have.
http://about.com/dogs/mentalhealth

**FREQUENT FLATULENCE?**

If your best friend can clear a room in minutes, you need to sit down and have a look at what the problem might be. Diet is often the cause of this dilemma, but there are solutions to this putrid problem.
http://about.com/dogs/flatulence

**PUSHING MAXIMUM DENSITY**

For the fat dogs in our lives, here are some healthy tips to taking the extra pounds off safely.
http://about.com/dogs/weightloss

## Chapter 4

# Your Dog's Diet

## Canine Nutrition

Good nutrition is essential to good health. Building strong bones and tissue early on in life will help to prevent many problems that commonly occur later on in life. Osteoarthritis, gastrointestinal disorders, and other joint diseases are all linked to poor nutrition. Good nutrition keeps your dog healthy by boosting his immune system, which helps him fight infections and illnesses.

There is some debate as to whether dogs are omnivores (can eat everything) or carnivores (mainly meat eaters). My own opinion is that they belong firmly in the carnivore camp and require a diet made of mostly meat products, supplemented with nutrients from vegetable sources, in order to stay healthy.

**Proteins are what will help your dog build tissue.** Proteins are made up of amino acids and are found in meats, poultry, and some plant matter. A dog's body produces some of the amino acids it needs, but it must get the rest of the ten essential amino acids from its food. Most meat proteins are complete, containing all of the essential amino acids; plant proteins are incomplete, so they can't be a sole source of protein in your dog's diet.

Dogs need different amounts of proteins at different stages of their lives.

### PERCENTAGE OF PROTEIN NEEDED

| Dog Age/Stage | Protein Amount |
| --- | --- |
| Puppy | 28% |
| Adult | 18% |
| Athlete | 25–35% |
| Pregnant or nursing | 28% |

*Proteins are necessary for your dog to gain strength and muscle.*

**Carbohydrates are part of what gives your dog energy.** Found mostly in cereal grains in dog foods, the starchy portions of rice, corn, oats, barley, and wheat are soluble carbohydrates that have been cooked or extruded and are easily digestible. Raw forms of these carbohydrates are slow to digest, or even indigestible in some forms. Most dry dog foods on the market are made of about 50 percent carbohydrates. Foods that are advertised as "high energy" contain higher percentages than foods marketed for weight control or seniors.

**Fats are also essential nutrients.** Poultry fat, cottonseed oil, and vegetable oils are common forms of fats used in most dog foods. Fats contain more than twice the amount of energy than proteins and carbohydrates and are a source of natural flavor. Fats provide insulation and cushioning for internal organs. Too much fat can lead to obesity, diabetes, and heart disease, but too little results in a dull coat and dry, itchy skin. Any reduced-fat diet should include a fatty-acid supplement to avoid those problems.

## PERCENTAGE OF RECOMMENDED FATS

| Dog Age/Stage | Fat Amount |
| --- | --- |
| Puppy | 17% |
| Adult | 10–15% |
| Athlete | 20–50% |
| Pregnant or nursing | 17% |

*Fats can make dog food taste better but can't replace proteins and carbohydrates.*

**Fiber is an insoluble carbohydrate.** Fiber comes from the cell walls of grains and plants, and it can't be absorbed by the body. Fiber in pet food comes mainly from corn, rice and soybean hulls, bran, beet pulp, and some starches that are indigestible. Fiber is essential to a dog's digestive system. It adds bulk in the small intestine and helps the stool pass normally, preventing both diarrhea and constipation.

## Age-Appropriate Foods

Just as human babies can't eat the solid foods adults eat, puppies require a different diet from adult dogs. The same principle applies to senior dogs, which have different dietary needs than younger dogs.

**Foods formulated for puppies are tailored to fit a growing body.** Puppies burn a lot of energy throughout the day from playing and growing, and it's important to keep up with their bodies' changes while not overloading it. Puppies grow incredibly fast

ELSEWHERE ON THE WEB

▶ If you live somewhere that you can't get a lot of dog food brands without traveling a fair distance (like me), then www.petfooddirect.com might be your answer. They have a large selection of dog food brands, even special order brands, and will ship directly to your door. Use the auto-ship feature to ensure that your dog food bin is always well stocked.

during their first year and it's no surprise they use up their bodies' resources quickly. A growing puppy needs a dog food that has a protein content of at least 28 percent, and a fat content of 10 percent or greater (but not more than 18 percent).

It's actually possible for a food to promote growth too quickly. Large-breed puppies can grow their bodies faster than their bones can keep up with. If this happens, bone density is compromised, which can lead to early osteoarthritis, hip dysplasia, and other bone disorders. Ask your dog's breeder, or your veterinarian, if your bigger-breed puppy needs to be placed on a special diet with less of the proteins and fats found in most puppy food. Some of the larger commercial dog food companies, such as Hill's Science Diet and Iams, offer a line of dog food made specifically for large-breed puppies that includes supplements like calcium for bone growth.

On the flip side of that, small-breed pups need to have food that is tailored to their size, in both the size of the individual pieces and in what those pieces contain. Because small breeds have small mouths, a dry dog food must be small enough for the puppy to easily chew and swallow. These pups also have stomachs that can't hold very much, so the amounts that they do eat must contain all the nutrients that the puppy needs. Foods formulated for small breeds have higher nutrient density in every bite than regular or large-breed puppy food.

**Your adult dog's needs change as his lifestyle changes.**
Dogs that are used for working or are in dog sports are going to need to a high-calorie food that keeps their energy up. Dogs that lead a more sedentary life won't need as many calories so their food is better off with more fiber and less fats and proteins.

Food formulated to help rotund dogs lose some excess weight is usually made with fewer fats and proteins, and more fiber.

▶ Suggesting that each individual breed has its own requirements, dog food manufacturers have come out with lines catering to specific subgroups of dogs. We've had "size" foods available for a few years now, but don't be surprised to see a breed-specific food on the shelves. A different offering for every dog breed is not available yet, but dog food companies are starting to target a few breeds in each group. Whether your dog needs its own breed food or not is something you'll have to discuss with your veterinarian or breeder.

Commercial low-fat and weight-loss diets are widely available, but most run-of-the-mill supermarket brands don't have enough of some nutrients your dog needs and are made mostly of corn with very little actual meat protein. Prescription weight-loss diets are available, but only when they are bought through a veterinarian's office. The bottom line is: Seek veterinary counseling about what your pudgy pooch actually needs for nutrition and work out a good weight-loss plan with your vet before resorting to weight-loss foods.

Performance dogs that work all day long, be it sports or jobs like dog-sledding, search and rescue, or herding, need to be on a diet that is full of high-energy proteins, fats, and carbohydrates. Their bodies will metabolize food quickly, and they'll use large amounts of energy throughout the day, so a diet geared for working dogs is best. Most of the better-quality dog food brands, such as Diamond, Eagle Pack, and Chicken Soup, all have foods made especially for the working dog.

Prescription diets are available from veterinarian offices to help control certain medical problems, or help prevent them if a breed is prone to a certain condition. Bladder stones can be controlled to a certain extent by the type of diet a dog eats. One of the prescription diets available through a veterinarian is made for dogs with bladder stone problems. A vet may also recommend a prescription diet if your dog is diabetic, has congestive heart failure, or has severe weight problems.

Pregnant and nursing bitches need all the extra calories and energy they can get, so feeding a dog food made for growing puppies will suit her needs better than a regular adult dog food.

**Senior dogs require different types of nutrients in their diets.** The aging body has started to slow down, and this changes what an older dog should be eating on a regular basis. Most senior dog formulas of dog food are made with less protein and additional nutrients and vitamins, such as glucosamine sulphate (to help joint tissue stay strong and supple), extra fiber, and other digestive aids to help your dog process his food better.

Unless he can keep up with it, your older dog has no need to be on a high-calorie, maximum-performance diet. Some older dogs still act like puppies, though, and if your dog is one of them, there is no need to put your dog on a senior's diet.

## How Diet Affects Your Dog's Health

It's true that dogs can eat just about anything, but just because they can doesn't mean they should. Dogs need a steady diet that covers all of their nutritional needs or their bodies start to fail, just like yours would. A lack of protein in your dog's food will cause his tissues to break down, and his immune system will not be able to fight off even the weakest of illnesses. Too little fat and your dog's coat will lose its luster; his skin will dry out, flake, and be more susceptible to painful skin disorders. He'll also lose the ability to adjust his body temperature, making him more prone to heatstroke or hypothermia.

**Your dog will tell you in loud ways that his diet isn't working for him.** Often a poor appearance in general is directly caused by your dog's diet, whether it is from a lack of essential nutrients or an overabundance of certain items.

A dull coat and eyes may indicate either a parasite problem (see Chapter 10) or a lack of fatty acids. If you are feeding a low-fat or weight-loss formula of dog food, add a fatty-acid supplement to the diet. Dry and brittle nails are also caused by a lack of fats. A lack of vitamins in your dog's diet can wreak havoc on his entire

**TOOLS YOU NEED**

▶ Most kids have a bad habit of feeding dogs right off their plates, or tossing them whatever they see in the refrigerator. If you have older children, or have somebody who comes on a regular basis to watch your dog, it's a good idea to keep a list of forbidden foods on the refrigerator where it's highly visible. Mushrooms, onions, chocolate, raisins, grapes, and milk (and other dairy products) can cause your dog serious health problems and possibly even death.

body, causing weight loss, a weakened immune system, respiratory problems, and heart and brain disorders.

**Changing his food could make a world of difference.** If your dog isn't doing well on his current regular dog food, it doesn't necessarily mean that the food is of a poor quality. It means that it's not the right food for your dog.

Unfortunately, dogs can't sample different foods the same way we humans can. They need to be gradually switched to a new food, which should be given a trial of at least two months to see if it makes a change in your dog's health. Most people get frustrated after only a couple of weeks and start to try several different brands, leaving them with a dog who is finicky, has regular soft stools, nearly fatal (for the humans) gas, and still not in the condition it should be in.

Don't make the same mistake. Your first order of business should be a trip to the veterinarian's to rule out any nondietary causes. Your vet may be able to recommend a diet that suits your dog's needs better. If you don't want to stick with what he recommends (although you really should), ask around for a food that is similar to what he recommends in both ingredients and the nutrient profile. Change over to the new dog food gradually, and give it at least two months before deciding that it's not working. Ask other dog owners to see if their dog may have suffered the same problems and what they recommend. You can also consult a veterinary nutritionist or holistic veterinarian, to help you choose a supplement that your dog may need to cover a hole in his food's nutritional content.

**Dietary supplements can confuse the average dog owner.** The most common supplements that are recommended

ASK YOUR GUIDE

*Are table scraps okay for dogs?*

▸ Some table scraps, in a moderate amount, will not hurt your dog, but it does encourage bad behavior like begging and digging in the garbage. If you want to give your dog your leftovers, make sure that it's food that is safe for him to eat (not all food is), and beware of gas later on.

ELSEWHERE ON THE WEB

▶ Here's a good article from the FDA *Consumer Magazine*: "Pet Food: The Lowdown on Labels" by Linda Bren (www.fda.gov/fdac/features/2001/301_pet.html). Offering an in-depth look at pet food labels, Linda covers just about everything a dog owner would want to know about the food he's buying and what he's putting into his dog. She also goes into health claims made by pet food companies and what they really mean to you as a dog owner.

by veterinarians are glucosamine and chondroitin sulfate for dogs with all kinds of joint problems. Even if your dog hasn't started feeling his age, your vet may recommend that your senior dog start taking these supplements. Both of these supplements promote tissue repair in dogs and prevent damage caused by stress and age. Omega fatty acids are good for the skin and coat, keeping skin soft, supple, and well moisturized from the inside.

Your dog may also require a supplemented diet if he is lacking essential nutrients in his regular diet due to dietary restrictions such as allergies or food intolerances (they are not the same thing). This is something your vet will tell you at your dog's check-up.

**Can dogs be vegetarians?**   Dogs in the wild don't eat much vegetation. Most of any plant matter they ingest comes from the stomach contents of the prey animals, herbivores like deer, birds, and other small animals. They may snack on the odd berry bush or fallen apple, but on the whole won't choose to eat fruits and vegetation on their own.

I do not believe that a strictly vegan (meaning no animal products at all) diet is a healthy choice for dogs. Not only does it not provide the complete proteins that a dog's body needs to reach its full potential, I feel that forcing a carnivorous animal to be an herbivore is denying its essential being. If a person does not want a meat-eater as a pet then that person should stick to birds, goats, and other herbivores. When it comes to responsible dog ownership, you should adjust to fit your dog's needs, not adjust your dog to fit your ideals.

There are rare cases of a dog having an allergy or intolerance to a meat source. Viable options in this case would be a fish-based food, such as Natural Balance Fish and Sweet Potato, or Halshan Fish With Vegetables. Often it is a type of meat that a dog is allergic or intolerant to, so switching to a different meat source may also alleviate the problem.

## Dog Food Labels at a Glance

The first thing you should look for when selecting a dog food is a Nutritional Adequacy Statement. This is the most important thing that should be on any commercially produced dog food. This guarantees the consumer that the food will meet his pet's nutritional requirements. Usually located next to the Guaranteed Analysis, the Nutritional Adequacy Statement should state that this food is "complete and balanced" and has been formulated to meet or exceed the nutritional guidelines established by the Association of American Feed Control Officials (AAFCO).

The second part of your dog food's label is the name. Let's say we have Bark Doggy Dog brand dog food and all its assorted flavors. "Bark Doggy Dog" is the brand name, not necessarily the manufacturer. Manufacturers often have several brand names that they produce. For example, Proctor & Gamble is the manufacturer that produces the brand names Iams and Eukanuba. You can usually find the manufacturer information at the bottom of the ingredient list, often as the last item in the label.

The AAFCO has certain rules regarding how a pet food is named and labeled. These rules give you, the consumer, some protection from blatantly misleading labels. As you can see in the following list, the difference in the wording is very subtle. One change in the order of the words in the name can mean a big difference in ingredients. The following rules exclude moisture content; they pertain to the solid parts only.

- **Chicken for dogs:** Chicken has top billing in this name, and it's not paired with any other words that throw the

**ASK YOUR GUIDE**

*I can't afford premium-quality food. Can't I just feed cheap stuff?*

▶ You can, but you'll probably spend the same amount of money anyway. Cheap dog food is made up mostly of fillers, like corn products, requiring your dog to eat a lot more of it in order to meet his needs. A better-quality dog food will meet those needs with less food, so you could be buying two or three bags of cheap stuff to match one bag of better stuff.

▶ For anybody considering a raw diet for their dog and thinking of making it themselves, I recommend the book *Dr. Pitcairn's Complete Guide to Natural Health for Dogs and Cats*, by Richard H. Pitcairn, D.V.M., Ph.D. and Susan Hubble Pitcairn. It goes into great detail about the benefits of feeding a natural diet, and it has recipes that are properly balanced and meet your dog's nutritional requirements.

meaning off. In order to meet the AAFCO regulations, this dog food must actually be 95 percent chicken.

- **Turkey and chicken dog food:** By calling it turkey and chicken dog food (and nothing else), you are safe expecting that this dog food is made up of 95 percent turkey and chicken combined with the chicken content being slightly less than the turkey (as turkey is listed first).
- **Chicken nuggets for dogs:** Things get a little tricky here. Because this name has the word nuggets in its title, the chicken in the food is going to be less than 95 percent of the total ingredients, but it must be at least 25 percent. Nuggets is a qualifier that many dog food companies can use. Other qualifying words that let companies get away with less meat are dinner, formula, and platter. It's really important to watch the ingredient list; you may notice that a food with this name doesn't even have any chicken in the top three ingredients!
- **Chicken-flavor dog food:** The word flavor makes all the difference here. According to the AAFCO regulations, there must only be enough chicken to add an actual flavor to the dog food. It could be chicken fat or chicken broth, or chicken byproducts, and it could be a very small amount.
- **Dog food with chicken:** Dog foods "with" anything must only contain 3 percent of that item. So a dog food with chicken or with beef must only have at least 3 percent of chicken or beef in the ingredients. What a difference the order of words makes!

## Choosing a Dog Food

There are four main types of dog food available for the discerning dog owner. Your dog can eat raw food, home-cooked meals, grocery store fare (canned or dry), or special-order gourmet meals (home-cooked meals that you buy from a supplier). Most of these will keep your dog growing and healthy. Commercially prepared dog food that is presented as a "complete and balanced" meal will have met the pet food standards that are regulated by AAFCO.

It's an oft-repeated truth: You will get out what you put into your dog. If you put in time and effort, you will get a dog that shows that you put in time and effort. If you put in cheap, filler-laden food, that's what you will get back out of your dog, only—lots of it, complete with lots of smell. There are hundreds of dog food manufacturers out there, so how do you sort out the cheap from the haute cuisine? It used to come down to price: If it was cheap, it was cheaply made and worth exactly what you paid for it, and the more expensive it was, the better it was, period. It's not like that anymore. Now you have small family owned businesses preparing and marketing their own brand of dog food, and these mom-and-pop businesses may be able to sell their product at a low price while still using quality ingredients. Other companies are using alternative meats that may be cheaper than the standard beef, chicken, and lamb.

**Ingredients in dog food are listed by weight.** The heaviest item is listed first, and each subsequent item weighs less than the item before it. So you just pick whichever food has meat listed first, right? Well, it's not quite that easy. If chicken is listed first, followed by corn, corn meal, and corn flour, then the corn products probably outweigh the chicken by quite a bit. Try to find a dog food that has meat as the first ingredient with at least two of the next four ingredients a meat product, too.

Don't be fooled by a meat "byproduct." Those are the leftovers after the meat has been stripped off a carcass. Byproducts usually consist of hooves, feet, eyes, skin, and heads. This should never be the first ingredient of a dog food.

ELSEWHERE ON THE WEB

▶ Making your own dog food is a tricky business and not an option I recommend for the beginner. You'll need to learn what is nutritionally required by your dog at each stage of his life and how to incorporate those elements into a daily diet. This link has a good starting recipe for an average dog: www.charles loopsdvm.com/dogdiet.htm. In addition, I really recommend reading the entire Pet Grub Web site at www.pet-grub.com if you want to learn about how and why people feed their dogs "people food."

ELSEWHERE ON THE WEB

▶ Jane Anderson's Raw Learning Web site ([www.rawlearning.com](www.rawlearning.com)) is a fantastic resource for anybody who wants to learn more about the raw food diet. She has quite a few important pages for the beginner, including information on feeding fish to your dog and supplementing your dog's food. Raw feeding is such a controversial subject, and she acknowledges this fact with a section of articles that oppose raw feeding and her responses to their claims. I found this to be the most interesting part of this Web site.

**Is dry dog food better than canned?** Canned dog food looks better, smells tastier, is easier to eat, and I'm willing to bet that it tastes better than dry dog food too, but that doesn't make it better for your dog. He may think so, but luckily, we humans aren't that easily swayed by a pair of pleading brown eyes.

Nutrient for nutrient, canned and dry dog food are generally pretty equal. But canned dog food is expensive, and your dog needs to eat a lot of more of it in order to meet his required daily intake since canned dog food consists of a lot more water than actual solid food. For this reason, and the fact that dry dog food is just easier to handle and store, I prefer dry dog food over canned any day.

**Semidry, or semimoist, dog food is another food option.** Dogs like it because it tastes better than other foods, and owners like it because it lasts longer than wet dog food and is often sold in single-serving packets. The convenience factor is nice, but these foods are often high in sugars and preservatives, making them less than ideal to feed on a regular basis. The price is often prohibitive, too.

**By making your own dog food, you know exactly what goes in it.** However, it's hard to get the right balance of ingredients. Commercial dry dog foods have a wealth of vitamins and minerals added that your dog needs to be healthy. Any diet that you cook for your dog will have to have these additives as well, and if you don't know what you are doing, you could make your dog very ill.

Raw diets are mostly made up of raw, meaty bones, specifically turkey and chicken. Yes, the dogs eat the bones too. Cooked bones can splinter easily, so never give your dog a cooked bone. Raw bones are soft and chewy and are easily ground up in your dog's teeth. It is believed that a diet resembling a wild canid's improves a dog's overall health and well-being. Dogs certainly enjoy eating a whole lot more when there are a variety of tastes and smells to go along with their dinner; who wouldn't get sick of the same thing, day after day? In general, natural foods are just better than foods that are loaded with preservatives and chemicals, as many commercial dog foods are.

Fear that a dog will suddenly develop a "taste for flesh" and the squeamish factor prevents a lot of people from investigating the raw, meaty diet for themselves. Old beliefs die hard, and the thought of a bone puncturing a dog's intestinal wall is also a huge fear of many dog owners. It is a valid fear, and it's a risk that many are not willing to take. Unfortunately, there are no hard statistics to waylay this fear either, so it continues its hold in people's minds. As with most things, we hear about the few dogs that have died from punctured bowels, but not the many that lived long and happy lives on a raw diet.

If you can't or don't want to make it yourself, you can buy it. There are a number of small "kitchens" that make and sell both home-cooked dog foods and raw diet foods.

## Feeding Your Dog

Every dog is different. I have been repeating this mantra since my second dog came to live with me and I discovered that food couldn't be left out. No more free feeding; I had to pick up the food bowls or Loki would eat his food and Oscar's (and the rest of the bag, too, if it happened to be within reach).

Some dogs want to graze throughout the day, grabbing a mouthful of food every now and then but never overeating. These dogs would prefer to be free feeders. Some dogs will scarf down an entire meal in one sitting and be satisfied until the next meal, while others will eat whatever isn't nailed down.

**Your dog should be eating a whole meal all at once.** If he's a grazer, you should condition him to eat full meals by removing

**TOOLS YOU NEED**

▶ I recommend a good cookbook, like *Dog Food: A Canine Cuisine* by Kathleen Stacey, Kathleen Lepage, Deborah Lepage, and Stacey Lepage, if you are planning to feed your dog homemade meals. You will need to know which foods are toxic to dogs and what elements should be in every meal. This book tells you which foods to avoid, has a variety of easy-to-cook recipes, and provides a few cookie recipes, too.

*Should I worry that my dog is not eating?*

▶ Dogs do decide to skip meals on occasion for no reason that we humans know of. One or two skipped meals are not a big deal. It's not a cause for concern unless he goes for several days without eating at all, at which point you really need to bring him to a veterinarian.

the food bowl after twenty minutes. Don't give it back to him until it's time for the next meal. It's best if dogs eat actual meals as opposed to free-feed grazing. This way you can easily tell if he is off his feed. It's easier to adjust how much food he gets as well if he starts to become over- or underweight. (See Chapter 3 for weight control help.) If your dog loses weight, your veterinarian needs to see him. He may need to just eat more or more of a higher-quality food, or he may have a serious health problem.

**Your puppy should be fed three or four times a day.** These should be small meals, no more than he can eat in about five minutes, spaced at regular times throughout the day. Your pup is growing fast and needs frequent feedings to keep up with his body's demands. Feeding on a strict time schedule will help you housetrain by creating a predictable elimination pattern. Approximately twenty-five to thirty minutes after your pup has eaten is prime time to bring him outside for a potty break. Don't forget your treats to reinforce his elimination in the right place. (See Chapter 7 for housetraining tips.)

**Your adult dog should be fed twice a day.** Try not to feed right before bedtime; your dog needs a chance to use up the energy the food gives him. Higher-quality dog food made of real meats is digested faster than a cheap variety made of mostly corn and grains, which means your dog gets the energy sooner. Adjust your dog's feeding schedule accordingly, and you won't have a dog that wants to go for a marathon run at two o'clock in the morning. A good dog food may have your dog invigorated two or three hours later, whereas a poorer quality may not energize your dog until ten hours later.

**Don't let your dog get picky.** If he refuses to eat there may be a legitimate reason, but he may also just be waiting to see if something better is going to come along. Leave the food out for a day, and if he still does not eat, it may be time for a checkup. Even picky eaters will eat if they get hungry enough, so a continued refusal to eat is a sign of trouble.

**Dogs that eat too fast are in danger of bloating.** You can slow your dog down by spreading his dry kibble out on a cookie sheet, instead of a bowl, so he can't grab large mouthfuls at a time. You can also place a heavy ball in the center of the bowl that he will have to eat around.

Bloat is caused by air trapped in the stomach that your dog can't properly eject. Eating too quickly is one way your dog can swallow a lot of air, but slowing him down isn't the only way you can help prevent him from bloating. Don't exercise your dog immediately after he has eaten. Always wait at least one hour before taking him out to play, and don't jump right into vigorous exercise, build up to it gradually. Raising your dog's dishes off the floor if you have a tall dog will also help prevent him from gulping air.

**Don't change your dog's usual food more than necessary.** Whenever you decide to change your dog's food, do so gradually. Switching foods without a weaning off of the old will give your dog an upset stomach, diarrhea, and gas. Mix a little bit of the new food in with the old food until it has gradually replaced the old food over a week's time.

In general, rearranging your dog's feeding schedule won't cause much trouble. Just make sure that you remember to adjust your exercise and potty-break schedules to match. If you change the usual time you feed your dog, you'll need to remember to take her outside at the appropriate times for this new schedule.

**Your dog may choose his own location to eat.** Raider picks up his entire food dish and carries it to wherever I am so that he may bask in my gloriousness while he eats. Well, really he just likes the company. Usually I'm in the same place the kids are, and he always hopes we'll drop something tasty in his direction. Your dog may do this, or he may choose Kari's method, which is to bring over a mouthful of food at a time and drop it on the carpet by your chair to be eaten at his leisure. If your dog chooses either of these methods or something similar, you should just give in gracefully and feed him wherever you are. Some dogs just like to have dinner company.

## Get Linked

*Dog food is a complex subject that sometimes reads like a foreign language. If you're looking for more in-depth information on the topics covered in this chapter, check out the following links to my About. com site.*

**THE DOG FOOD INDEX**

An alphabetical index of dog foods from commercial companies, holistic suppliers, and more, listing the ingredients and analysis of each brand name. Foods are constantly added as I find new information.

 http://about.com/dogs/foodindex

**STORING DOG FOOD**

If you buy in large quantities to save money, you need a good place to store your dog food to keep it safe from bugs and moisture. These are the cheap and practical solutions for storing dog food over long periods of time.

 http://about.com/dogs/foodstorage

## Chapter 5
# Keeping Fit

## Canine Exercise Needs

Every dog needs daily exercise. Even dogs that are billed as couch potatoes need to get outside and run around at least twice a day for a half hour. For most dogs, a walk around the block a few times isn't going to be enough. Enough exercise will keep your dog out of trouble, and in peak condition.

Dogs love to run, even the little ones. The average dog needs an hour of good, vigorous exercise every day. That's only an average, though; some breeds and mixes will need a good deal more than one hour, and some dogs will be content with less. Hunting dogs that are bred to track game over great distances will need a good hour of hard exercise at least twice a day. Great Danes, however, are happy with a short run twice a day, with a good-sized walk in between.

Regular and vigorous exercise every day strengthens your dog's muscles, and keeps his joints limber and strong. By keeping your dog's body healthy now, you will help prevent many problems when she is older:

▶ If you work long hours and
can't get home to give your
dog a good run and playtime
every day, you may want to
look into the many pet care
and dog walking services that
will do this for you. DogOn
Fitness at www.dogonfitness.
com is just one of many pro-
viders available all over the
country. This isn't a cheap
option, though, and you miss
out on fun times with your
dog. Still, it's there if you
need it.

- Keeping bones and joints strong and healthy will help prevent osteoarthritis and other joint diseases.
- Increasing her heart rate gets the blood flowing faster throughout her body and helps prevent later occurrences of heart disease.
- Physical exertion forces her lungs to expand fully, strengthening them, and better oxygenating her blood as it flows throughout her body.
- By maintaining a healthy weight, your dog won't put extra stress on his joints and bones, possibly saving her from arthritis in the future.

**Dogs need exercise to stay happy.**   Proper exercise will not only help your dog stay physically fit, it will also keep your dog content and emotionally and mentally healthy. Physical exertion releases endorphins into the body that give the dog a natural high and make her happy.

A lack of sufficient exercise can cause a lot of trouble for your dog, and you too. Believe it or not, boredom is what lands a lot of dogs in shelters. Bored dogs dig up yards, bark constantly, and even rip houses apart. A bored dog can cause all kinds of problems for his owners. Aside from the destruction of the owner's personal property, there are complaining neighbors to deal with, too. More than half of a dog's behavior problems can be helped by making sure the dog has enough exercise and things to keep him occupied throughout the day.

**Lack of exercise is at the root of some physical problems as well.**   Dogs aren't born lazy and overweight, but they can grow that way. Some breeds are more prone to laziness if they aren't used to getting a lot of exercise from the start. Basset hounds and dachshunds are two breeds I frequently see with severe weight problems.

Dogs that have joint problems really need to be watched carefully and kept on a strict exercise regimen. Once they start to gain weight because they aren't moving enough, it becomes a vicious cycle. The extra weight puts added pressure on their joints, which causes them pain. The pain makes it harder for them to get up and be active, and we owners feel bad about making them move so we don't. And the weight goes up. And we don't want to make him hurt by forcing him to exercise. Until one day you're trying to justify your dog's weight to your veterinarian when he tells you your dog had a heart attack that could have been prevented, if he had had enough exercise.

## Different Exercise for Different Ages

"A tired dog is a good dog." A very true saying, but too much of a good thing, or the wrong types of exercise, could bring injury to your dog. What size your dog is, how old he is, and what breeds he is made up of will all dictate what type of exercise he should and should not do.

**Puppies should avoid strenuous activity of all types.** Don't laugh! I know they run, jump, and generally play hard, but too much stress on growing bones can cause them to grow incorrectly and cause joint issues that will affect them throughout their lifetime. Jumping off of surfaces that are higher than the puppy's belly, jogging, leaping, and twisting movements can all damage your growing pup's bone and joint structure. Save these exercises until your veterinarian assures you that your dog has stopped growing up (dogs reach their adult height at different ages but continue to fill out overall for a time after). For larger dogs this may be as late

**TOOLS YOU NEED**

▶ Floating dog toys are great for the dog that likes to retrieve and swim. I particularly like the Combat toys from Bamboo Pet. We use the Combat Extreme Toss n' Pull Dog Toy on our outings at the lake. The tethered ball on the end of the floating bar makes it a breeze to throw a good distance, and the bright red color makes it easy to spot on the water.

as eighteen months of age, but patience now will reward you with a physically sound and stable dog later.

**Even adult dogs need some thought put into how they exercise.** Size and shape play a large role in your dog's capabilities. Very small dogs can break bones and strain muscles just from jumping off of a sofa, or out of people's arms. Dogs that are that small can't handle jogging beside you, or leaping over hurdles taller than they are. Long and low-slung dogs, like basset hounds and dachshunds shouldn't be doing any serious jumping either. Dogs that are tall and leggy, like borzoi, are built to run short distances at high speeds and can leap over obstacles as tall as they are with ease. Stocky, muscular dogs, such as an Alaskan malamute or an American bulldog, have the stamina to handle long distances, but at a moderate pace.

**Older dogs may start to slow down and experience some discomfort during exercise.** If your older dog is reluctant to jump up to play right away, it's time to tone down your usual playtime. Jumping games and long runs might not be a good thing for her at this stage of her life. You'll need to watch your dog for signs that your regular activities are getting to be too much. If they are, it doesn't need to signal the end of your recreational time, it just means that something less vigorous is desired, like longer walks instead of short and fast runs, or more swimming instead of hurdle jumping.

## Weather Concerns

Match your dog's activity to the weather. A marathon run on the hottest day of the year is asking for trouble. Dogs can overheat quickly when it's hot out, so be sure to keep any activity moderate but more often, and have plenty of shade and water on hand. Playing fetch in the water at a lake is the perfect thing to do when the temperature rises. It will keep you both cool—your dog as she swims to retrieve what you have thrown, and you when she comes out of the water and shakes her coat dry all over you.

Winter has its own special hazards. Running over ice can cause momentary slips that will strain muscles and joints. Cruciate ligament ruptures can occur when your dog twists his leg, and it requires expensive surgery to correct. Ice can gather and stick to the fur between the pads on the bottom of your dog's paws, making walking uncomfortable. Sharp edges in the ice and hard snow can cut up the pads of your dog's feet, too. These things can really make your dog reluctant to walk or play in the snow. Specially made dog boots will protect your dog's paws, and it won't take your dog long at all to get used to wearing them. They will also provide better traction if you walk in icy conditions.

Always supervise your dog when she's playing outside, no matter what the weather, and be sure that she has plenty of fresh water to drink at all times. You also can't expect that your dog will be able to run a marathon after lounging around and taking only sedate walks for a month, or even during the week. Dogs need to build up gradually to strenuous exercise. If your dog goes from zero to sixty right away, she can wind up with sprained joints or arthritis, and it will increase her chances of coming down with canine hip dysplasia.

Swimming is a great activity that works well for staying fit without straining muscles and joints. This makes it an ideal activity for all dogs, young and old. Dogs do drown though, so you need to take some precautions. Dog lifejackets are available from most sports outfitters and online retailers, and you should never take your dog swimming in fast-moving rivers or areas of the ocean with a strong current.

**ASK YOUR GUIDE**

*Are dog sweaters just for looks, or does a dog actually need to be kept warm?*

▶ Items like dog sweaters are both cute and useful! Dogs with very short coats don't tolerate cold temperatures very well, so getting enough outdoor exercise in the winter can be tough—frostbite is a real danger. Keep your dog warm with sweaters made just for dogs and her paws toasty with dog booties, and she won't be so reluctant to go outside in the snow. Keep her moving and she'll stay warmer too; don't let her just curl up in the snow and wait for you to let her back in.

You'll find that an off-leash dog park is an excellent way to exercise your dog. A dog park offers a securely fenced area for dogs to play off leash, and it provides a chance for them to play with other dogs as well. Fresh water and shade are readily available at dog parks, as are benches for the owners to sit and relax if they aren't playing with the dogs, too.

Exercise can be too much of a good thing if you don't recognize when your dog is tiring. Your dog has had enough if you notice hesitation, a slowed gait, and if he isn't on his feet bouncing in place and waiting for you to throw that stick again but is instead sitting or lying down. If you notice he has started limping at any time during your play, call a halt to his activity and see what's up. He may have tripped over something and wrenched his leg, or he may have something lodged in between toes or a torn nail. Further activity will only make things worse. Give your dog a good drink of fresh water, lots of praise and petting, and bring him home to rest if he has hurt himself. If he isn't better by morning, schedule a vet visit for as soon as possible to have his leg looked at.

Time of day is another consideration. In the summer months early morning and late evening, before the sun gets too high and after the temperatures peak, are better times to head for a good run. In the colder seasons, afternoons are better.

## Outdoor Fun and Games

There's no better place to be when the weather is nice. Most dogs love being outside, even if it's only in the backyard. Even if your dog isn't much of a runner, or prefers the sofa to the sand, he can still enjoy these fun activities.

**Hiking is one of my favorite activities to do with my dogs.** Any running is strictly voluntary on your dog's part, so if he's more of a couch potato than a star athlete, he can meander along with you at a slow and steady pace. Plan your hike a good week in advance, and have the exact route written down and mapped out to leave with family. Whether you go for just a day or a weekend-long hike, there are some things that should be done no matter what:

- Make sure your chosen route allows dogs. Many state parks and game preservations do not.
- Make sure your dog has identification and that the information is up-to-date.
- Your dog should be fully vaccinated and in good overall health.
- If you plan to and are allowed to let your dog off leash, he must respond quickly to voice commands. If your dog does not respond to commands well, then do not let him off leash.
- Always pick up after your dog, even if it is in the forest. Other hikers will notice if you don't.
- Always follow the posted rules for every hiking trail you take.
- Do not let your dog bark at people or wildlife.
- Do not let your dog chase other hikers or wildlife.

Remember: You and your dog will represent the dog-owning population everywhere you go, even in the wilderness.

Whenever you leave civilization behind you should have a few essentials. Adjust the amounts for however long you plan to be gone. Here's a handy checklist to help you plan your hike:

- ○ A spare leash and collar in case the one you are using breaks, or if you need to tie anything up
- ○ Enough water for both of you

▶ Dog packs are the perfect thing for hikers. You don't want to carry the dog's food and water—your pack will be heavy enough. The Palisades Pack II from Ruff Wear (www.ruffwear.com) does it all. It has an integrated hydration system for your dog's water, packs that detach from the harness for crossing water without the hassle of undoing the whole harness, and has extra pockets that are separate from the main compartments.

- Enough food for your trip, plus another meal's worth just in case of emergency if you are gone a full day or longer
- Plenty of treats for your dog to reinforce good behavior
- Bring plenty of poop bags to pick up your dog's piles
- A tent if you are spending the night, or not if you prefer to sleep under the stars
- A sleeping bag for the same reason as above
- Collapsible food and water bowls for your dog to eat and drink out of
- A mini first-aid kit containing tweezers, antiseptic ointment, antihistamine, and styptic powder

**Camping is a great summer pastime.** I like to be as far from civilization as possible, so we spend a lot of our time camping out far from home. Similar to the list for hiking, the camping list of "must haves" needs more of everything for your dog, plus these other items:

- A blanket or bed for your dog to sleep on
- A collapsible crate just in case it is needed, or for your dog to sleep in
- A chain or rope to secure your dog to your campsite so he doesn't go wandering off and visiting other campers
- A muzzle in case your dog barks. Everybody has a right to peace and quiet when camping
- A basic first-aid book in case there is an accident
- Dog toys to keep him occupied when you aren't out playing with him
- Garbage bags to collect your poop bags and any other garbage you may accumulate

**Think boating is just for humans?**  Think again! Most dogs learn to love being in a boat, even the ones that aren't too sure of it at first. The wind in their fur and the many different sights, sounds, and smells—all enchant the curious canine.

However, going for a boat ride is one thing; sitting in a stationary boat on the water while Mom fishes just isn't as fun, and a bored dog in a boat in a lake is a recipe for disaster. You'll have to wear your dog out before you take him fishing, or make sure he has plenty of toys to hold his interest, so he doesn't get restless.

## Thinking Games and Indoor Play

Dogs like to use their brain a lot, just like their legs. Thinking games can expend some of their energy as well, and they are good to play when weather or other circumstances make it hard for you and your dog to get outside. Having two healthy dogs that liked to get out and play hard in all weather, and one with hip dysplasia who couldn't tolerate the cold for very long periods, we developed a few games that could be played indoors after a short walk in the snow.

**Search and Rescue is a great game for any dog.**  My dog Raider has a fascination with empty toilet paper roll tubes. He never does anything with them, but he loves them. One of our favorite games involves hiding the tube in the house where it can be seen or smelled but not easily grabbed, such as in shirt pockets, on bookshelves, in piles of laundry, or under sofa cushions. One of us would have Raider sit in one room while the other hid the tube in another room. "Find it" meant the game was on. It usually doesn't take him long to "rescue" his tube, unless it is hidden in an unfamiliar room. Make your own version of this game using one of your dog's favorite things. You can even hide dog treats.

**TOOLS YOU NEED**

▶ Even if your dog can swim, she still needs a lifejacket in the boat. An accident can happen farther away from shore than your dog can swim, or she may be injured and unable to swim properly. When fitting your dog for a lifejacket, be sure it is snug all the way around and cannot slip over her head when her fur is wet.

**Hide and Seek is another fun dog game, and it's one kids really enjoy.**   Hide and Seek is like Search and Rescue, only it uses your dog's favorite people instead of toys. Best played in a larger arena like a backyard or the whole house, somebody can keep your dog in one room while another hides someplace in the house (under the bed, in a closet, in a box, etc.) until the hiding person calls the dog's name. Time your dog to see how long it takes him to find his person each time.

**Keep Away is fun to play with dogs, as long as you remain in charge.**   It's more fun when both participants are playing than when your dog is playing this game and you need to get something back from him. Dogs just naturally try to make a game out of it when they have something in their mouths. If your dog knows the "trade" command it will be easier for him to distinguish between a game and a real need to get something from him.

To start the game, wait until your dog has something he finds valuable. Make a move for him, telling him in an excited voice: "I'm gonna get you!" This will be his cue that it is now a game you are playing and he is free to try to run, dodge, and hide from you. Feint to the left and then to the right, grabbing (but not connecting) at the toy in his mouth in order to get him dodging.

**Soccer is like Keep Away in that it doesn't let you have the prize.**   This time, though, the prize is a ball too big to be carried. He needs to learn to push it around with his nose and paws. Usually all it takes for him to learn this is realizing that he can't pick it up in his mouth. If he doesn't quite get it, roll the ball back and forth between you and your dog for a while first, encouraging him with praise every time he noses the ball.

**Teaching your dog to do little tricks is a fun way of exercising his mind (and yours too).** Dogs love to learn new things and live to please you. You can teach your dog to do anything, from turning off the lights and shutting doors to bringing you things that you point to.

For example, Bring It Here is another of Raider's favorite games. I started out by teaching him to take things from my hand ("Take it!"). I'd use things he was inclined to grab anyway, like his toys and empty toilet paper tubes, saying "Take it" as soon as he reached for it. A reward for taking the item was a petting session and the item itself. After a few days of him taking things that he would have grabbed anyway, I started with different objects: his food dish (he was used to picking this up), an ice cream bucket (by the handle), and a hat.

Raider is the type of dog to baby things (except squeaking toys), so I wasn't worried about him gnawing on the items I gave him. If your dog is the chewing type, start with something hard and train him not to gnaw as he carries it (a "No" should work for the start, and reward your dog for holding items without chewing).

Once he started taking all types of different things from my hand on cue, I started to teach him to bring things to somebody. My husband, Dave, would be waiting at one end of the room while I gave Raider his hat. Dave would call him over, at the same time telling him to "Bring it here." Once Raider reached Dave, a trade ensued: Dave's hat for a tasty treat. A repeat of "Bring it here" followed as Dave took the hat.

Once Bring It Here was well established, in between delivering remote controls and carrying items around the house for me, I would randomly point at things and tell Raider to "Bring it here." Like any dog, this confused him, but in an attempt to please me, he would go and pick something up. If it was the wrong item I told him "No," and waited until he dropped it. Then I would start again. When he grabbed the correct object, I acted like he just solved world hunger, heaping tons of praise and a pocketful of treats.

As you can see, you can make a game out of almost anything when you're indoors. Just be careful; there are a few activities you should avoid. For example, one of the things people think is a good indoor activity for dogs when their owner is housebound is throwing a ball down a flight of stairs for the dog to chase. This is a really, really bad idea. One little slip, one missed stair, and your dog could land at the bottom much differently than intended, with several broken bones and internal injuries. Yes, the dog loves it, but the risk is too great. Try one of the other activities you've read about in this section instead.

## Organized Dog Sports

Dog sports are a great way to keep yourself and your dog in good shape, and you can meet with other dog enthusiasts. You can enter fun competitions that are there just for the pleasure of it, or you can work toward actual sporting dog titles.

**Agility is the obstacle sport.**  Border collies, Australian shepherds, and other herding breeds excel at this sport, although any breed or mix can compete. An agility dog must have basic obedience training as a foundation, and it will need to learn other commands that will guide him through an obstacle course. A handler can issue as many verbal commands and body cues as needed but is not allowed to touch the dog or the equipment. Dogs must complete the course before the time limit runs out. A standard course time, SCT, is set by the judges before each competition begins.

▶ Click-a-Trick cards are a great little tool to have on hand for indoor afternoon fun. These little plastic cards with a miniature clicker fit on your keyring and give you step-by-step instructions for teaching your dog many tricks. There are nine cool tricks you can teach him in one afternoon each, and once your dog has learned them all, pass them on to a friend! You can buy Karen Pryor's Click-a-Trick cards almost anywhere online and in some retail pet stores.

An average agility course has tunnels (both collapsing and open), weave poles, jumps, and climbing obstacles like an A-frame that a dog must run up one side of and down the other. An agility course is run by the dog entirely off leash and under voice control. This is a physically and mentally demanding sport not recommended for puppies. Any physically sound dog can participate, even mixed breeds, but AKC-sponsored events are restricted to registered dogs.

If you want to get your dog started in agility, check these Web sites for events and courses near you:

- Agility Association of Canada (AAC): www.aac.ca
- North American Dog Agility Club (NADAC): www.nadac .com
- United Kingdom Agility: www.ukagility.com
- United States Dog Agility Association (USDAA): www .usdaa.com

**Flyball is the ultimate dog sport for ball-driven dogs.** A relay race run by a team of four dogs, flyball is a straight course of hurdles with a spring-loaded box at the end of the track. The dogs run one at a time, jumping the hurdles (height is determined by the smallest dog on each team) and bounding off the spring box to release a tennis ball. The ball is shot of the box and the dog must grab it and return to the starting point, taking the hurdles on the way back as well. If you think flyball might be the sport for you, visit the North American Flyball Association's (NAFA) Web site at www.flyball.org for training information, courses, and events near you. This sport is open to all dogs regardless of breed and size.

**ASK YOUR GUIDE**

*How old should my dog be before starting in sports?*

▶ Your puppy can start in age-appropriate activities as soon as he has been fully vaccinated (around sixteen weeks). Puppy agility classes have puppy-sized, easy setups and classes for the young ones so they can get used to the equipment. Competitive obedience is a nice, low-impact sport for puppies, too.

**ELSEWHERE ON THE WEB**

▶ To keep abreast of all the sporting events in your area, join a local dog sport or breed club. They will have a schedule of events that are of interest to the breed. They may even host their own. To know when AKC-sanctioned events are held or televised, see the American Kennel Club's calendar of events online at www.akc.org. If you miss one, you can still find out who took the top honors when the results are posted.

**Weight pulling competitions are a real sight to see.**  Large, powerful breeds like Alaskan malamutes and pit bulls do really well in this sport, but any dog can compete, even small ones. Harnessed to a sled or wheeled trailer, a dog can pull an astonishing amount of weight, even as much as fifteen hundred pounds! Dogs must be in prime physical condition, over one year of age, and have a desire for working their muscles to their fullest potential. If you want to start your dog in weight pulling competitions, check out the information at International Weight Pull Association's (IWPA) Web site (www.iwpa.net).

**Musical freestyle is a new sport that is very entertaining to both watch and participate in.**  Freestyle is a choreographed dance routine performed by you and your dog, set to music. It's a fun sport, and a great stress relief even if you aren't competing. Again, obedience training is the foundation for freestyle, and your dog must be able to follow verbal and nonverbal cues. Freestyle is open to all dogs; size, shape, and breed do not matter. For more information, check out the Canine Freestyle Federation, Inc. at www.canine-freestyle.org.

**Lure coursing is the cream of sighthound activities.**  It's not quite the same as racing, even though it is sometimes a timed event and the dogs do follow a simulated rabbit, portrayed by a while plastic bag, or strips of rabbit fur. A lure operator pulls the lure through a series of loops in a zigzagging pattern to simulate escaping prey. Check out the American Sighthound Field Association for more information on lure coursing (www.asfa.org).

**There's even a sport for dogs who love to leap into the water: diving.**  Leaping off a long dock into a pool of water to retrieve a thrown toy sounds like a dream sport. I remember watching this sport debut at one of the big dog sport shows on television. It was won by a black Labrador retriever that was entered on a whim of his owner's, with no preparation at all. Some dogs are just naturals.

It's not quite as easy as that though. A dog does need to be well versed in the act of diving off structures, and he needs to know how to use his back legs to launch himself into the air. Your dog might be a natural at this and still need some fine tuning. If you want to look further into this sport, Sport Mutt has a great page on getting started (www.sportmutt.com/training/getting_started_new.htm).

**Most dog sports are put on by the local breed clubs, the American Kennel Club, or a sport club, like the NADAC.** Some events are open to mixed breeds and others are restricted to purebred dogs, possibly even dogs of a specific breed.

If you have a purebred dog that has never been registered with the American Kennel Club and still want to compete at AKC sporting events, you can apply for an Indefinite Listing Privilege (ILP). An ILP allows purebred dogs to compete in these events:

- Tracking tests
- Agility trials
- Junior showmanship
- Rally trials
- Obedience trials
- Lure coursing
- Earthdog trials
- Hunt tests
- Herding trials

ELSEWHERE ON THE WEB

▶ Earthdog is a performance event, and it's the sport that terriers were made for. They get to follow a rodent scent down a tunnel in the ground to find the rodent (it's safely caged). This is what terriers were originally bred to do as vermin dogs. Check out the AKC's Web site for more Earthdog information (www.akc.org/events/earthdog/index.cfm). Earthdog is limited to dachshunds and some terriers.

The ILP program allows purebred dogs that have never been registered, or are ineligible for registering, to compete in companion and performance events as long as the breed is recognized by the AKC. To obtain an ILP number, download the application form and follow the instructions on the AKC Web site (**www.akc.org/reg/ilpex.cfm**) for applying.

### Get Linked

*My About.com site has some more information on fun fitness for you and your dog. Check out the following links.*

**GO AND PLAY!**

Playing with your dog isn't just fun, it's a great way to keep in shape and relieve stress, too.

 http://about.com/dogs/playwithdog

**GO SWIMMING!**

It's low impact, and it gives your dog's whole body a workout—swimming is the perfect exercise for the summer.

 http://about.com/dogs/swimming

## Chapter 6

# The Most Important Commands

## Beginning Training

Everybody wants a well-trained dog that responds to commands instantly, but it doesn't happen overnight. Training your dog to do even the most basic of commands will take a couple of days for your dog to really understand what you want from him.

Before you start, you need to know if your dog is familiar with a leash. Believe it or not, some sheltered pets have never had a leash on before, and puppies need to be **desensitized** to their leashes, too.

Let your puppy get used to the collar first. A collar should be tight enough that it won't slip over his head easily, but loose enough for you to stick two fingers under it when it's on his neck. Give him a few days of wearing it before you go and attach a long, snaky thing to it. Make sure you make a habit of grabbing his collar, sticking your fingers under it, and moving it around on his neck so he's used to you playing with it.

Once he's accustomed to the collar, go ahead and tie a short rope that's about the same weight as a short leash to his collar. Two feet is a good starting length. Let him play with it. Let him drag it around and detach and reattach it numerous times. Praise him every time he lets you take it off and put it back on. Keep him like this for about two days, but take the rope off at night because you should not leave him unattended with it tied on.

When the short rope has become a commonplace thing to your puppy, take it off and replace it with a six-foot-long one. This may bring about a big change in your dog. Now the rope has gone from intriguing to almost threatening. It's three times the length of what he was used to, and the way it follows is downright scary. Instead of just letting your puppy get used to it, now you'll need to take a more active role. And watch your step carefully. A six-foot lead trailing behind a puppy is a pretty big tripping hazard.

Start by picking up the other end of the rope and just holding it. I don't know what your puppy might do; he might come to see you (good), or he might sit down (also good), or he might even growl at the leash (not so good). For every good reaction, praise him and give him a treat. You want him to associate the leash with good things (treats and praise). As odd as it sounds, you may need to talk to the leash in a calm voice, so your dog sees that it is nothing threatening.

After your dog has accepted the rope, switch it for a regular six-foot leash. As long as your dog shows no signs of trepidation over this new one, you can now start to randomly pick it up, step on the end, and give it little tugs so your dog is reminded that it's there and that you are on the other end of it. It won't take long at all until your dog accepts that the leash is an extension of your arm.

**Use of a release word is how your dog will know he has been let go.** Pick a word or phrase you don't use every day and use it to signal the end of whatever command you have given your dog. "Good job" might work if it's a saying you don't use around your dog regularly, or come up with something else as long as you use it consistently. Make sure you praise your dog for a job well done all the time.

**The best rewards to use are small, soft chunks of food.** Most dogs are food motivated, and even the ones that aren't will be for the right treat. I like to use small cubes of cheese or bits of hot dogs. This makes the reward highly desirable, smelly enough that he knows it's there without getting close to lick it, and easily chewed so that his valuable (but short) attention span isn't spent on chewing up a hard treat. Praise is an effective reward but is not as precious as food. Your dog will eventually graduate to where you can praise more than a food reward, but you should still reward with food once in a while even when your dog has been trained for years. It will keep him sharp.

**A puppy obedience class is a great way to learn how to work with your new dog.** These types of classes aren't just for training your dog, but also for teaching you, the human, how to relate to your dog, and how to train effectively. Check the yellow pages or search Google for classes in your area. You can also ask at the local Humane Society or veterinarian's office if they know of any classes starting in the near future. Look for a class that teaches using a positive reward system, and don't be shy about asking other dog owners for recommendations either.

**There is a wide variety of training collars available.** Most, like the prong collar and choke chain, should be left in the hands of experienced dog trainers. Head halters are user-friendly training collars, but beware of letting the halter take the place of actual

**WHAT'S HOT**

▶ The clicker training craze is still going strong. Training dogs using a small device that clicks loudly to mark the correct response really is as simple as it sounds. Dogs have been taught to do hundreds of different things using this method. If you want to learn more, check out http://about.com/dogs/clickertraining. Clickers are available at most pet stores for just a couple of dollars. Just don't click it too near your dog's ears or you may have just ruined your dog for clicker training altogether.

*What about those shock collars with a remote?*

▶ I really think they should be banned completely. In the hands of the average dog owner, these collars can do more harm than good. Designed to deliver a correction from a distance, people tend to think these collars are a quick route to a well-behaved dog. It's not true at all; in fact, it's almost abusive. The lowest shock setting may feel mild to you, but it left burns on the neck of my mixed breed when I tried one.

training. You want your dog to obey all the time, not just when he wears the halter.

**I recommend coupling every verbal command with a nonverbal hand signal.** It's important that dogs learn to use physical as well as verbal cues so that you don't always have to stop or start talking in order to get a response out of your dog. Just remember to be consistent, and use the same commands and the same actions for the same desired result every single time.

- For "Sit," snap your fingers.
- "Down" is a point to the floor.
- "Stay" has your hand up, palm out.
- A beckoning hand signals "Come."
- A wave of your left hand by your side means "Heel."

These are merely suggestions, you don't have to use the same signals I use, but you do need to use the same ones you choose with your dog all the time.

## Sit

Usually the first command a puppy learns, "Sit," is also going to be the most important command in your arsenal. "Sit" will get your dog through a stressful situation, or have him waiting somewhat patiently while you get through a stressful situation. Using positive reinforcement, you will find that "Sit" is also the easiest command to train. Even an untrained adult dog will pick up "Sit" in a matter of minutes, and from that point on it's just a matter of reinforcing the behavior throughout her life.

Catch your dog's interest first. Use your leash if you have to bring her and keep her in front of you, but make sure she focuses on you. Hold a small chunk of treat just above her nose so she can smell it. Let her smell it, and one you've caught her interest with it, raise it up over her head. Don't raise it too high, but hold it more over her head so she has to lift her head back to smell it. With your other hand, push down on her hindquarters and issue your command in a firm voice. Her hind end will drop, and as soon as it hits the ground, give her the treat and praise her loudly.

Once she's devoured her reward, you'll want to do it again. Do it again after that, rewarding for each successful "Sit." After the first two or three times, maybe even less, your dog will have the basic idea and you should not have to push on his hind end to get him to drop his back end. Remember though to keep these sessions short, about five to ten minutes long, so your dog doesn't get bored and let her attention wander. Stop before she fails to complete a "Sit" as well. If you have six successful "Sits" out of her, stop there. It's very important to always end a training session on a positive note so that training remains a fun experience for your dog.

Repeat these short and fun training episodes with your dog three or four times a day for the first week.

Want her to sit for visual cues, like a wave of the hand or a pointed finger? Use your signal along with the spoken command until she responds well to both used together. After she is sitting like a professional, remove your spoken command and just use your visual cue. Remember to reward heavily, and praise lavishly. You may need to attract her attention first however, but once you have eye contact, your hand signal should be enough to get her sitting. If it's not, you need to go back to the beginning and start over again with both cues. Don't let her get away with ignoring your signal once you have her attention. She'll only learn that you mean it sometimes, and that can be disastrous for future training. If she ignores you, grab her collar, give the signal, and make her sit with your hand on her backside again.

**TOOLS YOU NEED**

▶ Use hollow, polypropylene rope, and modify it to fit a swivel snap (like on the end of leashes) for easier attachment while training on a long lead. About two feet from the end, take six inches of rope between each hand, then push your hands together while holding the rope to puff it out (you may need to twist it a bit). You'll notice it looks like a cage now. Have a friend insert the end of the rope through the snap ring, thread the end of the rope through an opening, and push it up inside the rope along the length of it, not exiting, until you have a loop at the end about four inches long. Now pull on the loop to tighten it.

In fearful situations, issuing a firm "Sit" will give your dog something to focus on, and something specific to do. A dog with a job to do is a more confident dog. Likewise, a well-taught "Sit" will save your guests from your dog's overexcitement.

## Down, Up, and Off

Teaching your dog "Down" is the next step after "Sit." It's not hard, although getting him to stay down may be a bit trickier. Maybe your dog is a kangaroo dog like mine are. Down they go, letting their bellies touch the floor, but they are back up in less than a second. It's like watching somebody on a trampoline. Luckily the "Stay" command is what we teach them next.

Get your treats handy again, and bring your dog to sit in front of you. Get down on your knees and take a treat out for him to sniff quickly. Put the treat on the floor in front, still in your hand, so that he can touch it with his nose but not take it. Issue your command in a firm voice, then move the treat away from him so that he is forced to try and follow it. As his upper body lowers itself to the floor, you may need to encourage his shoulders a little bit by pushing down on them gently. Once he is completely down, give him the treat and praise him lavishly. Repeat three or four times until your dog is dropping on his own. Some dogs are stubborn; it may take a lot longer. Don't mistake this for lack of intelligence, as intelligence does not equal trainability. Keep your training session short, but go back and repeat the entire session in a couple of hours. Keep it up for about two or three days, and your dog should have "Down" down pat.

So now you've taught her to lie down, but what about "Up"? This is a great command to use when you're trying to get your dog to jump into the car or onto a raised deck or porch. She doesn't need to be leashed for this one unless you take her outside to

ELSEWHERE ON THE WEB

▶ Perfect Paws is a great library of dog training tips. Dog trainer and behavior expert Gwen Bohnenkamp writes with an easy-to-understand style and doesn't assume that you already know half of what must be taught (thereby leaving out essential information). She is also the author of *Manners for the Modern Dog, From the Cat's Point of View,* and *Help! My Dog Has an Attitude.* Check out her library of training articles at www.perfectpaws.com.

work on it, but you do need to locate some surfaces you're willing to train your dog to jump on. And it needs to be a low enough height that your dog can get onto it easily with no strain and a large enough surface for her to get up and sit on.

Hold a treat just above the surface you want her to jump onto, and using your other hand pat the surface and tell her "Up." She may try to take the treat with just her front legs up on your chosen surface, but don't let her get away with that. Hold the treat higher. You may need to physically lift her rear end onto the surface. Once she's up, give her praise but not the treat yet. Make her sit first. Now give her the treat and more praise. Repeat for a short time. For your next session in a couple of hours, use a different surface.

Similar to "Down" and "Up," "Off" is a really good command to have in your arsenal. Attach her leash, and put your dog on something you can command her off of: a sofa, bed, in the car, or even a park bench if you have nothing else. Make sure it is a surface that she can jump off of without threat of injury. A tiny dog like a Chihuahua shouldn't be jumping off of a park bench, so use a stair instead. Once she is up on the object, tell her "Off" in a firm voice, point to the ground, and pull on the leash so that she has to jump down from whatever she's sitting on. When she's on the ground, reward and praise her lavishly. Like all training sessions, keep it short and make sure you end on a positive note. One thing with "Off" though, it will help you a lot if you use a variety of different surfaces during training, otherwise she may come to think that "Off" is only good for the sofa and nowhere else.

## Stay

In my experience with my dogs, "Stay" was the toughest command to teach and have them perform reliably. It was a very simple problem; as soon as I turned the corner, they would come looking

▶ A ramp might be just the thing to help your dog get into and out of your vehicle if it's a tall one. Even if your young dog can actually make the jump, it's not necessarily a good idea. Small dogs can easily fracture bones by jumping off of things that are too high, and your dog won't know how high "too high" is.

**My dog is not food motivated. What do I do now?**

▶ You'll need to find your dog's motivator. Some dogs crave affection, so praise, petting, and cuddling will be your dog's reward. Other dogs have a favorite toy they want to play with all the time (that toy may be you, by the way). You can still reward your dog, just use his motivator, even if it means tossing the ball to her a couple of times when she does a good job.

for me. Thankfully, they eventually figured out what I was trying to teach them.

It's easiest to teach your dog to stay if she is in a comfortable position she can maintain for long periods of time. Attach your dog's leash and put her in a down. Once she's down, praise her and tell her to stay. Don't walk away. When she starts to get up, without repeating "Down," put her back down with your hands and repeat the word "Stay." If she stays down for a few seconds, praise her and give her a treat. We are only looking for thirty-second stays at this point; it's too early to ask for more.

Right now your dog should be up, wagging her tail and wondering what she did right. You have to show her again. Put her in a down, and tell her to stay. Again, if she starts to get up, use your hands to put her back into a down, repeating the "Stay" command. Repeat this action, without rewarding her, until she stays for about twenty seconds. Issue your releasing order, then reward her lavishly. Remember that you still haven't left your position right in front of her yet. Increase her stay time slowly over several short training sessions.

As her time gets better and she can stay for five minutes, start to distance yourself from her, beginning with just a couple of feet. You may have to rush back and put her back down if you see her getting up to follow you. Don't make her hold her stay for as long though. Release her after thirty seconds again. Gradually increase this time again over several short sessions. Again, once she hits the five-minute mark, move another three or four feet away.

You can get a good distance away just by increasing your distance a few feet at a time once your dog has stayed for five minutes at each interval. But once you are out of sight, things may get harder. Some dogs will have figured it out by now, but some dogs will just naturally get up to follow you without a further thought. For the latter type of dog, we'll have to greatly reduce the time, starting out at just five seconds. Give the command, then walk out of the room, but turn around and come back almost immediately. Before she even has a chance to get up, you'll be back and praising her for staying. And the next time you walk out of the room, count to ten and then go back and praise her.

Don't set her up for failure by trying to rush this and increasing your time too quickly. Add to your time out of sight in very small increments, and remember to not over do the length of the training session either. Scatter sessions so you are training her for roughly five minutes every couple of hours. Or do a "Stay" here and there throughout the day.

Once you've worked your way up to a minute, the times will start to increase faster. Don't forget to release her after! What she will eventually be doing is waiting patiently for a reasonable length of time in the spot you put her until you come back.

## Come

The best way to get results and a reliable recall is to teach your dog that no matter how much fun he is having, it's more fun at your side. Make his every return to you worthwhile. Because this is such an important command, I suggest rewarding for every single return, even years later, so that he will always come, no matter what.

Some dogs just naturally gravitate to your side without much effort on your part. If this describes your dog, be sure you reinforce that behavior well. It's something your dog needs to know is correct and desirable. If your dog is of the other persuasion, as in you have to persuade him back to you all the time, then this is for you.

Tie the rope onto your dog's collar and let him go, keeping the other end for yourself. Let him wander around and explore, and wait until he looks engrossed in something. Call his name loudly. When he looks up at you, holler out some praise. If he starts toward you, speak your "Come" command in a firm voice.

TOOLS YOU NEED

▶ A really long length of rope will be your best friend while you're teaching him to come. Try to get one fifty feet or longer. You want your dog to have a lot of roaming room before you start to reel him in. Hang a sport whistle around your neck, too, as you might need to grab your dog's attention when he's farther away from you.

Hopefully he continues his journey and makes it to your side with little trouble. Reward and praise him silly. And he may come to you immediately for the first few times.

But stubborn, playful dogs rarely keep to a pattern, so don't start thinking he's ready for the next step yet. While this game seems new and exciting, and it's one he always wins, your dog may get bored of it very quickly. When he does, you'll be ready.

This is what the fifty-foot length of rope tied to your dog's collar is for. When he gets a mischievous urge and instead of coming when you call he takes off in the opposite direction, don't take it laying down! Use that rope, and when you give your command, reel him in. But don't reward him for this. He only gets rewards for coming on his own volition. Despite what you may think, it won't take him long to figure this out either.

Keep this up for a long time. You need this command to be as firm as a brick wall in his mind. Once he's been at it for a while, and you've started to get a fast response every time you call his name or holler your "Come" command at him, you can take him somewhere else for practice.

Remember that up until now you've been able to enforce your command by reeling him in when he doesn't listen. Now that's going to change. Arm yourself well; go for the liver biscotti, cheese chunks, or even small bits of raw hamburger, and get ready to go in. You'll need a securely fenced area for this, something like a tennis court with a closable gate or your backyard if it's fenced in completely. It can't be too big or you could have trouble when it's time to fetch your dog.

Now turn him loose! Chances are he already knows what you have in your pockets or treat bag; it's why I like to use smelly treats for rewards. Wait until he's engrossed in something around the perimeter of the enclosure, then call his name. Does he look at you and go back to what he's doing? Try to issue your command in that split second between looking at you and him looking away.

If he comes running, reinforce that behavior with everything you've got! Well not everything, try to save some rewards for the next time. But seriously, give him a ton of praise, and petting, and a few treats too. This is the big one that you want your dog to keep doing.

If he just gives you that look, you know the one, like he's asking what it is you plan to do about it, and goes back to what he was interested in, you must go and get him. These are the hazards of training your dog to respond while off leash. But unfortunately, it's the only way he'll know you mean business.

If you have to go and get him, even just once, attach the rope and begin again.

Once he starts coming reliably in a small enclosed area, it's time to cement it in your dog's head that you are where he wants to be at all times. Keep a pocketful of treats on you at all times, and distribute them liberally. Call your dog to go for a walk and reward him when he reaches you. Call your dog to go for a car ride and reward him enthusiastically. Create a dozen other situations that your dog will enjoy and call him to you. Or just call him to give him a treat for no other reason.

Always call your dog with an upbeat, happy voice. Always call your dog for good reasons and to do something or go somewhere he enjoys. If you have to take your dog someplace he does not like, such as the vet's, or if you are angry, do not call him to you; go and get him. Your dog will learn that it is worth it to run to you every single time when you call him.

Even after your dog races to your side, I still don't recommend letting her run loose except in designated off-leash or fenced areas. Remember that every dog has a mind of her own, and the one time you let her off near traffic may be the one time she disregards

**TOOLS YOU NEED**

▶ There a couple of nifty treat dispensers that hang on the belt loops of your pants for easy, one-handed dispensing. Make sure the dispenser opening is big enough for your regularly used treats or you may have to switch. One thing to keep in mind is that most dispensers aren't good for moist treats like cheese or wieners. You may need to find a dry version, or you could dry up your own cheese by leaving the blocks in the fridge overnight with no covering. Wieners can be baked to dry them out.

▶ I keep mentioning small, easily dispensed treats that are fast for your dog to chew so his mind will stay on your training session and not what's in his mouth. Liver biscotti dog training treats are the ideal reward for short training sessions. They are smelly, and though they are crunchy and not soft, you can fit a dozen or more in your pockets without much mess.

your call. Once your dog is older, or has lived with you for a long time, and you can predict your dog's actions accurately, you can use your own judgment regarding your dog and his off-leash activities provided you obey all the laws of your town and follow dog etiquette. My dogs are older and have come reliably for years, but I still won't let them off leash where there is traffic or a lot of other people. It just is not worth the risk of something bad happening.

## Walking on a Leash

This skill sounds like a given, but even adopted adult dogs may need to be taught to walk nicely on a leash. Some dogs will pull on the leash, nearly tearing your arms out of their sockets. Others will wander off the path you're following into the woods to investigate a smell or another animal. It's important that you teach your dog to walk with you when he's on the leash so that he doesn't slow you down, knock you off balance, or get into some kind of trouble.

There are several methods of training a dog to walk nicely on a leash. I'll share my favorite and most effective with you and I hope either (or both) work for your dog. I was never able to train my first dog. This isn't surprising since the method I chose to use was the old "jerk your dog back to your side" method. What a waste. It really does not work. Luckily, I learned other methods with my other dogs later on. You can do this without a special training collar as long as you are strong enough to stop your dog from gaining ground.

Take your dog out into your yard. You'll want to do this without distractions at first, but it still must be in a place where he will pull to go where he wants. Take her out and let her pull for a second, then stop her. That's it. Just stop and stand immobile without letting her get any further. Wait until she stops to look back at you; if she doesn't, call her name, and resume walking only when she starts to come back to you. You know she wants to go forward; therefore, your forward motion is her (early) reward.

If she starts to pull the leash again, do the same thing. Stop, wait for her to notice, and when the leash gets a little bit of slack in it, step forward again. You can see why I suggested doing this in your own yard at first. I should also point out that when you stop, don't give your dog any leeway. Keep your arm tight against her pulling and allow her no give at all. Don't even lean in the direction she's pulling.

It sounds like you'll look ridiculous, but it does work over time. Your dog will quickly learn that she only gets to move forward when the leash has become loose.

You do realize, of course, that I gave you the dignified methods first, right? This next method is somewhat more vigorous than the first.

Using a plain buckle collar and six-foot lead, start off outside and move forward at a brisk pace. As your dog gains momentum and starts to get ahead of you, turn without stopping and walk in a different direction. Once he's turned with you, and starts to move ahead again, turn and go in another direction. Keep it up until your dog has learned to focus on what you are doing, not what's up ahead. You'll notice the time stretching between turns in no time at all. Add in distractions as you go along, rewarding your dog for ignoring anything that isn't you.

To heel ("show heeling" to be more precise), your dog must walk at your left side at a distance you are comfortable with but neither forging ahead nor falling behind. Getting a comfortable heel is a long and slow process.

To begin, hold the leash in your right hand and a small smelly treat in your left hand. Call your dog to a sit on your left side, and show him your smelly treat. Now you have his attention. Or rather, your left hand has his attention. This is good, so give him his treat

ELSEWHERE ON THE WEB

▶ The Association of Pet Dog Trainers (APDT) has great information on choosing a dog trainer and how to become one. There are pet memorials, a calendar of obedience events, and information on the sport of rally obedience. You can use this Web site to help you locate a trainer and classes as well, and it's not limited to the United States. Visit www.apdt.com and see what else interests you.

(but don't let him jump for it) and your praise, then let him go play. Repeat this again.

Call your dog to your left side and sit him again. Give him a word you'll want to use to get him to focus on your left hand ("Focus" is a good command, as is "Here now"). Give your left hand, with treat inside, a little shake to catch his eye.

Once he's focused on your hand, wait about ten seconds and give him the treat. Get him focused again and step forward two paces, just far enough that your dog has to move forward as well in order for him to reach your hand. If he moves with you and stays focused, give him his treat. If he doesn't, give your hand a little shake and gently pull him forward with the leash until he's back in position, telling him "Heel." Focus him on your hand and step forward again, giving your hand a little shake. If he gets up to follow your hand, walk forward a few more paces and then dip down to reward him. If you have to pull him forward again, don't reward him until he is moving on his own. Make sure you have a lot of those little treats with you!

Increase your walking distance each time you give him a treat. Every time you stop, start by focusing him on your hand again and then give the command "Heel." Stop rewarding him for focusing, but continue rewarding him for walking beside you with his attention still focused on your left hand. If he gets distracted, give your hand a little shake to bring his attention back to you and continue walking. Don't forget to reward him for walking beside you nicely, and end the training session before he gets bored of this new game.

## Get Linked

*Visit my About.com Dogs site for even more basic training help and puppy-specific issues that you may need to deal with.*

**FINDING THE TRAINING COLLAR THAT'S RIGHT FOR YOUR DOG**

There are a lot of training collars available these days. Here is my take that's Right for Your Dog on four of them that I've used in the past and still use today.

 http://about.com/dogs/trainingcollar

**WHAT MOTIVATES YOUR DOG?**

What motivates your dog to do the things that you want him to do? Not every dog is food motivated, mine certainly aren't. Here's what I do to motivate my boys when food doesn't work.

 http://about.com/dogs/motivation

## Chapter 7

# Early Training Challenges

## Beginning Housetraining

Housetraining can be the most frustrating part of dog training. Puppies sometimes pick this up very quickly. In fact, I've noticed that puppies that were raised outside seem to grasp the concept much quicker than puppies that were raised inside and eliminated inside for the first weeks of their lives. Adult dogs from shelters or rescues may need to be retaught housetraining, or they may have never learned it to begin with. Again, like puppies, I've found that adult dogs that spent most of their lives outdoors will often keep eliminating outdoors, as it's what they are used to. This is like my old dog that had to back up to a tree to defecate. It was what he was used to, and not having a tree available made him anxious if he needed to go.

**Your first step is to remove opportunities for him to go inside.** You need to restrict his freedom inside until he's fully housetrained. I'm a big advocate of crate training dogs of all ages.

When you cannot watch your dog, he will be in his crate. (Revisit Chapter 2 for information about choosing a crate.) When your dog is out of his crate, he'll be with you and you should be watching him. Add tethering to crate training and, if done properly, you'll have the two most powerful housetraining tools you can get.

**It's time to get your dog used to the crate.** Your dog may already be used to the crate, in which case you have half of your work done for you already. All you'll need to do is continue to reinforce his acceptance of the crate and make it a safe place for him to run to when he needs time apart. You can do this by establishing rules with the other family members: If the dog is in his crate, he is not to be disturbed by anyone except yourself.

Pick a spot for your crate somewhere in the house that is a quiet, out-of-the-way area. Your bedroom is a good place to put it, since your dog will be sleeping in it as well (unless, like me, you've opted to let him sleep on the bed with you). It's quiet during the day and close to you at night.

If your dog hasn't been introduced to the crate before, it's up to you to do it. Prepare to devote a large chunk of time to this. Before putting your crate in its place in your room (or wherever you decide to put it), take the top and door off, and leave the crate in a busy spot that your dog frequents (the kitchen is good). Encourage him to sniff it, play with it, and get in and out. Every time she gets near it praise her, and if she steps in (even if it's just for a second) reward her.

You're going to want your dog to go into his crate himself, on command. Put her in a sit, inside the crate with the lid off, reward her, and release her. Wait just a few minutes, then go and get your dog and place her inside the crate again, issuing your new "Crate" command. Make her sit, then reward her. Now put her leash on so that you can tell her, "Crate" throughout the next few days at random intervals and take her by the leash to her crate if she doesn't

## ELSEWHERE ON THE WEB

▶ The Humane Society of the United States has a Web page that offers great advice, tips, and reassurance about housetraining puppies (www.hsus.org/ace/13112). Print it out and hang it somewhere prominent in your home so you can reference it as you go through this trying, early stage with your new dog.

start to go on her own. Once she catches on that the location (in her crate) is the correct response to your command, she will start to go in on her own. If she seems to not be making the connection, move the crate to different locations, and start to reward once she's inside, even if she isn't sitting.

When your dog starts to run to his crate on command, put the lid on it but leave the door off. This will throw him off a bit, so you'll have to up the reward to match his trepidation. Or he may decide this is the greatest thing ever. Some dogs just naturally gravitate to small, dark, enclosed spaces. If you aren't so lucky, you can put a treat inside the crate itself. Command your dog to his crate, and he'll be able to smell the treat in it. Hopefully that will be enough to lure him inside, at which point you'll shower him with praise. If you have to, you may need to physically put him inside the crate the first couple of times. Don't forget to reward him and give him a lot of praise for going in the crate.

Keep it up, giving praise and rewards for going to his crate on command. When he does it on his own for a while, shut the door on him. Don't leave him in too long, just thirty seconds or so, and when he comes out, lavish him with praise.

You're almost finished, now you just need to increase the time he spends in there with the door closed.

**Your dog should be in his crate when you cannot watch him.** His crate is going to become his den, his little safe haven. Never use the crate as a punishment.

Put your dog in his crate after you've taken him for a walk each morning on your way to work. Your puppy can last for one hour for every month of his life. If he's four months old, don't make him wait longer than four hours in the crate. If you work a full day, you'll need to arrange for somebody to come and let your pup out during the day.

Now that you understand crate training as a concept, it's time to put it into practice.

Wake up in the morning and let your dog out of the crate. Some dogs will let their bladders go as soon as their feet hit the floor outside the crate, so be ready for that. If your pup is one of those, physically pick him up and carry him outside before putting him down. When he pees outside, praise him heavily and give him a treat. If he actually pees on you on your way out the door, don't panic, just deposit him in the grass and praise him for finishing the job on the grass. That's very important. He must actually get some urine on the grass in order for you to praise him for it! Don't make the mistake of praising him for peeing on the floor (or you).

**Tether your dog when he is out of the crate.** This will allow you to go about your regular life while still keeping your puppy close to you so you can catch him in any accidents. Supervision is really the best housetraining tool there is. I'm a practical person and I know we can't really follow our puppies around all day, nor can we stuff them in the crate and forget about them, hoping they'll train themselves. Tethering is a happy medium between those two extremes.

Take a long leash and loop it around your waist. Now attach the other end to your dog. As you go about your daily routine, your dog will have to follow you around the house. Because she is so close to you, you'll notice immediately if she starts to urinate or defecate on your floor, and you'll be able to stop her and take her outside immediately.

**A strict schedule will make this process easier.** Puppies thrive on schedules, just like babies do. A structured lifestyle will make your dog's inner workings conform to a pattern as well, and this will make housetraining much easier on you.

Feed your dog at the same times every day. Take him outside approximately fifteen to twenty minutes after he's eaten, and after every drink. You'll find it is easier to restrict his water at first until you can recognize his body language.

He'll need to be taken outside after every length of time in his crate. As I mentioned before, don't dawdle bringing him outside. Chances are he really needs to go, and any delay just makes an accident more likely.

Your very young puppy may also need to go once or twice through the night. This is why I recommend keeping the crate in your bedroom. Take him outside, give him ten or fifteen minutes to do what he has to do without playing, and then put him right back in the crate. Praise him for peeing outside, but don't turn these middle of the night jaunts into a time for play. Potty, praise, and back to bed.

**Never punish your dog for accidents in the house.** Dogs don't assign the same value to your carpet as you do, so punishment just confuses your dog, and he'll be left bewildered by your anger. Or worse, he'll start hiding his mistakes. Most accidents are owner errors, mostly from failure to supervise your puppy when he's loose in your home, or not recognizing that he needs to go outside.

**Your dog's body language will tell you when he has to go.** Watch carefully for the first few days; you will recognize the signs that your dog is ready to urinate or defecate. Thankfully, the signs are pretty obvious once you know what you are looking for.

Watch for excessive sniffing of the ground in a circle. Your dog will shift his balance to either cock his leg or squat down (almost to a lying down position) in order to urinate.

Impending bowel movement will be preceded by a tight circling with his back end tucked up near his stomach. It looks like he is going to sit but is not quite making it.

**TOOLS YOU NEED**

▶ Dogs will always return to a spot they've used before, so you'll need to really clean any accidents. A great enzyme cleaner for those little accidents is Nature's Miracle. Once you remove the dirt, use Nature's Miracle to remove all traces of smell so your dog won't return to the same spot again. You can use a black light to find all of the spots your dog may have marked in the house.

## The Second Stage of Housetraining: Going on Command

It may sound silly, but training your dog to eliminate on command can be a very useful trick, especially during traveling or if you are in a hurry. It's also surprisingly easy. I've found it especially useful when I was in the city with my dog Kari for a month. We are both somewhat uncomfortable in cities, and being able to take him out and command him to do his thing helps him relax enough to do his job before we would go for a walk to the park.

Once your dog is housetrained and she's eliminating outside where she should be on a regular basis (barring the odd accident that will happen in the early stages of training), you can now start to teach your dog to go in only one spot.

Because dogs will almost always go in the spot they have marked before, training your dog to use one area of the yard is a lot easier than you may think. Start off right away by bringing your dog to pee in the same spot all the time.

If you don't take your dog out on a leash but rather just let him out into the yard, you'll need to do a little work. You're going to have to "mark" a spot for your dog. Pick up your dog's waste and move it to the new area. Don't remove it from your yard for a few days.

Like with basic housetraining, timing is everything. When you see your dog start to investigate the area you've moved his potty spot too, praise him wildly. He probably won't catch on right away, so you'll have to keep moving his piles to the potty spot so it always smells like the right place to go.

If you see his body start to ready itself, you can catch him in time and move him to the designated potty spot. Praise wildly when he starts to go in the right place. Designating an area filled with gravel or sand may actually look better in the long run as you won't have to worry about the grass burning.

As your dog goes outside more reliably, you'll want to think hard about a command for him to urinate to. It will have to be something you rarely use, or there might be a few accidents in your future. A word in a foreign language is a good choice, as long as you or other people around you don't routinely converse in this language.

Bring your dog outside as usual and wait until she gets into the posture she uses to urinate. As soon as you see her get ready to go, issue your chosen command. She'll be there ready to go anyway, and you'll be ready with the lavish praise to heap on her when she seemingly goes when you told her to. This was just timing. And it will be just your timing for the first few times, but gradually your dog will start to hold back her urine until she hears you give the command. Always praise your dog and give her a good reward for going.

## Chewing Everything in Sight

Puppies and adolescent dogs are terrible chewers. Teenage dogs in the midst of teething, especially Labrador retrievers, can cause the most patient owner in the world to lose his cool. I have lost a frightening amount of items to teething puppies over the last decade, and looking back on it now it is enough to make me decide to adopt an older dog and leave the puppies for other people this time around.

Puppies start to lose their milk teeth at about five months of age. Unlike humans, a puppy's first teeth appear at roughly three weeks of age. These are sharp, temporary teeth that aren't much good for grinding up meat yet.

Redirection will be your best bet for teething puppies. If you catch him gnawing on your bookshelves, tell him "No," give him an appropriate chew toy, and praise him for making the trade. The key, of course, is catching him in the act. One Beauceron had eaten

▶ Toys, toys, toys. Lots and lots of chew toys are what you need to get through this horrific time. Find the ones your dog likes best and stock up on them. Teething can last for a full year in dogs, and as they get bigger the damage they can do to your bookcases gets greater. Don't sacrifice your valuables to the puppy; redirect her to a new and hopefully more exciting chew toy.

**_Why do puppies like to chew on shoes so much?_**

▶ Shoes are a fun shape, they are often made of soft materials like leather, and they are usually right in harm's way on the floor. And though it may sound gross, your puppy is also attracted to your shoes because they smell like you. So keep those shoes hidden away in boxes or closets; he can't resist them when they're on the floor!

a substantial chunk of the underside of my chair while I was sitting in it when he was a puppy.

Never give your pup something of yours to chew on, like a discarded shoe, sweater, or slipper. Some dogs may be able to distinguish between their shoes and everybody else's, but I'd hate to see the shoes that were sacrificed along the way. Avoid this headache altogether and put shoes firmly on your No list. If he decides he wants a shoe anyway, take it from him immediately—don't delay even just a few seconds. Once you catch him, give him a firm "No." Redirect him to a toy he can chew on.

If he is really getting on your nerves, chances are his teeth are really getting on his. Try to give him something to soothe his poor gums. You can wet a small towel, just enough to harden it when you freeze it, and give this to him if you suspect he's in some pain.

Some puppies like to play with ice cubes. While it can be a little messy, it's just water. Not only will this entertain him for a while, it may help cool his gums down, too.

Teething aside, chewing is just fun for your dog. Make sure he has plenty of things that are good for him to chew on, like greenies, or dog-safe chew toys. Pig ears are great, chewy treats, but they are very fattening so don't overdo it. Bully sticks are also great chewies to let your dog gnaw on.

## Settling the Anxious Dog

The biggest causes of destruction in dogs are separation anxiety and boredom. Boredom can be solved easily enough when you step up your dog's exercise regimen, but anxiety is something altogether different. As human beings, we have to leave our homes at times and we have to leave our dogs behind at some point. Most of us have to go to work outside the home, and coming home after a long day of work to a destroyed house is a nasty shock.

We've discussed crate training as a tool for housetraining, but it is also the most effective way of preventing destruction when you aren't home. If your dog is crated when you aren't there, he can't get out to eat the baseboards or urinate on your slippers.

You can also try to get your dog used to your absence by desensitizing her to your extended absences. Start slowly and build up the time you're absent from ten seconds to twenty minutes then to an hour or longer, making sure your dog is never aware of when you'll reappear.

Another big part of desensitizing your dog to the empty house is to not make any kind of a fuss as you walk out the door. If you don't get excited, and treat the outside door the same as you would walking from the kitchen to the living room, your dog will not realize that there is anything to get excited over.

After you have been at this for a few days, and you have the timing down pat, you should be able to extend the time between leaving and returning to a fair amount (twenty minutes at least). But don't take that long every time. Be gone for twenty minutes once, ten minutes twice, and five minutes three times, in no particular order. Throw in a couple of thirty-second walk-outs as well just to keep your dog guessing.

As long as you don't make any fuss over leaving, and don't give your dog any nonverbal cues about how long you will be gone, like packing a suitcase or filling three water bowls for her, the separation anxiety should get much better.

## Common Mistakes Dog Owners Make

Dog ownership is fraught with pitfalls. You can easily reinforce the wrong behaviors, or discourage the right ones by missing a crucial moment in time. Dogs are creatures of the moment, and if you yell at the precise instant she does something right for the first time,

**WHAT'S HOT**

▶ Bitter Apple Chewing Prohibitive works wonderfully during those trying teething times. Spray it on your valued possessions and spots, like table legs, and the taste will turn your dog away before any damage is done. It's also great for keeping an injured dog from chewing off his bandages, and it's good for use on hot spots as well. It does not irritate the skin and does not damage real wood furniture.

she won't want to do it again. In this way, much of dog training is precision timing.

Reinforcing bad habits is one of the most common mistakes dog owners make. It's such an easy thing to do—most of us do it without even realizing it. It's as simple as letting your dog in the house when she barks, or giving her any attention when she's jumping on you when you get home from work. Recognizing what you are doing is the very first step. Because so many of us do this without realizing it, it has usually gone on for a long time unchecked. And unfortunately, that means you're going to need a lot of patience, and possibly earplugs, too.

Let's take a look at what behaviors you are inadvertently reinforcing that you want to stop and how to stop them. Check out the following list for some good advice.

**WHAT'S HOT**

▶ I have a step-by-step guide for helping your dog overcome separation anxiety on my About.com site (http://about.com/dogs/separation anxiety). Prepare to devote at least a week to this exercise, but the end results are more than worth it. Your dog will be a much calmer pet, and you will be much happier with your dog when you aren't coming home to a destroyed house anymore.

- **Whining needs to be completely ignored.** As long as you are sure your dog's needs have been met and you know she is not in pain, don't give her any satisfaction or attention when she's whining. Wait until your dog is completely quiet before rewarding her with the action she wants. Any reaction from you, whether it is letting her outside or in, or yelling at her to be quiet, will be attention that she is looking for.

- **Comforting a fearful dog tells it that it is correct in being afraid.** By petting her and making soothing noises to your fearful dog, you are reinforcing her fearful reaction to something that should bring her fright. Fearfulness, for the most part, should be ignored. If ignoring her extreme reaction is not an easy thing to accomplish, give her something else to focus on, like a command that takes her attention away from whatever is making her afraid.

- **Barking is a behavior that needs to be ignored. Timing is crucial.** You want to reward her the minute she shuts up for longer than ten seconds, but you don't want to miss that window and give her attention when she starts barking again.

- **Punishing an action that is natural to a dog sends the wrong message.** Dogs aren't people, and they don't assign the same value to things that people do. If you yell or punish your dog for soiling in the house, she is only going to learn that you don't like to see it. Now she'll try to make you happy, and part of that could mean she'll hide her messes.
- **Punishing a dog for growling is a really bad idea.** All it really does is teach your dog not to warn, and if you do that, your dog could bite with no warnings at all. A growl should never be ignored or corrected, but the cause of it should definitely be explored.

In general, it's good to be mindful of the message you're sending your dog. She will take all of your reactions to her behavior very literally, so you want to be sure you're giving the correct reaction. When in doubt, just observe what works and what doesn't. If something isn't working out and your training isn't sticking, break it down, piece by piece, until you find the problem. If you put in the time and effort early on, you'll reap the rewards for years to come.

## Get Linked

*Early training can be incredibly frustrating, and a lot of dog owners start to wonder if having a dog in their lives is actually worth all this hassle. I assure you it is, and this period will be over shortly. When things get really bad, take a break and find something fun to do that both you and your dog can enjoy that is stress free.*

**DOGS ARE GOOD FOR US**

We have to spend a lot of time playing with our dogs, and a lot of money on making sure our dogs stay healthy, too. But it is worth it.

 http://about.com/dogs/goodforus

**THE WONDER OF MUTTS**

It's easy to forget all the great joys of owning dogs when we are in the middle of training a teenage dog. Take a break and read some of these heartwarming stories of Wonder Mutts when you get overly frustrated.

 http://about.com/dogs/wondermutts

**Chapter 8**

# Petiquette:
# The Well-Mannered Pooch

## The Socialization Process

Socialization is a lifelong process for both you and your dog. A well-socialized dog is a dog that can be taken anywhere, into any situation, that reacts in a predictable manner almost every time. The socializing process is your foundation for training and will affect every aspect of your dog's life.

Before your pup is fully vaccinated (at roughly four months old) you should introduce it to people around you. Invite people over, and reward your puppy for interacting appropriately with people. Growls, barks, and jumping up on visitors should be discouraged by ignoring the behaviors and redirecting his attention to you. Reward your dog for sitting nicely and behaving in a manner you want to encourage.

Behaviors you want to reward include:

About.

- Sitting calmly
- Sniffing at his surroundings
- Greeting other dogs or animals politely
- Allowing people to approach and greet him

Behaviors that you should ignore and redirect your dog's attention away from include:

- Jumping up
- Barking
- Growling
- Hiding
- Grabbing/nipping
- Whining

**Once your dog is fully vaccinated, start his public education.** Consider enrolling your dog in obedience classes that focus on positive training methods. These classes benefit dogs at any age and are an important step in socialization and developing a bond between a dog and you, the handler. Not only are these classes great for teaching you and your puppy how to relate to each other, but they also involve close interaction with other people, and sometimes other puppies. Regular obedience classes as your dog grows will strengthen all that socialization and keep your dog in top shape for social interactions. They are also the perfect place to nip any potential problem behaviors in the bud.

**Take your dog into posted dog-friendly locations.** These may be stores that cater to the dog-loving public, parks, beaches, or even outdoor cafés. While in these places your dog should sit patiently or stand at your side as you are browsing or having a cup of coffee. Do not allow your dog to wander. Keep her leashed at all times, and when you stop, put her in a down-stay and reward her for holding her position. You can allow her to greet other dogs, but out in a public place is not the right time to play. If she starts to get rambunctious, put her in a down immediately.

Through steady exposure, you should notice that your dog is relaxing more as things become more familiar. Make every outing fun. If you take him down a busy street and he is scared, take him to a park to play or a walk down a quiet street so that he does not fear the outings, just the situation. While he may never learn to like being out in busy areas, he will tolerate it, if only to get to the "good" part of the outing at the park after.

Most pet supply stores allow well-behaved pets inside with their owners. This is a great place to bring your dog once he's a little older and listens fairly well. Perfection isn't expected of young dogs, but dogs with no training won't be tolerated for long. Make sure your dog is on his leash at all times, and that he doesn't harass other store patrons or eat the displays.

The socialization process is never really over. As long as new situations arise, and new people are met, socialization will never be finished.

## Manners in the Home

Dogs need to learn to behave according to the rules of your home in order for you both to live in harmony. Every home is different, and for the rehomed dog, the rules of his former home might be very different from his new one. You, his new owner, need to understand that as well and give your new dog plenty of time to adjust to both the new home and the new rules.

Training a dog to stay off the furniture from puppyhood is fairly easy: Never let your puppy on the furniture. Give him a comfortable spot on the floor by your feet (it's nice if you have a rug there),

▶ Getting your dog his own comfortable resting spot, aside from his crate, may help reduce his desire to use yours. My dogs are more inclined to take over all of my favorite places when there's nothing comparable for them to lie on. There are hundreds of dog beds on the market today—from utilitarian bean-bag-style pillows to fancy daybeds and settees. Even an old, soft rug or comforter will do if you don't want to fit the price of an actual dog bed into your budget.

and keep his crate only for when he wants to go to sleep. Don't pick him up to cuddle him when you are on the upholstery. If you want to cuddle him, get down on the floor with him. When your puppy jumps up and puts his front paws on the sofa or you, put him back on the floor with a firm "No." Repeat as necessary. Never pick your dog up when he jumps up on your legs or the furniture as this will reward his actions.

If your dog is a preowned model, he may be used to using the furniture as his main parking spot. If he is, you'll know it by the nonchalant lounging on the sofa, the unworried curling up on the easy chair, or the bed he's used to taking over. At this point you'll need to decide if you want to allow him to continue as he is or if you want to change that behavior and restrict him to the floor only. There's no magic trick to help you accomplish this quickly, and a lot of owners simply give up and let the dog have its way. You don't have to be one of them. Every single time your dog lifts a paw to get up onto the sofa, give him a very loud "No!" If you enter a room and your dog has already made himself comfortable, take him by the collar and put him back on the floor with an "Off" command. It won't take him long to get the idea, and always reward him once he is on the floor, either with praise or a small treat. Persistence and a refusal to allow any exceptions to the rule will be what ultimately wins you compliance.

Even once he is retrained and follows the rules to the letter when you are around, he may make himself comfy on the furniture when you aren't at home to observe it.

## Meeting New People

From the first moment you bring your new dog home, there will be all sorts of people hoping to get a glimpse of him. Family, friends, and neighbors will all be clamoring to see the new dog, pet him, play fetch with him—you name it. And while you might be eager to show off your new pup to everyone you know, you need to keep in mind that the first few weeks in your home will be a somewhat stressful time for both of you. In addition to his new family, he will also have to get accustomed to his new house, a new yard, new rules, new food—everything will change for him. And if you weren't a dog owner before, there will be lots of changes in store for you, too. Take it slow as you introduce your new dog to all your best pals, and be sure to look out for signs that your dog is frightened, overwhelmed, or otherwise uncomfortable with a new situation.

**Some dogs are just naturally suspicious of strangers and are antisocial.** That's not necessarily a bad thing, in fact, it's a trait bred for in many breeds. But your dog does need to learn to tolerate new people if he is one of those dogs. The other end of the spectrum has the dogs that just love people. Big people, small people, lots of people, this dog loves them all, maybe too much. Both of these types of dogs, and every dog in the middle, need to learn how to greet and visit with people they aren't used to.

**Antisocial dogs should be tolerant of new people—not afraid of them.** There's a fine line between fear and distrust, and you don't want a dog to react to every new person he meets with fear. You can't make a dog like people, just like you can't make people like your dog. You can only train your dog to behave around people even if he's not happy about them being there.

Thankfully, training antisocial dogs to greet people calmly is pretty easy. It's just a matter of reinforcing a sit and stay when new people come up to her. While a person approaches your dog, hold her with her leash and put her in a sit. While the strange person proceeds to pet her, reward your dog for sitting calmly. It's important for dogs to get used to being handled by strangers; it will make all veterinarian visits and grooming a whole lot easier.

▶ Throwing a puppy party is a great way to socialize your dog with new people and other dogs. Have your friends bring their healthy, vaccinated dogs to your home for a meet-and-greet party. Your dog will have a chance to play with other dogs, and you can start the important job of training your pup to greet people with decorum.

Warning growls from your dog should be heeded by you, and it is your job to tell people not to approach if your dog is growling. You can't punish a dog for growling. If he isn't allowed to warn people off, your dog may bite without warning.

If your dog growls at new people for no discernible reason, except that he doesn't know the person, you need to step up your socialization of him and desensitize him to strangers.

**Overly enthusiastic dogs need to learn control when making new friends.** A hyper, jumping dog that slobbers all over your visitors isn't going to be viewed with much patience. As a puppy it may be cute, but puppies grow up to be dogs, and a jumping dog makes people not want to come back. Submissive urination tends to turn people right off, and you may never see them again. That might be a good thing in some cases, but you need to realize that training has to be consistent and enforced for everybody, even the people you wouldn't mind driving away.

This is not an easy thing to train. You need the cooperation of everybody that comes through your door in order for it to be effective. If just one person lets your dog jump on him or her, and encourages it by greeting your dog, petting him, and giving him the attention he wants, everything you have done up to that point has just been undone. I seriously recommend posting a note on your door telling your visitors that your dog is in training and to please ignore everything he does to try and get their attention. And be prepared for the people who think they know better anyway and will still give your dog attention for jumping up.

**Submissive urination is a frustrating habit.** It's also, unfortunately, one that many owners make the mistake of reinforcing. Any type of negative attention for this behavior will only make it worse, as will any coddling of your dog.

▶ Sometimes large crowds of people entering your home can overwhelm your dog, even once he has learned to greet people properly. If you suspect your dog is getting stressed out by all the company, make sure he has a safe spot to run to, or just put him in his crate in a quiet room to help him calm down until things are more settled.

You need to completely ignore this behavior, and treat every exit and entrance as something unworthy of note. As most submissive urination occurs when you return home after a time away, or when somebody comes over for a visit, you need to get everybody in on the act. Any type of excitement on your part will increase hers, and as she gets more excited, things get soggier. So if you come in the door and act like nothing has happened, she will eventually stop with the waterworks and calm down to greet people properly.

Ignoring improper greeting behavior works for almost any undesirable greeting. For your own returns, you just have to ignore anything from your dog until he has calmed down enough for you to command him to sit. Once he's sitting down, you can greet him with praise and affection. If you establish this as a pattern, no greeting from you until he is sitting, he'll start to sit as soon as he sees you walk in the door. Remember, though, that old habits are hard to break, so it could take a few weeks. Don't deviate from your plan either, or you'll be right back where you started.

Recruit other people to help you train your dog this way as well. You'll need to accomplish two things with their help: make visitors a commonplace thing in your home and not an exciting time, and teach your dog that a nice sit gets a reward, even if he's really happy to see somebody.

**Not every puppy is made for children.** Kids can be frightening with their constant and quick movement and lack of volume control. To a small puppy, even young children can tower over them and seem like out-of-control giants capable of great harm. Your pup needs to get used to children too, so introduce him to as many calm (if possible) children as you can but not a lot at once.

Pick a friend who has a child or two (or start with your own) and explain to the children about safe puppy handling first (see

**ELSEWHERE ON THE WEB**

▶ So why do dogs jump on people? The ASPCA's Web site has a great article on this unwanted behavior. It offers four different proven methods of stopping your dog from jumping on people; if one doesn't work, try another. (Just remember, you really need to give a method time to work. Some dogs are stubborn!) Check them out at www.aspca.org/site/PageServer?pagename=pets_jumpingup and try these on your dog today. The list of "don'ts" is a great tool for us owners too, as it tells where we've gone wrong before.

Chapter 2). Settle yourself in to supervise all interaction between your pup and the child very carefully; even a small puppy can damage a small child.

Have the child sit quietly and still while the puppy explores the room around them. Instruct the child to let the puppy come to her, and show her how to call the pup over using his name and a treat in her hand. When the puppy comes to take the treat from her hand, praise him and see if he'll let the child pet him gently. Praise and reward your pup (and the child) for every positive interaction.

Once things progress to the point of actual play, make sure that both participants know how to play carefully. This is the point when problems usually happen. All grabbing of clothing and ears must be firmly discouraged, and jumping around is a bad idea when little dogs are underfoot.

You need to make it a point to introduce your pup to all of the children he will be interacting with on a regular basis. After he has met a few of them, you can move on and have a couple of kids around at the same time, letting them chatter and make the normal amount of noise that groups of kids do. Don't forget to enforce the no jumping rule, though, and watch carefully. Be prepared to remove either the puppy or the children if things get out of hand.

## Meeting Other Dogs

Most puppies learn puppy etiquette while they are with their littermates, before (or after if left longer) eight weeks of age. They learn some bite inhibition, what is fun to play, and what hurts during rough play. Momma's corrections play a big role during this time as well. Puppies that leave the litter too soon or are orphaned may lack essential doggy social skills. Your dog may need to be taught basic dog etiquette by other dogs. Don't freak out if your exuberant puppy is nipped into submission by an adult dog that has had enough of your pup's playing. Mild corrections from older dogs,

**How can I tell if my dog is afraid or aggressive?**

▶ Your dog's body language will be your clues to his frame of mind. If he is afraid, his tail will be tucked against his body, his ears will be laid back close to his head, his head will be held closer to his body, and he may be trembling. An aggressive dog will hold his tail high (and it may be wagging), and his ears will be back close to head but not flattened. His head will be held high and he may curl his lips without outright snarling.

such as a nip here and there when your pup gets out of hand, will help your pup grow into a well-mannered dog.

**Dogs need to play with other dogs.** It's an essential part of the socialization process, and continuous exposure to other dogs will help your dog grow into a well-adjusted pet. Off-leash dog parks are the perfect place for socializing your dog with other dogs. Your dog will learn how to play with other dogs, how not to play, and you will be able to see how he interacts with other dogs to determine if he's a submissive sort or if he has a more dominant personality.

Official dog parks have strict rules of conduct, such as the following:

- **Aggressive dogs are not allowed.** This is what makes it safe for dozens of dogs to get together and play en masse without a big fear of dog fights. The odd fight may happen, especially when two dogs with strong, dominant personalities start posturing, but it is pretty rare.
- **All dogs must be vaccinated and free of communicable diseases.** It's just common sense, of course, that if your dog is sick you don't take him around other dogs. This is especially important if he's contagious or has fleas or worms.
- **Watch your dog, but don't keep him leashed.** These parks are off leash for a reason. Not only does keeping your dog on a leash rob him of valuable play time and socialization, but it could be the cause of aggression in your dog. Some dogs don't react well to other dogs when they can't get away and are tied in one spot. Remove the flight option from your dog's fight or flight instinct, and all you have left is fight. Don't force your dog into a cornered position and you will see that he is just fine.

When dogs get together they will sort themselves into a ranking order with no help from their humans. Dogs will growl, posture, and maybe even nip other dogs while sorting their rank. One dog will generally retain the top spot and all others will fall into line behind him. More submissive dogs will be sorted quickly, falling to bottom rank, while more dominant personalities may take some posturing and growling to figure out who's on top. Unless things get overly violent and injuries are imminent, it's best if you do not interfere.

**Dog fights are serious situations—not only for your dog, but also for the others involved.** If the posturing between your dog and another at the park escalates into a full-fledged dog fight, you will need to separate them before permanent damage is done. Whatever you do, do not get between the dogs, you will be bitten! Most dogs will not turn on you if they are intent on your dog, but if you get in the way of their teeth, all bets are off. Your best bet is to immobilize the dogs one at a time. Early stages of a dog fight are quick snaps and a lot of snarling, so you have a few minutes to work out a plan.

If you aren't alone and have another adult with you, each of you will need to get behind a dog and grab a tail. Pull the dogs apart slowly (do not yank) until they let go of each other's body parts voluntarily. Work them backwards until you have a good distance between them, and loop the leash around your dog's head. Don't bother trying to clip it on to his collar at this point, let him get settled first. The other adult with the other dog should be doing the same to his battle participant. Secure him with his leash to a stationary object (a fence post, or even a street sign), or put him in his kennel or your vehicle right away.

If your dog doesn't have a tail, loop the leash around the dog's entire back end (this could be tricky). If you can, if the dogs haven't connected yet, loop it over his head and pull him back to a secure location. If you are alone, secure your dog first, then go around and do the same to the other dog. Leave both dogs secured until you can locate the other dog's owner.

**If you suspect your dog is dog aggressive, do not take him to off-leash play areas.**   In fact, you really shouldn't take him anywhere that he'll be bound to run into other dogs until you have had him evaluated by a professional. Some of dog aggression is dominance, and some of it may be bred into his genetic makeup. In either case you'll need more help than a book can really give you, and a professional dog trainer will be the way to go.

## Scary Situations

Even dogs that are confident in everyday situations may find themselves afraid of things that are unusual or excessively loud. Fireworks, thunderstorms, traffic, or even overly crowded places are common fear inducers. And then there are the things that cause you anxiety. Your dog will pick up on your fear, and what would normally not bother a well-socialized dog may cause it to be fearful if you are. I'm terribly uncomfortable in crowds, and because I'm anxious about them, my dogs are too. It has taken a lot of work to desensitize my dogs to crowds when I can't even tolerate them well myself.

**A lot of dogs are afraid of loud noises.**   Fireworks and thunderstorms are pure torture for these dogs. The fear of loud noises can put your dog in serious danger if he's outside when the noise happens. Dogs have been known to break down gates and jump over tall fences when the fear is strong enough. After any fireworks displays animal shelters see an increase in the number of dogs that are found wandering the streets, and being hit by a car is a serious possibility.

ELSEWHERE ON THE WEB

▶ The Pit Bull Rescue Central Web site has a page on preventing dog fights. Visit www.pbrc.net/fightinfo.html and www.pbrc.net/breakfight .html for information on preventing fights from starting in the first place and how to break them up using a break stick if your pit bull is in a dog fight.

▶ If you're having trouble recording the noise from a thunderstorm (because nature doesn't always cooperate), you can buy recordings of loud noises just for desensitizing your dog at some of the bigger pet stores. You may even be able to find recordings of gunfire and fireworks that you can download to your computer on the Internet and play through your computer speakers.

You can try to train your dog to sit still during a thunderstorm or provide a hiding spot to run to, but it's much better to desensitize him and remove the fear of loud noises since you can't control when the noise occurs.

Try to figure out what kind of noises drive your dog into a fearful frenzy. If it's all sudden, loud noises, you'll have a bit of work ahead of you. If it's just one or two types of noise that do it, like thunder or gunfire, things will be a bit easier on you.

Using a tape recorder, record the noises your dog responds negatively to. Pick a nice calm day, and play back the tape (or disc) of scary noises. Start off playing it at a low level of volume, low enough that your dog isn't reacting to it yet. Gradually increase the volume.

Once your dog starts to react to the sounds, put him in a down-stay, then reward him for staying in the face of fear. Keep the recording at this volume level until your dog starts to relax. As he relaxes make sure you heap praise on him, but do not make the mistake of comforting him if he shows fear by shaking, drooling, or whining.

Keeping the same volume level that he is now relaxed at, play your recording at different times during the day and at night. After a couple of days the noise shouldn't affect him at all, and it will be time to increase the volume.

Turn the volume up just loud enough for your dog to show fear again. You don't want to overdo it and strike terror in your dog, but you do want it loud enough that he's reacting negatively again. The idea is to gradually increase his tolerance for the volume and suddenness of the noise so that he will no longer fear the real thing, not terrify him into hiding.

**A fear of crowds is a harder thing to fix.** You'll need to step up your dog's socialization, repeatedly taking her places that involve other people. Take care not to encourage fearful behavior, like petting her when he's frightened or otherwise offering comfort. This will only reinforce her fear. Instead, give her a specific job to do, such as sit, heel, or stay. Reward her for focusing on her given task. Gradually increase her exposure to people in various situations and locations.

If you recruit your friends, start off with just one or two friends in your house (it's best to start in a familiar place), and have people come in one at a time and mingle, making conversation and generally behaving like people in a crowd would behave. Don't allow your dog to escape, but put her in a down and make her stay for the duration. As soon as she starts to show signs of relaxing, reward her. Watch for the easing up of tense muscles or a move to get more comfortable and out of a rigid position. Her breathing will also become more regular and her ears should move forward, not laid back against her head. Note that by attracting your dog's attention to you when you reward her she may tense up again, but she should settle and relax much quicker this time around. Bring in another person or two to repeat the process.

**Car rides can also cause your dog a fair amount of trepidation.**   Not every dog was born to ride. Some need to learn to love the car, if only for the ending destination. A dog that is relaxed and happy in the car will just look happy about being there. His body will be relaxed, his tongue may be hanging out but not panting excessively, his tail may wag, and his ears will be pricked forward, not laid flat against his head. A relaxed dog will have no problems settling into a sit and holding his position or laying down to get comfortable.

A dog that is afraid will be twitchy, jumpy, and have trouble settling into one position. His ears may be plastered against his head, and he'll pant excessively and drool. He might even vomit as a result of his fear.

So why does your dog fear the car? Where do you take him in it? Part of it may be that the only time he's actually in the car is because he's on his way someplace less than fun.

It's important to understand before starting that some dogs just get car sick and there's nothing you can do about it. It's not fear but actual motion sickness. Your dog may be excited and happy to be going somewhere, but he'll still get sick and barf all over your back seat halfway there.

Cars are scary objects that vibrate and make a lot of noise. Like any other object of fear, you can desensitize your dog to a running vehicle. He may never be a cruising buddy, but he may see the car as a means to an end and cease to be afraid. Kari is not my shotgun dog. He's okay and even enjoys it a little for short, slower car rides through town, but longer trips, even a twenty-minute drive at highway speeds, turns him into a frothing, shaking wreck.

Your first day of car desensitization begins with your car sitting in your driveway with its engine off and all the doors wide open. Walk your dog around the car in circles, and every time he sniffs at the vehicle, tires, or in the doors, reward him. Do this four or five times during the first day.

On the second day, with your vehicle still silent and doors opened, lure your dog into the car. Have him jump through and exit out the other side. If he feels up to exploring, let him, and be sure you praise him lavishly. Instead of pushing on to phase two, continue this for two days instead of one. Remember to reward your dog for every step he takes on his own.

On the fourth day, start your car. With all the doors opened and the engine running (leave the radio off though), let your dog explore. Now is the time you may see more reluctance to get close to your vehicle.

Using treats and the leash, lure and coax your dog into the vehicle. Even if he only sticks his head in, give him a reward. As with the first day, slowly get your dog closer to the car and reward him for every step he takes that brings him closer to the running vehicle. Make it sound like jumping in the car is the greatest game you have ever played.

Once your dog willingly enters a running vehicle, put him in a sit inside the car and close the doors with both of you inside. Reward him for sitting with you quietly. Do not comfort him if he shows any fear. After just a minute or two, open the door and let your dog out. He may bolt out of the car, or he may opt to stay and sit with you. Either outcome is fine at this stage. After a couple of hours, lure your dog into the car with you again. Gradually increase his time inside the car with you until he can sit quietly beside you for five minutes.

It's time to get your car moving. Since you need to correct your dog and issue commands, you'll need to get somebody else to drive the car. Put your dog in the car, in the spot he will always use, and secure him in place with a seatbelt device. Sit as close to him as you can, and as the car starts to move, tell him to sit, then stay. Before he starts to tremble, reward him for sitting. If you can't catch him before the shaking starts, then you'll have to ignore it. If there is room, have him lie down and reward him for laying down on command. Remember that you cannot comfort him if he starts to shake, drool, or whine. In fact, you'll need to ignore these behaviors completely.

Be relaxed yourself, yawn (to show you are unconcerned), and talk with the driver in a calm voice. Show that this ride is nothing to be afraid of. It may help your dog even more if you show that you are happy and excited about going somewhere. Use a high-pitched voice, and laugh with the person driving the car.

Make this first trip and every trip for the first few weeks have a fun destination. A trip to the veterinarian's office is a not a good first trip in the car. Take your dog to a place where he can run

**TOOLS YOU NEED**

▶ Get a friend to help with desensitizing your dog to vehicles. Have your friend hold your dog on the leash on one side of the car while you stand on the other side so your dog can see you through the open doors. This will make it easier for you to coax your dog through the car, and it beats trying to climb in first or trying to push him in the car first and you following. Make sure your dog knows you have a tasty treat waiting for him when he jumps through the doors.

around and play, or drive him around the block and back home where you should have plenty of treats and praise waiting.

If every trip in the car is to go someplace less than fun, then your dog is right to fear the drive. Make sure you go plenty of fun places in between the necessary trips to the veterinarians or other undesirable locations.

### Get Linked
*On my About.com Web site you'll find lots of information on socializing your dog and desensitizing him to strange noises. Check out these great links.*

**THE NOISE DESENSITIZATION PROCESS**

A long and slow process, desensitizing your dog to his fear triggers is the only sure way to cure your dog of his fears for good.

 http://about.com/dogs/noiseanxiety

**PLACES AND WAYS TO SOCIALIZE**

Here are some great ways to socialize your new dog. Make sure you ask for permission before bringing your dog into other people's homes and businesses first.

 http://about.com/dogs/socialize

## Chapter 9

# Is Something Wrong?

### The "Ick" Factor

Everything that comes out of your dog is a clue, no matter what end it comes out of. One of the most interesting facets of dog ownership is the wealth of information found in the worst places. Poking through dog poop on a sunny afternoon to find out if your dog is infested with worms is nobody's idea of a picnic, but it's one of those things that we sometimes must do. Poop can tell us an awful lot about your dog's internal well-being. If you suspect your dog is ill, your dog's fecal matter could be your first clue as to what is wrong with him.

**Blood is always an alarming sight when it comes from any part of the dog.** Unfortunately, it takes on a whole new dimension when you see it in the stools of your dog. Bloody diarrhea is one of the first signs of parvovirus in puppies, and it foretells other serious illnesses. Intestinal tears and a foreign object lodged in the anus will also cause blood in your dog's bowel movements. How much blood and what color it is will be something your vet will want to know, so gather up a sample and bring it in with you at your appointment.

**TOOLS YOU NEED**

▸ A few pairs of nonlatex gloves and a strong stomach are important items to have when poking through a dog pile looking for clues. If you don't have any gloves, you can stick your hand in a plastic bag (one with no holes, I hope). You don't need any special instruments for gathering samples, just a clean plastic container and a stick will do fine.

**Some varieties of intestinal worms can be seen by the naked eye in a dog's stool.** Isn't that a pleasant image to contemplate? Roundworms are the most common and often noticed immediately. Long, spaghetti-looking roundworms can be found in the stools of heavily infested dogs and puppies, but eggs can be detected early on by a routine fecal exam at the veterinarian's office. Roundworms are passed from mother to puppies in utero and to adult dogs when they ingest feces from an infected animal.

**Tapeworms are long, segmented worms that live in an infected person's or animal's intestines.** These are most often noticed when the worms start to shed segments full of eggs, which are often found around the anus or in stools. These segments look like grains of rice when dry, but they are squishy and may be moving when fresh. Tapeworms are spread by ingesting fleas that have eaten the eggs.

**Diarrhea is a common ailment in dogs.** The cause can be from something as simple as an upset stomach from too many dog cookies, or it can be something serious like parvovirus. Alone it may not be alarming, but if you add it in with other symptoms present, it can mean big trouble. Not to mention that diarrhea for any significant length of time causes dehydration. Make sure your ill-feeling pal has plenty of fresh water to drink at all times. If he is not drinking at all, it's a sign of a serious problem and he needs to be seen by a veterinarian right away.

When my dogs have diarrhea but are otherwise acting normal, I will put them on a bland diet of boiled hamburger meat, plain, cooked rice, a couple of teaspoons of yogurt, and lots of water. Usually it only lasts for a day or two at the most, and the bland diet helps the output slow down.

**Loose stools are a common problem with some dogs that have digestive tract issues.** If your dog has diarrhea on a regular basis, you should book him in to see the vet and ask about what might be causing it. It may be something as simple as switching to a different food. And on the flip side, switching your dog's food abruptly can also cause gastrointestinal distress and diarrhea.

**Vomit is another wonderful substance that can tell us many things.** Dogs can vomit at will, which makes things much easier on all of us. If something is sitting wrong in their stomachs, they bring it back up, although it's often in a most inconvenient spot.

Foamy, clear vomit is a symptom of serious illnesses like parvovirus and coronavirus. An inability to keep anything down, including water, is a serious sign of something wrong. Don't wait too long to see if it passes. If watery vomit lasts longer than one day, or if it happens every time your dog eats or drinks, or keeps happening, your dog needs to see a veterinarian as soon as possible.

## Where to Look for Health Problems

When a person is sick, you can probably tell right away. This is not only because of any physical symptoms the person may be displaying, but also because she can tell you she feels ill and can complain of any aches and pains. Dogs, on the other hand, can't communicate how they're feeling. You'll have to be extra observant to

**ASK YOUR GUIDE**

*My dog throws up a yellow liquid almost every morning. What causes this?*

▶ Throwing up yellow stomach bile every morning isn't as alarming as it sounds. If it happens roughly the same time every morning, and your dog eats at the same time every night; he may just be going too long with an empty stomach. Try feeding your dog a small amount of food (not a full meal) directly before bedtime to help settle his stomach.

notice changes in your dog's health, and this also entails knowing where to look.

For example, a glossy, clean-looking coat is not just a testament to your grooming skills. Likewise, a dull, dingy-looking coat may be your first warning that your furry buddy isn't feeling well. A healthy dog also has a vibrancy and vitality in her bearing, a steady gait, and only vaguely stinky dog breath (face it, nobody finds dog breath pleasant). Knowing how your dog looks healthy will make you more adept at noticing when she looks a little off. A change in appearance for the worse, added to any other symptoms, no matter how commonplace, can spell trouble.

**Dull, dingy-looking fur is a sure sign that something is just not right.** Either your dog is in desperate need of a bath and a brush, or you need to look deeper.

Internal parasites can cause a normally beautiful coat to look dull and unappealing. Mites on his skin may also be the culprit. Some are clearly visible to the naked eye, looking like small flakes of dandruff walking around in your dog's fur, and others need a microscope at your vet's office to diagnose. A poor-looking coat is also a symptom of overall ill health, so a trip to your vet's office along with a list of any other symptoms she is experiencing is in order.

**If your dog's just not her usual, exuberant self, then it is time for a checkup.** It could be something as simple as her having eaten something that didn't agree with her at the moment, or it could be an early warning of bigger trouble. Either way, it will save you some serious time and money if you catch any issues early on rather than letting it escalate into something that might not be so easy to fix.

ELSEWHERE ON THE WEB

▶ If you're looking for more in-depth information on health issues, be sure to visit www.thepetcenter.com. It's a large Web site created and maintained by veterinarians, and it's designed to help the average pet owner better understand the general health and well-being of their pets and health-related issues. Go on a photo tour of a neutering, a femoral head ostectomy, and many other surgical procedures. You can also view x-ray photos of common dog problems such as broken bones and bladder stones.

**Dogs aren't known for having nice breath.**  Still, if your dog's breath has a truly awful, offensive odor, you can be pretty sure that something is amiss. Often it is something relatively simple to fix at the vet's, such as an abscessed tooth or even just tartar buildup. But if his teeth look clean, white, and healthy, you'll need to look deeper. Foul and odd-smelling dog breath is a symptom in all of these issues:

- Kidney failure
- Liver failure
- Intestinal disease
- Intestinal blockage

## Choking and Ingesting Poisonous Substances

Let's face it: Dogs like to eat things they shouldn't. From the plants in the garden to children's toys, the average dog will take a taste of anything and everything. As a dog owner, it's smart to have a general idea of what to do if your dog starts choking, and you should know how to handle a dog that has ingested a poisonous or caustic substance.

**The doggy version of the Heimlich maneuver is an easy thing to learn.**  Dogs tend to mouth a lot of things, so choking on something is a pretty common scenario. Signs of choking are:

- Pawing at the face and throat
- Gagging
- Bulging eyes
- Coughing
- Struggling to breathe

**ASK YOUR GUIDE**

*My dog's breath doesn't smell bad; in fact, it smells rather sweet. Is this normal?*

▶ No, this isn't normal at all. A sweet or fruity-smelling breath is a symptom of undiagnosed diabetes, and it is definitely worth a trip to the veterinarian for further investigation. Be sure to take note of any other odd behaviors happening at the same time, such as drinking more water than usual and sudden weight gain.

If you are sure your dog is choking, first try to remove the object with your fingers or pliers if it's lodged high enough in your dog's throat. If you are unable to reach it, the Heimlich maneuver is your best bet. Grasp him from behind around his waist below his ribs. Put your fist in the hollow just underneath his ribs, and give three or four hard thrusts upwards to dislodge what he's choking on.

Once the object has been removed, check your dog to make sure he is breathing freely. Bring him to a veterinarian's office right away to check for any damages.

**If you suspect your dog has ingested a poisonous substance, call your veterinarian immediately.** Toxic substances can do a lot of damage in a short amount of time, and poisons travel quickly through a dog's system. If you suspect your dog has been poisoned by something, you will need to bring him in to an emergency vet clinic.

Here is a list of the most common household toxins and the symptoms your dog might exhibit if he ingests them:

- **Acetaminophen (Tylenol):** excessive drooling, vomiting, weakness, abdominal pain
- **Antifreeze:** stumbling, staggering, vomiting, seizures
- **Chocolate:** staggering, labored breathing, vomiting, diarrhea, abdominal pain, tremors, fever, heart rate increase, arrhythmia, seizures, coma, death
- **Coffee/cocoa:** staggering, labored breathing, vomiting, diarrhea, abdominal pain, tremors, fever, heart rate increase, arrhythmia, seizures, coma, death
- **Grapes/raisins:** vomiting, diarrhea, abdominal pain, lethargy
- **Household cleaners** (toilet bowl cleaners, pine oil cleaner, bleach, detergents): skin irritation, vomiting, diarrhea, internal organ damage, bloody vomit, bloody stools

**TOOLS YOU NEED**

▶ Keep the phone number and address of your veterinarian and the emergency clinic as well as the ASPCA's Animal Poison Control Center phone number, 1-888-4-ANI-HELP (1-888-264-4357), posted on the fridge. This will save you time in a true emergency. It will also be there in plain sight if you have somebody coming in to care for your dog while you are out.

- **Insecticides:** excessive drooling, weeping eyes, excessive urination, diarrhea, muscle spasms, weakness, difficulty breathing
- **Mushrooms:** abdominal pain, drooling, liver damage, kidney damage, vomiting, diarrhea, convulsions, coma, death
- **Onions:** hemolytic anemia, labored breathing, liver damage, vomiting, diarrhea, discolored urine

But your home isn't the only place where potentially dangerous substances hide. Your landscaped yard may also hold a number of plants that could be toxic to your dog. Pretty to look at but painful to eat, the following common plants and trees should be kept out of your dog's reach. This list also contains the corresponding symptoms of ingestion.

- **Amaryllis:** stomach upset, lethargy, shock, death
- **Asparagus fern:** vomiting, respiratory problems, kidney failure, tremors, abdominal pain
- **Caladium:** mouth irritation, stomach upset, asphyxiation, tremors, seizures
- **Calla lily:** stomach upset, mouth irritation, asphyxiation, seizures, death
- **Christmas rose:** stomach upset, diarrhea, convulsions, death
- **Colocasia (elephant's ear):** mouth irritation, stomach upset, asphyxiation, tremors, seizures, death
- **Crocus:** stomach upset, liver failure, lethargy, shock, death
- **Daffodil (bulb):** stomach upset, tremors, seizures, lethargy, heart failure, death
- **Dieffenbachia (dumb cane):** mouth irritation, stomach upset, asphyxiation, tremors, seizures, death
- **Easter lily:** stomach upset, kidney failure

- **English ivy:** stomach upset, hyperactivity, labored breathing, drooling, fever, thirst increase, pupil dilation, staggering
- **Foxglove:** stomach upset, tremors, seizures, lethargy, heart failure, death
- **Jessamine:** seizures, respiratory failure
- **Peony:** stomach upset, staggering, tremors, seizures, heart failure, death
- **Philodendron (devil's ivy):** upset stomach, convulsions, asphyxiation, death
- **Narcissus:** stomach upset, staggering, tremors, seizures, heart failure, death
- **Umbrella plant:** vomiting, respiratory problems, kidney failure, tremors, abdominal pain

Burns in and around the mouth and nose may indicate that your dog has ingested a caustic substance. Do not induce vomiting as it will cause further exposure and damage to the throat and mouth. This is a list of the most common caustic chemicals:

- Battery acid
- Bleach
- Carbolic acid
- Dishwasher soap
- Drain cleaner
- Fertilizer
- Glue
- Household cleaners
- Kerosene
- Laundry detergent
- Motor oil
- Paintbrush cleaner

- Paint thinner
- Pine cleaner
- Plaster
- Putty
- Nail polish
- Nail polish remover
- Sidewalk salt
- Turpentine

If you suspect your dog has ingested one of these or any other caustic substance, seek veterinary care immediately.

## Emergency Signs

A lot of dog owners tend to treat things at home as much as they can, or they put off a trip to the vet in the hopes that whatever is plaguing their dog will resolve itself before too long. Sometimes that decision can end up costing them a lot more money, and in some cases the life of their dog, than it would have had the dog seen a veterinarian sooner. Don't let this happen to you. If you see any of the symptoms described in this section, get your dog to the veterinarian's office or animal hospital as soon as possible.

**Rapid swelling of the abdomen is a sign of trouble.** Even though it most often occurs in deep-chested dogs (such as basset hounds, Great Danes, and other large breeds), bloat can occur in any dog. Abdominal swelling is its primary symptom, and it must be treated immediately by a veterinarian. Bloat is a fatal condition that kills a dog very quickly unless it is corrected within hours of occurrence. It causes the stomach to flip around and cut off the blood circulation to your dog's internal organs.

Because bloat is essentially gases that build up in your dog's stomach that he can't release, it is thought to be preventable to some extent. Raising your dog's food and water dishes might help prevent him from gulping air into his stomach as he eats, and make sure he does not do any vigorous exercising for at least an hour after he has eaten.

**Bloody diarrhea is an ominous sign.** Just a little bit of bright red blood might not be a big problem, but if you add it to diarrhea it spells trouble. This is one of the primary symptoms of parvovirus, coronavirus, worms, ulcers, and other serious illnesses.

On that same note, vomiting blood (hematemesis) is a scary sight. This could indicate a variety of problems, including a foreign object in the system, blood disorders, poisoning, ulcers, and even cancer. Vomiting blood is a sign that your dog needs to see a veterinarian in order to get the proper diagnosis.

**In the case of any trauma, your dog needs to see a veterinarian immediately.** If your dog has been struck by a heavy object or hit by a car, don't wait and see if he develops problems before taking him to the vet. Fractures, internal bleeding, and organ injury while invisible to the naked eye can be the death of your dog if left untreated for even a short period of time.

**Sudden lameness and a refusal to walk or rise requires immediate investigation.** Broken bones are not always obvious, and if you see one of your dog's limbs suddenly facing the wrong direction, get him to the veterinarian as fast as you can. Some dogs will rise with a fractured leg but will hold it as high as they can while hobbling around. If your dog favors a leg and you can see that it is more than the usual limp a dog gets when he trips over something, take him in. By the way, your dog's tail can also break. If there is a visible bend and it is swollen and painful, he needs to have it seen by a veterinarian.

**Outside of diagnosed epileptic seizures, any convulsions are cause for an emergency vet visit.** Seizures are caused by a number of problems, including head trauma, tumors, and poisoning. Seizures that last longer than a couple of minutes will cause brain damage and can bring on heart failure, so it is essential that your dog is seen by a veterinarian immediately. The first time my dog, Loki, had a seizure I didn't even know what it was; it looked like he was choking until he fell over.

**An inability to urinate requires veterinary assistance.** Often caused by bladder stones or urinary tract infections, difficulty urinating is one sign that your dog needs to see a vet as soon as she can. Both require medication: infections need antibiotics, and stones need to broken down into a passable size or surgically removed. If your dog's urinary tract is blocked by a stone, this could actually kill her if left for any length of time.

**Any time your dog has trouble breathing it is an emergency.** There are dozens of reasons why this is happening, and you need a veterinarian to get to the bottom of it. Labored breathing inhibits oxygen from reaching the brain and can cause brain damage if it lasts for an extended period of time.

**Lethargy is another one of those things that need to be investigated right away.** This is a symptom that is often overlooked. If your dog is conscious but unresponsive, it could be a sign of a serious or life-threatening illness, such as poisoning, brucellosis, rabies, blastomycosis, and many more. On that same note, any time your dog is in an unconscious and unresponsive state, she needs emergency veterinary care. Almost all dogs are easily disturbed when sleeping, and if yours suddenly isn't, and she is not hard of hearing or infirm, bring her to a veterinarian immediately.

▶ I admit it; I'm in love with the Doggie Dooley Waste Management System. It's a miniature septic tank for dog waste. You just scoop the waste up and drop it in the tank that is embedded into the ground. The tank doesn't take up a lot of space either, or smell bad. In fact, it's the perfect solution for dog owners who like to have a dog-doo-free yard with little fuss. Check out www.doggie dooley.com and see it for yourself.

**Swelling of the face and neck area is an extreme allergic reaction.** Most often a reaction to a bee sting or other bug bite, swelling of the neck area can suffocate your dog quickly if his throat swells shut. It could also be caused by a foreign object that may have become lodged in his mouth or throat. Both of these problems can be treated successfully with no lasting harm done to your dog, but only if they are treated immediately.

**Thick mucous discharge from the anus that does not produce a bowel movement is an emergency.** When unaccompanied by a bowel movement, this is usually a sure sign of a bowel obstruction, and it is often accompanied by a high fever, lethargy, and an almost hunched-up posture. If your dog is exhibiting these signs, emergency veterinary care is needed as soon as possible. Bowel obstructions cause hypovolemia and shock and are fatal if left untreated for even a short amount of time.

**Uncontrollable bleeding must be dealt with.** Dogs can die from blood loss very quickly. Minor cuts can usually be treated at home, but if you cannot control the bleeding from an injury, you must have the dog's injury treated by a veterinarian.

**Knowing the signs of shock could save your dog's life.** If your dog has gone into shock, you must get him veterinary care immediately. Look for these signs:

- Pupil dilation
- Sudden weakness or lethargy
- Body temperature decreases
- Pale lips and gums
- Tremors

- Weak pulse
- Shallow breathing

Wrap your dog up in a warm blanket to conserve his body heat, and keep him still while you transport him to an emergency clinic.

**If your previously healthy dog suddenly can't get up from a prone position, don't hesitate to bring her in.** Extreme pain or muscle weakness in a normally healthy animal is a definite cause for concern and could be caused by a number of different problems from spinal cord injury to complete organ failure. Any delay will not only worsen your dog's condition, but could limit treatment options or cause permanent damage.

**Any sudden change in your dog's behavior is a cause for concern.** If your usually placid and easygoing dog has suddenly turned into a snarling, crabby, and irritable wreck, your first action should be calling your veterinarian. Dogs generally don't have "bad hair" days, at least not to extremes, so if your dog does a complete turnaround in personality, there is likely a very serious health problem. Pain can turn the happiest dog in the world into an unstable mess who'll bite and snarl at anything, so please don't disregard your dog's unusual mood swings.

## Alarming but Normal

Dogs are just strange animals, and a lot of what they do, they do because they are dogs and nothing more. Keeping in mind that any sudden behavioral changes ought to be investigated, these behavior quirks and personality perks are just part of your dog's being.

**Eating grass is one behavior that stumps a lot of dog owners.** It looks like something dogs do because they are ill, and when they regurgitate it later, it looks even more alarming. There are a number of theories about why dogs do this. One reason may be because grass winds itself around items in the stomach cavity, making it easier for the dog to vomit it up later. However, it also seems to be something that dogs just do, possibly because they like the taste of grass.

**Though it will repulse you as his owner, your dog will probably try to eat his own or another dog's feces.** Some sources suggest that it indicates a lack of certain nutrients, but not what those nutrients may be. By its very nature we try to assign it as a symptom of a larger problem, but in reality it's just something that dogs do because their tastes are vastly different from ours.

But even though it's a natural thing for dogs to do, there are ways we can put a stop to it. Direct supervision while outside with a sharp "No" and removing him from the area when he attempts to eat feces is one method that will prove successful over time if it's coupled with strong praise and rewards as he leaves the tempting snack behind. However, immediate removal of the offending material is really the best solution. He can't eat it if it's not left for him to go back to.

**Snacking out of the cat's litter box is another big gross-out habit of dogs.** Cats are obligate carnivores, and their stools are full of good-smelling and tasty proteins that dogs just love because cat food is almost entirely made of meat. You can put an end to this habit easily enough, though. Putting the litter box up on a shelf where an agile cat can still jump to access it is one solution. You could also place a cover on the box or even use one of the newer self-cleaning litter boxes.

▶ Eating "kitty crunchies" and a lot of other habits that make a dog owner cringe are behaviors the dog has taught himself where the very action the dog takes results in a reward with no human intervention. Counter surfing, garbage eating, and food stealing are a few of these unwanted behaviors that are self rewarding. You can read more about these behaviors and how to stop them on my Web site (http://about.com/dogs/selfrewarding).

**Luckily, you can train your dog not to do these things.** "Leave it," "Stop," or just plain old "No" are the commands for these situations. It's our hope that your dog will be told enough to stop when you are around that he will eventually end the behavior altogether, but that may be expecting too much.

There are a few ways to train your dog to leave things alone on command. All involve a negative stimulus and a positive reward for stepping away from forbidden objects. You can use any command you like, from "Drop it!" to "Step away!," as long as you use that command consistently and don't confuse the dog by having more than one command mean the same thing.

You'll want to start by baiting your dog with something you know that he wants. In my Raider's case, it was an orange (he loved the juice squirting out when he sunk his teeth into it, but he didn't like to eat the actual orange). Your negative stimulus will be your loud voice issuing your command of choice and the leash pulling him away.

Attach your dog to his leash and let the session begin. Allow him to get right up close to your bait. Issue your command, then pull him away firmly (do not jerk him away). It's actually better if you walk a bit of ways away. As soon as he focuses on you, and not the bait, lavish him with praise and a tasty treat. It does help if his reward is more valuable (to him) than your bait is. If you issue your command and he stops without you pulling him away, reward him immediately.

Keep your training sessions very short, but have several throughout the week, four or five times a day. Don't end a day with a failure either. If your dog manages to get hold of the bait, get it back as soon as you can (see the section on trading in Chapter 11). Start from the beginning again in a few minutes, and physically pull him away from the bait.

**ASK YOUR GUIDE**

*Why does my dog eat poop?*

▶ Coprophagia, or dung eating, is very common. Most of the time dogs do it just because it smells tasty to them. You can try putting Tabasco sauce on the piles, but honestly, if you are right there, the best solution is just to pick it up right away. You can buy a powder called Forbid that has the effect of rendering the rendered food distasteful.

Once your dog is listening well to you on a leash and steps away from the bait without your correction, trade the leash for a long rope. Start with a twenty-foot rope at first, and begin again with the tempting bait. Your dog needs to learn that he has to respond even if you are not standing directly next to or in front of him. Gradually increase the distance between you and your dog.

When you think your dog is ready, drop the end of the rope. Within a week of starting this exercise you should be able to remove the rope altogether, leaving your dog to "leave it" off leash.

## First Aid

Every dog owner should have a well-stocked first-aid kit in the home and a smaller version in the main vehicle. Every first-aid kit should include a small booklet on emergency first-aid procedures for common emergencies. Ask your veterinarian if she sells them or if she can recommend one. You can buy a prestocked kit from any number of online retailers and outdoor sports stores, or you can use this list to help you populate one yourself.

- A laminated card with emergency phone numbers: your veterinarian, the emergency after-hours clinic, your emergency contacts, and the National Animal Poison Control Center's number (1-888-264-4357)
- A muzzle: Even if he would never in a million years bite you, all bets are off when pain has taken over
- Benadryl or other veterinarian-approved antihistamine for allergic reactions
- Scissors
- Tweezers
- Digital thermometer (a dog's normal body temperature is between 101°F and 102°F)

- Sterile eye wash to wash out any foreign objects
- Rubber gloves
- Antibiotic ointment
- Styptic powder to stop bleeding
- Gauze bandages
- Spare leash: This can be used to tie up a splint, or anything else you can think of, even securing your dog to an inanimate object
- Pliers: for use in removing objects from your dog, such as fish hooks or thorns
- Hydrogen peroxide
- A mild disinfectant soap

Keep your first-aid kit in the same spot in your home at all times, and make sure that your family members and any other of your dog's regular caregivers know where to find it.

Every dog owner should also keep a veterinarian-approved first-aid manual in their home. This is not the small booklet that stays in your first-aid kit, rather, it is a full-sized manual that stays on your bookshelf. I have and recommend *The Dog Owner's Home Veterinary Handbook* by James M. Giffin, M.D., and Liisa D. Carlson, D.V.M. It covers all the common emergencies often encountered in your dog-owning years, some not-so-common scenarios, and first aid for out in the field as well.

It's important to have a first-aid kit for your vehicle, too, along with a blanket made of strong material and a spare collar. You can use the blanket to keep your dog warm if needed, and to help you move and lift him safely without causing further injury. Gently slide the blanket underneath your dog (do not roll him onto it). If you have somebody else with you, pick up one end of the blanket and have your friend pick up the other end, creating a hammock with

**ELSEWHERE ON THE WEB**

▸ Check out www.doglogic.com/firstaid.htm for information on emergency first aid for different situations, artificial respiration, and canine CPR. It's a good idea to have read the information long before you take your dog out in the field, since you won't have your computer with you. You may even wish to print the pages and keep them in your car if your dog is prone to one of the conditions listed.

your dog inside. You can safely carry your dog to your vehicle and transport him to a veterinary hospital for treatment.

If you are alone and far from your vehicle, fold your dog into the blanket as above, grasp an end in each hand, and with your back to your dog, heft him up onto your back like a sling.

For a splint, you can use any strong, straight, and long object, like a stripped tree branch, and secure it to your dog's damaged limb using the spare leash. It's very important for you to study a first-aid manual if you spend a lot of your time outdoors and away from home with your dog to learn the proper techniques of splinting and lifting and carrying an injured dog.

## Get Linked

*The medical side of dog ownership is no fun, but luckily there are ways to make it easier. There are some great ways to make things easier for you on my About.com Dogs site. Here are just a few articles that will help you along.*

**HOW TO MEDICATE DOGS**

Not every dog owner is blessed (or cursed) with a dog that looks at everything as a tasty treat. For the rest of us, we need to disguise the drugs in drool-worthy treats.

 http://about.com/dogs/howtomedicate

**COLLECTING A URINE SAMPLE**

You may feel ridiculous doing this, but I have found it to be the most hassle-free way of bringing dog urine in to the vet's office.

http://about.com/dogs/urinesample

## Chapter 10

# Common Problems and Their Solutions

## Shedding, Drooling, and Goopy Eyes

There are two issues that dogs are well known for that turn a lot of people off of dog ownership: shedding and drooling. If one isn't bad enough, the other will seal the deal. Goopy eyes is another less obvious issue, but it is one of those lovely dog traits that all dog owners have to deal with.

**Nearly every dog sheds.** It may only be an amount so small as to be unnoticeable (single-coated breeds), or it may be enough to make another dog (or two or three), but almost every dog sheds something. Even hairless breeds have tufts of fur that lose a hair here and there. There really is no escape from it; it's something we just need to accept as part of a dog being a dog. If shedding is a big problem for you, then you should choose a dog that sheds very little. For the rest of us, we can only do damage control.

▶ A shedding blade is just the thing for medium- and long-haired dogs. It digs deep into the undercoat and pulls out all the loose hair with little effort on your part. Removing the loose hair prevents matting and helps to prevent hot spots as well. One size fits all; a shedding blade comes apart at the handle to tackle the bigger dogs.

Shaving won't save you. It may actually make your problems worse in the long run. A dog's coat protects it from the sun and wind. The insulating fur does double duty: In the winter it keeps your dog warm, but it also keeps your dog cool in the summer. Once shaved, sometimes the hair doesn't grow back properly, leaving you with either a funny-looking dog, or one you need to keep shaved.

Dogs will shed all year round, losing hair every day. If you let it build up you'll notice it more, finding clumps of hair whenever your dog gets up off the floor (or sofa). Daily brushing of your dog's coat, even if he's a short-haired dog, will keep most of his shedding under control. There's still the summer blowout to look forward to though. When your dog starts to blow coat, you may need to brush him three or four times daily. Longer-haired dogs need more care to remove the loose hairs. If the loose hairs aren't removed from their coat they'll form mats that can be painful to remove and may actually rip hair out of the skin. A good bath and rub down with a rubber bath glove will loosen the hair underneath the top coat so you can brush it out easily after. Don't brush your dog before his fur is dry though, or you'll end up pulling out a bunch of hair that wasn't ready to go and your dog won't be so complacent about brushing the next time.

If your dog has mats that have been growing for a while, are large, or too close to the skin, don't risk injuring him. Take him to a professional groomer and have them taken care of by somebody who knows what to do. Once the mats are removed, you may need to take your dog to the veterinarian for ointment if there are sores on his skin. Infections are very common in skin lesions and an antibiotic ointment is probably all that is needed to clear it up.

Even short-haired breeds can lay a fur carpet. Dobermans, Dalmatians, and Great Danes are all equally guilty of the shedding phenomenon. Every single hair won't be as glaringly obvious like a long-haired dog's would be, but the dust puppies can still build up pretty quickly. If you aren't expecting them, the sheer volume that can appear overnight can be shocking.

**Drool is a most unpleasant aspect of some breeds.** But it is a very easy characteristic to avoid when you are selecting your dog breed or mix. Dogs with tight lips, like huskies, collies, and shepherds, are minimal droolers, while loose-lipped dogs will let more saliva slip. The looser your dog's lips are normally, the more drool you may be dealing with. Some dogs are only partial droolers. My Beaucerons have a tendency to grab mouthfuls of water and drip it throughout the house, and they drool quite a bit when nervous, like most dogs do.

While some drooling is pretty normal for most dogs, it can also be a sign of illness or injury. So if your tight-lipped dog suddenly starts to drool excessively and he has no reason for anxiety, he may have a serious problem. Check his mouth for foreign objects that may have become lodged between his teeth or stuck in the roof of his mouth. If there is nothing there, watch for other signs and symptoms of possible illness, like diarrhea and vomiting (could be anything) or swelling of his face (insect bites).

While excessive and foaming drool is a sign of rabies in dogs, you shouldn't automatically panic if your dog is drooling a ridiculous amount, especially if he has been vaccinated against rabies. If he hasn't come into contact with any other animals and he has been vaccinated, it's unlikely that rabies is the cause of his oral ooze.

**Eye goop is really easy to deal with.** Just a damp washcloth is all you need for this. Carefully wipe around your dog's eyes, picking up any dirt or discharge, and take care not to touch the eye itself.

**ELSEWHERE ON THE WEB**

▶ Check out www.eartheasy. com/article_natural_flea_ control.htm for different ways of preventing fleas using natural ingredients and herbal supplements, including information on the use of garlic and brewer's yeast as a flea repellent. This page will even tell you how to control the flea population outside, the hardest place to get rid of fleas, and the biggest reason dogs become reinfested.

Some breeds have looser eyelids, and there are a few eyelid conditions that can make the eyes goopier than usual. For example, ectropion is a condition where the lower lid of the eye sags loosely. Raider had this problem, and it made it easier for dust and dirt to collect inside the eyelid, causing irritation. A simple stitch in the corner of his eye tightened it up when he was under anesthetic for another procedure. Entropion is the opposite condition where the lower lid is turned inward against the eye. This can also be corrected with a simple procedure under anesthetic.

## The Ins and Outs

I don't think there's anything worse than bugs and worms. And to think of bugs on my furry pals that sleep on my bed every night is enough to give me nightmares. It's best if you don't read the rest of this chapter while eating.

### We'll start with the more commonly known bugs: fleas.

Fleas are caught by an animal coming close to a flea source, either another animal of any species, a person, or even stepping on flea eggs on the ground. Fleas bite, make your dog scratch like mad, can carry diseases, and worst of all, they spread tapeworms.

Fleas are also incredibly hard to get rid of if you don't get them all in one fell swoop. Eggs are left on upholstery, bedding, in vehicles, and in carpets. They can even be all over your yard, and they may not even have come from your own animals.

Puppies under twelve weeks of age should not be given any over-the-counter flea prevention or flea-killing medication. Combing them out, flea by flea, is your best option for young pups. Use a good metal flea comb and a bowl of soapy water to dip the (hopefully flea-ridden) comb in after making a pass in your puppy's fur. Comb him every day, two or three times daily, for a good week to be sure he's free from the little bloodsuckers. Treat all the other furry members of your household as well as your house itself.

There are both flea repellents and flea killers on the market for dogs. Applied topically, these solutions are said to work for at least a month or more. Advantage and Frontline are two of the better known brands of flea killers that kill adult fleas on contact.

Killing fleas on the dog won't stop them for long if you don't get rid of them in the dog's environment. Treating the yard will require the use of pesticides, and possibly an exterminator, but the house you can do cheaply although it's still a lot of work. Mule Team Borax (found in the laundry aisle of grocery stores) will dry out and kill fleas and eggs in your carpets and upholstery. Sprinkle it liberally and let it sit for a couple of hours before vacuuming it up. Don't forget to get rid of your vacuum bag right away, too. Put it in a garbage bag and seal it up so none of the fleas escape. Wash all sheets, bedding, and removable covers in hot water with as much bleach as you can get away with (without ruining the items).

Flea prevention is really your best bet. You can use medicated flea preventatives, like K9 Advantix or Advantage, to prevent infestation on your dog, or you can use natural substances to repel fleas. Garlic and brewer's yeast are two natural flea repellents used in your dog's food. Because garlic has some unpleasant side effects if too much is used, make sure you contact your veterinarian about how much to use.

**Mites are nearly microscopic bugs that hang out on your dog's skin.** Cheyletiella dermatitis is a small mite that resides on the outer layer of skin in both people and animals. This mite is easily passed through contact with an infected animal and can cause scratching, fur loss, and scaling of the skin.

**ELSEWHERE ON THE WEB**

▶ The Dog Owner's Guide on the Web (www.canismajor.com/dog/intestin.html) has a great informational page on stomach upsets of all kinds—diarrhea, vomiting, and symptoms of poisoning. It offers practical and easy solutions to diarrhea and information on when it becomes a problem. If you suspect your dog has been poisoned, don't hesitate to call your veterinarian.

Sarcoptic mange is caused by scabies mites that burrow under the skin to lay eggs, which hatch then work their way up during their various life stages that last about three weeks. Scabies mites cause itching, redness, and flaky skin in dogs and are highly contagious.

Demodicosis is the other form of mange that you may have heard of. This type of mange is not contagious; it is actually caused by regular inhabitants of your dog's skin. In their usual numbers, demodex mites do no harm, but if a dog's immune system isn't up to snuff, these mites can become numerous and irritate the dog's skin causing fur loss, flaking skin, and oozing sores.

Ear mites are itchy, irritating little mites that like to hang out in your dog's ears. These are highly contagious, though it is sometimes hard to tell if your dog has them. If your dog is scratching his ears bloody, if they are painful to touch, and if they smell bad, please have his ears checked for mites.

**Worms are a common and unpleasant problem.**  Signs of a worm infestation are usually dull coat and eyes, diarrhea, blood in your dog's stool, vomiting, and weight loss.

The most common of internal parasites beside tapeworms, roundworms frequently infect pets. They look suspiciously like thin spaghetti noodles and can often be found in feces with the naked eye. I can't describe how grossed out I was when I found one in my dog's stool. Luckily, treatment is an easy thing with medication from your veterinarian.

Tapeworms are a very common problem, and a very obvious one. Tapeworms are spread by fleas that have ingested tapeworm eggs. The flea is ingested by a dog, and the tapeworm larvae escapes the eaten flea and matures inside the dog's intestine. Once it's mature, egg-filled segments are released from the tail of the

ELSEWHERE ON THE WEB

▶ This is one place you won't want to visit if you plan on eating anytime soon, but knowing what intestinal worms actually look like will be a big help if you think your dog has them. The Pet Center has a page of detailed information and photos of actual worms (www.thepet center.com/exa/worms.html). It's not pleasant, but it's a fact of dog ownership and one we have to deal with.

worm and find their way out of the dog through its anus. If you see rice-looking things that move around your dog's bedding, in his feces, and stuck to his fur by his anus, then your dog has a tapeworm problem. Tapeworms can't be treated by regular over-the-counter deworming medications; they need a special drug available at your veterinarian's office.

Hookworms are nasty little creatures that feed off the intestinal walls. They are passed to other animals through soil where eggs have been laid. These are incredibly easy to contract. The larvae that live in the soil can enter the body through the feet and travel throughout the system until they reach the intestines where they stay to feed off of blood and lay eggs that shed once again in feces and contaminate the ground. These worms can kill young puppies. Humans are susceptible to hookworm infestations, too. Hookworm infections are usually noticed during routine fecal exams. These creatures are just one of the many reasons it is so important to pick up after your dog.

Whipworms are ingested either from the feces of infected animals or spread through other bodily fluids. They are found in the colons of animals and shed eggs through feces approximately three months later. Feeding on blood and tissue in the intestines of animals, a severe infection can cause weight loss, severe dehydration, and **chronic** bloody diarrhea. Most dewormers won't work on whipworms, so talk to your vet and see what he recommends.

Regular checkups and fecal examinations will catch worm infestations early before too much damage is done.

## Allergies and Hot Spots

Skin problems are terrible things to live with. Not only are they painful and itchy, but the sound of scratching all night will drive any

TOOLS YOU NEED

▶ Get the Scoop on Poop! contains everything you ever wanted to know about dog poop, and a whole scoop of things you probably would have slept better if you didn't know about. These are the reasons dog people harp on about picking up after your dog poops. Leaving it where it falls just spreads disease and dissent. Take a look at http://about.com/dogs/dog poop for the real scoop.

sane person over the edge. Most skin problems can be quickly sorted out with a quick trip to the vet's. The vet will take a scraping, which is exactly what it sounds like, and see what he can find under a microscope. Skin mites and yeast infections can quickly be diagnosed and treated with a skin scraping. A general checkup and your own observations about your dog's habits and problems will help your veterinarian determine the cause of your dog's misery if a scraping doesn't produce results.

**Dogs really can be allergic to things just like we can.** Unfortunately, they can't tell us if certain things give them itchy skin or watery eyes. It's up to us to try and figure it out on our own.

Some allergies are fairly obvious and easy to figure out. A lot of dogs have a flea allergy that causes them to break out in hives when they have a flea infestation. Clearing up the flea problem is usually enough to clear up the dog's allergic reaction, as long as the flea medication doesn't harm your dog's now sensitive skin.

Insect bites are another allergen that becomes obvious quickly with localized swelling after your dog is bitten. Ask your veterinarian about antihistamines that you can keep on hand for when it happens and what dose your dog should be getting.

Food allergies are another common problem that are hard to nail down. Itchy, red, and flaky skin and goopy eyes are two common symptoms. Corn, wheat, and soy products are three of the biggest offenders. If you suspect your dog is suffering from a food allergy, you'll need to try to put him on a diet that eliminates the suspected allergen. Beef, eggs, and milk products are also ingredients in dog food that should be eliminated if you think your dog is allergic. There are special hypoallergenic diets available online and at most veterinary offices.

Some dogs have it really bad and are allergic to things in the environment that they just can't get away from like dust mites, molds, and pollen. Allergy tests may be needed to determine the cause of your dog's misery.

If your poor dog is allergic to dust mites, pollen, and molds, you can help by washing his bedding in hot water once a week, and drying it in the dryer on the high heat setting. Don't hang it out to dry; it will pick up pollen and dust from the outside as it hangs. Vacuum his regular areas frequently as well to get rid of any pollen he may have brought in with him. There really isn't much more help for these dogs except for warm water rinsing every week (no soap; soap makes it worse), and maybe an antihistamine regimen from their veterinarian.

**Hot spots are oozing sores that appear on your dog's body.** Usually from licking in one area too often as a result of an insect bite or other irritation, a hot spot grows until it is a painful, oozing, open wound. These sores may require antibiotics, but you have to get the dog to stop licking at it first. An Elizabethan collar is the most effective way to accomplish this. Wrapping up a hot spot so the dog can't get at it will only aggravate it and make it itchier, but a cool compress or bath for a short period of time will soothe it for a while.

## Intestinal Gas and Diarrhea

These lovely parts of a dog's life carry two of the worst smells in the world. When a dog has gas, everyone knows it. Thankfully, gas is rarely of any real concern; it usually passes as the dog digests whatever he has eaten. When a dog has diarrhea it could simply mean he's eaten too much of something or part of his meal didn't agree with him. Chances are he won't be able to hold it in, though, and you might be stuck with accidents in the house. It's a good idea to always be aware of how your dog's bowels are working. Persistent intestinal upset or excessive, foul-smelling gas could indicate a bigger problem.

**Gas is almost always a byproduct of what a dog has eaten.** Dogs can't digest some things the same way we do, and eating them can produce some noxious results. Switching your dog's food to one without a lot of soy might make a big difference, and so will cutting out any people food your dog is currently eating. Dairy products are also a prime suspect when fumes are present.

If eliminating certain foods doesn't help, try a spoonful of plain, low-fat yogurt in your dog's main meal each day. Yes, I know I just said dairy was bad, but yogurt seems to break all the dairy rules. The bacteria cultures that make yogurt will help your dog's digestive system. Activated charcoal supplements will absorb the gases in your dog's stomach, making him a whole lot more pleasant to be around.

Eating too quickly can also give your dog gas. Get him to slow down by spreading his kibble out on a cookie sheet. Make sure he isn't eating too much, too. You know how uncomfortable and bloated we get when we overeat; your dog is the same way.

Additional exercise will also help your poor flatulent dog. Walk him around the block a few times after he's eaten to help move gas out of his system and into the open air (and not the closed space of your living room).

**Diarrhea, by itself, is rarely a big problem.** It's only when it's constant, and accompanied by other signs (like blood), that it represents a bigger health issue. Regular, run-of-the-mill diarrhea is usually caused by something your dog ate that he shouldn't have. It should run its course in a day or two.

The best thing to do is stop putting food into your dog so that it can stop coming out the other end. A few missed meals won't hurt your dog and will give his system time to recover from whatever it didn't like. Make sure he still has plenty of fresh water to drink though, as diarrhea can dehydrate a dog really quickly. A bland diet should follow the fast. Boiled ground beef or chicken and plain white or brown rice will be enough food for one day. If the problem persists past day three though, it's a sign of more trouble, and your dog needs to see a vet.

## Anal Sacs and Urine Issues

And you thought dog ownership couldn't get any grosser, right? Unfortunately, it does. If you haven't heard of anal sacs, this will be an informative section for you. Every now and then, a dog owner may notice his dog behaving in an odd manner. Biting at his hind end, dragging his butt across the carpet, urinating every twenty minutes or so or straining to make it happen—these are all signs of trouble down under. Things are about to get down and dirty, so grab a pair of rubber gloves and a roll of paper towels.

**What does it mean when he's dragging his backside across the floor?** As comical as this may appear, this could indicate a real problem. Unofficially known as "scootching," this amusing action usually has less than entertaining causes. Dogs usually only do this when their anal glands have become impacted.

Anal glands are located to the right and left of and slightly below the anus (positions 5 and 7 if they were on a clock's face). When a dog defecates, the stool squeezes out a substance that marks your dog's territory. If his stool isn't hard enough, the glands fail to empty and fluid builds up and hardens, leaving your dog in pain and in danger of infection.

Once his glands are impacted, they won't empty on their own—they'll need your help. Your veterinarian can show you how to do this safely, and with little mess at home. You might want to ask him about surgery to remove the glands altogether if your dog has a frequent problem with impaction.

**Urinary tract infections and bladder stones are fairly common in dogs.** If you notice that he's been asking to go outside every half hour or so, but urinates a very small amount or strains to go, your dog might have a urinary tract infection or bladder stones. The symptoms are the same for both of these problems, so it will take a veterinarian to figure out which problem he has. Blood in the urine and a foul smell are also signs of a problem.

Antibiotics will clear up a urinary tract infection, usually quite quickly. Make sure your dog has plenty of fresh water to drink so he can flush out the bacteria that is hanging out in his body. If the antibiotics don't work after a couple of days, take him back to the vet. The infection may have spread to his kidneys and bladder.

Bladder stones are also treated with antibiotics once it is determined that is your dog's problem. If there is a stone blocking the urethra though, your dog is going to need immediate surgery to have it removed. So if you see him straining to urinate but nothing is coming out, take him to the vet's right away.

If he has a number of large stones that the medication doesn't seem to be working on, then your vet may suggest surgery to have them removed. It is in your dog's best interest to have this done. Your vet may also suggest that you put your dog on a special diet, made especially for prevention and management of struvite crystals and urinary tract disease.

## Wildlife Woes

Our dogs love the great outdoors, but the great outdoors may not be so fond of our dogs. There are a lot of hazards for the intrepid dog that likes to explore the wilderness. And some of those hazards will come to your dog even if he's safely contained in your yard.

**Ticks are a real danger to your dog's health.** Aside from their affinity for blood and the infections that can arise at the bite locations, ticks also carry and spread serious diseases.

If you find ticks on your dog, pick off the ones that are not yet embedded in your dog's skin with a pair of tweezers and dispose of them in a jar of rubbing alcohol (do not flush them).

Embedded ticks should be removed very carefully. Grasp the body of the tick with the tweezers, as close to the head as possible, and slowly pull the tick out of your dog. Do not touch the tick or attempt to squish the tick as his body carries disease as well as his saliva. If the head doesn't come out of the dog with the rest of its body, give your vet a call and see if he will remove it for you. Don't go digging around for it yourself—you'll only injure your dog. After the tick is disposed of, put a dab of antibiotic ointment on the bite location and watch for signs of infection.

Lyme disease is often diagnosed when the dog is taken to the veterinarian with symptoms of lameness, high fever, and lack of appetite. A course of antibiotics is the treatment for Lyme disease. If you live in an area where Lyme disease is a common problem, ask your veterinarian about the preventative vaccine.

Another rickettsial disease that is transmitted through the bite of an infected tick, Rocky Mountain spotted fever can be treated successfully with antibiotics as soon as it is suspected. However, if it's not diagnosed and treated quickly, Rocky Mountain spotted fever can have serious and fatal complications. Symptoms of this

**TOOLS YOU NEED**

▶ Rubber gloves are going to become a staple in your house. Use them for emptying anal glands, pulling ticks off your dog, poking through poop to look for worms, and a whole lot of other unpleasant things that are now a part of your life. You can pick up a box of nonlatex gloves in any size at most drug stores.

illness include lethargy, appetite loss, high fever, weakening of the muscles, and labored breathing.

Tick prevention is your best defense against these bloodsuckers. Frontline, K9 Advantix, Revolution, and BioSpot (you may recognize these names from the flea section earlier in this chapter) are all popular tick preventatives. Applied to a spot of skin (topically) on the back of your dog's neck once a month, each works by killing the ticks as they come into contact with your dog's skin. At this point, K9 Advantix is the only one known to repel ticks as well as kill them, but I prefer Frontline myself, as its solid reputation as a trusted product has remained steady for years now.

**Raccoons will come to you, even in the city.**  They are feisty creatures that will fight with your dog if they meet. Raccoons are common rabies carriers, so make sure your yard doesn't hold a lot of attractions for them, and that your dog's rabies vaccinations are always up-to-date.

- Keep your garbage in tightly lidded containers in your garage or porch until collection day.
- Keep your dog in the house at night, and supervise his outside time after it is dark.
- Keep your yard well lit.
- Don't feed your dog outside. Even if you pick up the bowl after he has finished, the smell remains and there may be pieces of food that have strayed from the bowl.

**You can smell it coming a mile away: the aroma of a skunked dog.** And you shake your head in sympathy for the poor owner who has to deal with that smell at ten o'clock at night. Good thing your dog is safe and sound in the backyard, right? Right?

Wrong.

Here comes your dog out of the backyard smelling like he was just dipped in raw sewage. Maybe a skunk got into your yard or perhaps your dog found an escape route out of your yard, but your dog has been skunked. And at ten o'clock at night, the pet store is closed. Luckily, if your pantry is well stocked you can still deskunk him, even this late at night, if you're willing to let him back in the house, that is. Here are two tried and true recipes for getting the skunk out of your dog (and your clothes):

- 1 quart hydrogen peroxide (3 percent)
- ¼ cup baking soda
- 1 teaspoon Dawn dishwashing soap

1. Mix all the ingredients in a bucket (it will fizz).
2. Soak your dog's fur, but be careful not to get any in his eyes.
3. Use a sponge to clean off his head and around his eyes.
4. Knead solution into the fur and be sure to get every part of him with it.
5. Rinse thoroughly.

If this recipe doesn't do the trick, try this one as well:

- 1 pint hydrogen peroxide
- ⅔ cup baking soda
- 1 tablespoon citrus-based liquid soap

1. Sponge the mixture onto the dog's fur.
2. Let it sit for two to five minutes, then rinse it off with plain water.
3. A second batch may be needed. Use fresh ingredients.

When washing your dog off, always be careful not to get any mixture in his eyes. The peroxide in these recipes may cause your dog's fur to lighten a little, and if you wash your clothing with it afterward, be forewarned that it may bleach the clothes as well. If you notice that his eyes are red and swollen before you start washing him, rinse his eyes carefully with plain water and call the emergency vet for eye drops that will help take the sting out of them.

## Get Linked

*You can check out my Web site for more information on the issues that commonly plague dogs:*

**DECLARE WAR ON FLEAS!**

Are those irritating little bloodsuckers driving your dog and you insane? Don't despair! There are a lot of ways to rid yourself of these vampires, some natural, some chemical, and a cheap and easy trick to get rid of them from your furnishings for good!

 http://about.com/dogs/fightfleas

**RED, ITCHY, IRRITATED, OR FLAKY SKIN**

Irritated skin can make your dog miserable. It's no picnic for you either as you listen to your buddy scratch all night. Unfortunately, there's a wide range of health issues that can cause skin to be itchy, and sometimes pinning down the problem can be a lot of work.

 http://about.com/dogs/irritatedskin

**CORN, WHEAT, AND SOY-FREE DRY DOG FOODS FOR THE ALLERGY SUFFERER**

Corn, soy, and wheat are three of the biggest culprits as far as food allergies in dogs go, and finding a brand of dry dog food that is free of these ingredients can be tricky.

 http://about.com/dogs/foodallergies

## Chapter 11

# Bad Behavior

## Nipping, Biting, and Other Rough Play

Puppies nip a lot when they play, and some breeds will continue to be mouthy throughout adolescence. Left alone, this will only get worse and can escalate into outright biting. Some bite inhibition may have been taught while your pup was still in the litter, but it'll be up to you if your pup continues to consider fingers and limbs fair game as far as his teeth are concerned.

If you've already taught him "No," you have half the work finished already. If not, now is a good time (for instructions on teaching your dog "No," see Chapter 9). Use the "No" command liberally whenever your dog starts to get mouthy.

It's probably not going to be that easy, however. Biting can turn into a power trip really quickly for older puppies and adult dogs. In no time at all, your dog may learn that by biting at your arms and feet he can control where you go and what you do or don't do. He may bite to stop you from brushing him. He may bite at your legs

**What should I do if my dog begins to mouth and play too roughly?**

▶ Once dogs hit a certain size, their mouthy behavior ceases to be "play" and can become downright frightening. Redirection only works to some extent, and if your dog is out of control, it is time for you to seek professional help. Don't be afraid to call a dog trainer, even if you consider the matter trivial in comparison to other issues. What you'll pay for one or two sessions will be well worth the peace of mind you get in return, and your dog will be a better-liked addition to the house, rather than one that frightens people.

to get you to turn in a certain direction, or just to chase you away. This is a behavior that must be stopped early on in your dog's life.

If you are dealing with a nipping puppy, the easiest way to get him to stop is to shun him when he nips you. Yelp loudly, like one of his littermates would, when he grabs you, and as soon as he lets go, end all play, turn your back on him, and walk away. Don't look at him, don't talk to him, just walk away. If you turn your back on him often enough, your pup will learn that using his teeth puts an end to the fun.

Redirection is another great tool for training puppies not to play rough. It's less of a direct training method and more of a negative reinforcement, where you simply remove the item (or game) out of his reach. If he grabs your hand, use a toy to get his attention and praise him for taking the toy (and in the process, letting go of your hand).

Older puppies and adult dogs have a harder time learning that rough play and biting at their humans are unacceptable behaviors, but they will if you are consistent. Most adult dogs that nip and grab were never taught not to and continue because it gets a desired result. In addition to shunning your dog for getting rough with you, you can start with reasserting your own dominance, as some biting behavior in adult dogs is also a way of putting themselves higher in rank than their humans.

If you are quick to notice and can tell when your dog is about to grab you or somebody else, a sharp "No" may be enough to stop him from connecting. Just the command isn't enough though, you'll need to reinforce his failure to connect by rewarding him as soon as he focuses his attention on you and not his target.

If your dog is older and still nipping, he has been successfully grabbing and chewing people for a long time, so remember that it will take a long time to break him of the habit.

Beware of giving him a reaction that he wants. Any type of attention from you will give him what he's looking for, so don't holler, scream, or run off; that will only start the game. And if he grabs your arm to stop you from doing something? Get up calmly, grab his leash and a muzzle, put the muzzle on your dog, and continue what you were doing anyway. He must learn that biting at your hands will not get him what he wants.

If your dog starts to increase his grabbing, you may have to take harsher measures. A muzzle will prevent him from biting, but it's not an ultimate solution.

Use a head halter like the Gentle Leader that has a short, dangling tether, and keep it on your dog at all times. When your dog goes to grab your arm, you grab the tether under his chin and pull his nose down fast while telling him "No" in a loud, firm voice. Don't let any panic come through in your voice, even if you feel it. If he goes for your arm again, repeat this action but instead of just letting go, haul him off and shut him in the bathroom for five minutes. Don't let him out until you hear absolute quiet from him.

Repeat this as often as it takes. And in the meantime, start looking for a behavioral trainer. If he does not get the message and continues or worsens his behavior, your dog will need professional intervention.

## Barking

Nothing gets your attention faster than your dog's barking. And unfortunately, nothing gets your neighbors angrier faster either. Annoyance factor aside, some towns have strict noise ordinances, and a dog that barks may be violating them, which could result in hefty fines. Constant barking is one of the top reasons dogs tend to end up in shelters.

**ELSEWHERE ON THE WEB**

▶ Shetland sheepdog owners have a wide variety of ways to put an end to nuisance barking. Here is a Web page listing a large amount of them, including a few that weren't discussed here: www.dogpatch.org/sheltie/barking.html. There is some information on the surgical procedure known as debarking and what its outcome is like. I'm not a fan of debarking. I dislike the principle of it, but I have never met a debarked dog so I can't go on about what effects it might have on the dog's personality.

Barking, more often than not, is a boredom reliever. Dogs like to hear the sound of their voices, and it expends some of their pent-up energy. Barking relieves stress! Haven't you ever shut yourself in a room and yelled just to let it all out? I know I have. For all the same reasons, dogs will bark just because they can. If you have a problem barker, I have a list of methods for getting your dog to quiet down.

- **Exercise your dog more.** There's a saying in the dog world that a tired dog is a good dog, and you will find that it is an absolute truth. A dog that has been well exercised is a dog who is too tired to get into trouble. Barking takes up a lot of energy, which is why dogs who lack appropriate exercise are often problem barkers.
- **Crate your dog while you are not home.** When the barking happens when you aren't there to hear it, it's usually because your dog is lonely (or bored). You usually find out when your neighbor complains, so it's important to put a stop to the noise as fast as possible. Crating your dog will fix this problem, as he should already see the crate as "quiet time" if he has been crate trained. If he hasn't been crate trained, you might want to seriously consider it, and read Chapter 7 for more information on how to go about crating your dog.
- **Try doggy daycare.** If you are opposed to crate training, or your days at work are too long for crating your younger dog, doggy daycare is an excellent alternative. I urge you to give it serious thought, even if your dog is not a problem barker but you work long hours, even if it is just for a day or two each week. It's an excellent socialization tool, and your dog will be well cared for and exercised during the day.

- **Use thinking toys.** Even a well-exercised dog may bark just to entertain himself while you aren't there. It may take a bit of trial and effort to find the right toy that occupies your dog for more than two minutes at a time, but the peace in the end will be worth it. Toys that dispense minuscule treats as your dog rolls it around on the floor are good ones to have.
- **If your dog barks outside when you are home, wait until he is quiet before you let him in.** But don't let him in until he has been quiet for at least ten seconds, and don't let him in if you miss that window and he has started barking again. He probably just wants to come inside where you are. If you miss the mark and accidentally let him in when he is barking, you'll only have taught that the door opens on his command.

There is some thought that you can put an end to your dog's barking by getting him a buddy, another dog. There is a bit of truth to that; if your dog barks because he's lonely, another dog will certainly alleviate the loneliness. But now he'll have somebody to talk to. And dogs talk very loudly. In fact, it sounds almost identical to barking. I'm not sure your neighbors will be able to tell the difference.

## Digging

Another very distressing problem for owners to deal with is a dog that digs. It's destructive, sometimes hazardous if there are other animals or people that can trip in the holes, and seemingly impossible to fix. But digging, like barking, is an entertainment behavior, and most dogs do it because they are bored. Some breeds are more prone to this type of boredom relief than others. Yes, I'm looking in your direction, terriers.

**ELSEWHERE ON THE WEB**

▶ PAW Rescue's Garden Tips for Dog People is a great page full of easy, cheap, and practical tips on keeping your garden and your dog living together happily. They can coexist peacefully, without him ripping up the garden as he runs around the yard. Read it online at www .paw-rescue.org/PAW/PET TIPS/DogTip_garden.php and keep the gardener in your family happy.

Most digging can be stopped by direct supervision and sufficient exercise. But digging is fun, and for some dogs it's as necessary to their being as running is for others. If you can get her to dig in a spot that is out of the way and that you won't mind being dug up, it's a great form of entertainment for your dog (not to replace conventional play and exercise).

Find a spot for your dog to dig in your yard away from fences and flowers and out of the way of people walking. A corner by the house is usually a good place. Start out by filling in your dog's previous holes and starting one of your own in the digging corner. Leash your dog, then take her out to the digging corner. Show her where to dig by tossing some dirt around yourself. Yes, you'll look funny, so I recommend getting one of the kids to do it while you stand there and keep your dignity, though it might go out the window while you praise your dog when she starts to dig with your kids in the right spot.

You can encourage your dog to use this spot all the time by burying treats in the dirt for her to dig up. This will reinforce her digging in that area by rewarding her for doing it. You will likely have to also redirect her quite a few times at first. If you see her digging in an unapproved location, tell her "No" and physically move her to the appropriate spot. Don't forget to praise and reward her if she starts to dig around in the right place.

Digging to escape is a different thing from boredom digging. This digger has a specific goal in mind; she's not digging just to entertain himself. There will be more on escape digging later in this chapter.

## Begging

Big, soulful, puppy-dog eyes may be cute in photographs, but that look is usually directed at you when you're trying to eat in peace. It can be worse if your dog is a drooler. Great big gobs of doggy saliva dripping onto your lap just don't do a whole lot for your appetite. This is another bad habit that can take some time to break, especially if your dog has been able to get away with it for a long time.

If your dog does not beg, then now is the perfect time to tell you that you can prevent it from happening simply by never giving your dog food that you are eating. It will still smell good to him, look good, and he'll still want it, but asking for it won't even cross his mind if he's never given the same food you are eating. Separating foods into "dog" food and "people" food is a very effective method of preventing begging. But this is one of the things that must be done from the very first day you bring your dog home. Once your dog knows that you are a complete pushover (and most of us are), he'll try to get you to share every chance he gets. Don't give him those chances.

If your dog is already skilled at sucking in his stomach and giving you those pathetically cute puppy-dog eyes, you need to train him to leave you alone when you are eating. I admit it; I'm not fussy about how my boys don't beg, just as long as they aren't staring at me while I'm eating. I'm happy if they are at my feet pretending I'm not eating, or if they are across the room watching the paint dry on the walls not looking at my food.

This result really isn't as hard as it may seem, it's just very time consuming. And if you aren't consistent and allow him to get away with it, or worse, reward the begging, even just once, you've added another couple of weeks to the time it will take to break your dog of this habit.

Don't even let him get comfortable in front of you when you have food. Order him to his crate immediately, and tell him to stay. If he gets up and comes to you while you are still eating, send him off again. And again. And again until you have finished eating. If he refuses to go, put your meal down and physically place him in his crate (but don't shut the door; remember, it's just a destination,

▶ *Mine!* by Jean Donaldson is a book all about dogs that guard their food, their toys, and their people. Jean is a unique writer, and while some people take issue with how she words things, very few have anything bad to say about her training methods. *Mine!* is available for sale online through Amazon.com and at most bookstores and libraries.

not a prison). Repeat this procedure until you have pulled out all your hair in frustration and your dog successfully stays for the entire meal.

When he stops coming back out to see you eat and after you are finished, call your dog to you and give him a reward of his own (not what you were eating or anything remotely resembling that meal). Keep in mind that if you just crate him up for every meal with the door closed he won't actually be learning anything, he'll still beg just as much when he's out.

## Guarding Things of Value

A dog that guards his resources can be a lawsuit waiting to happen. And unfortunately, a lot of dogs get away with it simply because many dog owners don't seem to recognize this as a big problem. Instead, they'll encourage it by telling people to stay away from the dog that is eating or to not take the toy away from the dog.

Dogs guard for a few reasons. Often it is shelter dogs and other dogs that come from a place where they had to compete for food among other dogs or animals, but sometimes family dogs can develop guarding tendencies as well, especially if there are children in the home that might have bothered the dog or made off with his food at one point.

**Guarding food and toys is a common problem.** And it's often reinforced as owners repeat the old axiom "Don't disturb the dog while he's eating." A dog that is allowed to get away with guarding his food and toys can easily turn into a biting dog if his behavior is allowed to continue unchecked.

Getting your dog used to people taking things from him is a very important skill to work on. It's much easier to do when your dog is a pup, but many adult dogs have guarding issues as well.

There are two methods I have used that have proven effective on adult resource guarders.

**Teach him to trade.**   When your dog is eating, distract him with a tasty treat. When he stops eating to take the treat, issue the "Trade" command, remove his food dish, and praise him. After a moment give him back his dinner, but repeat this action again before he is finished eating it.

You'll want him to trade other things, too. Trade a toy of higher value for the one he is playing with, a treat for the higher value toy, and dinner for another toy. Always go up one step in value when teaching "Trade."

**Teaching tolerance is a good way to put a stop to food guarding.**   Food guarding can be the start of dominant behavior (see Chapter 12) and needs to be stopped immediately. If you notice he's not letting anybody near his food, you need to take action.

Don't give your dog his food in a bowl; instead, feed him by hand a little bit at a time, as long as he sits patiently. About halfway through his dinner you can give him back his bowl, but don't take your hand off it. Make him eat from the bowl in your hands. If your dog accepts your hands on his bowl while he's eating, reward him after he's finished with a tasty treat.

For his next meal, start off the same way but give him more of the bowl, and while keeping one hand on the bowl, place your other hand on his head. Ignore any minor resistance, but if he starts to growl, remove his food completely and go back to feeding bit by bit by hand. Your dog must learn to accept your hands wherever you decide to put them.

The next step you'll take when you feel your dog is ready for it is petting while he eats from the bowl in your hand. If he gives any

*What do I do if my dog bites me while I'm teaching him to accept my hands?*

▶ If he does bite you, then start from the very beginning again, feeding him each piece by hand. This time have one hand on a leash attached to the Gentle Leader head halter while the other feeds him slowly. If he starts to snap at any time, pull the leash down to close his jaws. Use the Gentle Leader for this entire training exercise until you are confident he has learned to accept your hands. If your dog now frightens you, feed him in his crate and seek professional help.

overt sign of resistance, go back to the previous step until he has earned a rewarding dessert.

After he has mastered this step, let go of his bowl and let him eat out of it without you holding it, but put your hand inside the bowl while he's eating. Don't let it show if you are afraid. This is crucial. Before you were merely holding the feeding vessel, now you have your hands in the food. To your dog, this is a big difference.

If you've successfully accomplished the prior steps, now you and your dog are ready for the final step: taking his food away completely. But not for long! After just one minute give it back to him, but garnish it with a high-value treat. What you've now done is what he has been afraid of you doing all along. But you gave it back, and gave back something better with it. Do this a couple of times, always making sure you increase the value of his dinner with a treat placed on top in plain smell. Eventually your dog will step back and wait for you to take his dinner. When this happens, you know you've won.

Always reward your dog heavily after a successful meal completion.

Because this is a very time-consuming process, I suggest breaking his meals up into three or four small meals a day instead of one or two larger ones (but keep the total volume the same). Not only will meals go by a little faster, but the extra sessions in a day will only help the training as your dog gets to practice more.

**Your dog's greatest resource is you!** A lot of dog owners don't pick up on this behavior; rather, they think their dog is being protective. He is, but not the way they think he is. Growling and menacing behavior toward people who approach you when you are relaxed and at ease are the actions of a possessive dog.

If your dog is guarding you, request the help of your friends and family to teach your dog to accept the presence of others around you. While you hold her leash, have your recruits approach you with treats in hand. Put your dog into a sit-stay, talk calmly with your friends, and if your dog starts to growl, order her to lie down and reward her quick compliance. By giving her other commands to follow and rewarding her compliance with the commands, you avoid punishing her for growling, and you are giving her something to focus on. When your dog is down and acting in a calmer manner, have your friend give her the rewards.

## The Escape Artist

Every breed has them. These are the dogs that no fence can contain, that nobody can trust off leash: the Houdini dogs. Houdini dogs will climb trees to get over a tall fence, or they will scale the fence itself. They will dig under gates, squeeze through a hole your daughter's hamster couldn't fit through, and slip out open windows. A maximum security prison would be nothing more than an afternoon's challenge to these dogs. Houdini dogs tend to end up in shelters a lot, either because their owners couldn't take the stress anymore, or they were picked up as a stray and never reclaimed. Many are hit by cars and killed in the streets.

Neutering will remove a lot of the desire to roam the neighborhood, but it probably won't cure your dog of his escapist tendencies. Some dogs, like my Ozzy, just like to go off on a jaunt, even after having been neutered since six months of age. He's six years old now, and he still sometimes tries to go off and tour the town.

**Your dog runs out when the door opens.** If he is the type to bolt out the door whenever somebody goes in or out, you're going to need to do some serious training. Eventually he'll need to learn to sit at the door before you open it and wait for everybody else to go through first. However, before you get to that point you need to prevent him from getting to the door in the first place.

**ELSEWHERE ON THE WEB**

▶ For a good long look at various types of aggression, including territorial aggression, from a behavioral standpoint read www. workingdogs.com/doc0182. htm. We'll get more into aggression in Chapter 12, but there are quite a few different types, and each one means something different to your dog and how you react to each one will be different as well.

Keeping your dog in another room or in his crate whenever someone comes in or goes out will work, but that will be hard to enforce on a regular basis. One delivery, or a kid's friend opening the door unexpectedly, is all it takes to have your dog gone again. Until your dog is trained, keep him tethered to you at all times. Set out some rules, such as the following, and make sure everybody understands them:

- Nobody opens the door until the dog is secured.
- Nobody lets the dog outside without having him leashed.
- All potential visitors must be alerted to the dog's tendency to bolt.
- The dog gets nowhere unless he is sitting.

The last rule will take a lot of practice. Have a stream of people walk in and out of your house while your dog is with you and on a tight leash and a head halter collar. Using the head halter, hold your dog in a sitting position as people come through the door. Tell him to stay. If he gets up, put him back down and tell him to stay again. This goes back to the basic obedience commands you read about in Chapter 6. It's not going to be as easy as training basic commands though. Your dog has a specific goal in mind, and his motivation is high. You'll need to heavily reinforce every moment that he looks at the open door and doesn't try to run through it. If he sits still, even for just five seconds, catch him before he struggles against the leash and reward him with one of the highest-value treats you have. Don't miss the mark and accidentally reward him for trying to get to the door! Count on practicing his sitting by the door at least ten times a day every day for a month or more.

**How does he get away?** Though you might not like to admit it, your dog's escapist tendencies could be due, in part, to some of your behavior as an owner. Dogs need guidance to follow, and if they don't get it, they will compensate by making up their own rules. While you may want to give up and declare him a "bad dog," this probably isn't the right answer.

Along those same lines, many dog owners like to believe that their dogs are better behaved than they actually are. Perhaps you consider your dog fairly polite and obedient (he knows basic commands, he doesn't beg at the table, he doesn't go on the furniture), so you often let him out into an unfenced yard "just for a few minutes," assuming everything will be fine. To your dismay, he keeps wandering off! It may seem more convenient for you to take these kinds of shortcuts, but it will prove detrimental to both you and your dog in the long run. Take the necessary steps to get the situation under control now—before it's too late.

If your yard is not fenced, then, please, seriously consider changing that. A solid fence is one hundred times safer than a chain or just letting your dog loose in the yard. Underground fences are better than nothing, but I'm not a fan of them for various reasons, and they don't measure up to a true physical barrier.

If your dog escapes his yard, and it seems to be securely fenced, you might have a challenge on your hands. Walk the perimeter of your yard, pushing on the fence as you go along, to check for loose boards or gaps in the chainlink that a crafty dog can slip through. What might seem inconsequential to you may be just big enough for your dog. Slightly larger gaps between the ground and the bottom of the fence might be your dog's route to freedom too.

**Observe your dog to find out his escape route.** If you can't find any way out, try to trick him into revealing it himself. Put your dog on a long lead, long enough to get him right out of your yard altogether but not long enough to get him into trouble like in the middle of the street, so that he will leave the yard. Now go and pretend he isn't being supervised so he'll try to make a break for it.

If you catch him in the act and you have one route blocked, don't relax your guard just yet. He may have three or four of them, so this could take some time.

**Foiling your dog's escape plans won't be easy.** Whether she digs, climbs, or squeezes free, you can stop her. It's just going to take a lot of work.

If she is a digger, you'll need to make it impossible for her to dig out. Attach chicken wire to the bottom of your fence, all the way along the perimeter, and bury it so that it is in the ground at least two feet deep. Your dog will stop digging when she hits the wire fence. If the wire fence isn't to your liking, pour a concrete barrier into the ground between your fence posts. It doesn't need to be as deep underground as the wire fence, only about a foot or so. Most dogs won't bother to dig further underneath such a solid barrier.

Climbers and jumpers can usually be stopped by modifying your original fence material. Dogs can scale chainlink fences fairly easily once they realize it is possible to do, and horizontal board fencing is just like climbing a ladder. You'll find that it's worth it to replace these types of fences with vertical board fencing or block walls. Take down or prune any climbable trees that hang over the fence or grow close enough to it that your dog can jump down to the other side from. If your dog can jump over your current fence, you'll need to build it higher. For the die-hard dogs that can some-how get themselves over an eight-foot solid concrete wall, mount a three-foot section of chainlink off the top of it at a fifty-degree angle.

**TOOLS YOU NEED**

▶ If your dog has run off, print up a checklist of places to search and things to do. It will help keep your mind focused and you won't forget an important step when you are stressed out. If you aren't sure what to put on your list, I have a printable checklist available online (http://about. com/dogs/lostdogchecklist) that I put together with the help of the Dog Park forum members.

**Find your dog as soon as possible—before something happens.** Think carefully. Are there any places nearby that might be especially attractive to your dog? Maybe there is a schoolyard full of kids if your dog likes children, a meat shop that might have a tasty garbage bin, or a neighbor who has his own friendly dogs. Arm yourself with a box of treats and a leash and check these places first. If you don't find her right away, drive around the blocks near your home and call for her excitedly. If your search is still fruitless, head home and start gathering search tools.

Remember that information file for your dog I keep mentioning? One of the things in it should be a couple of recent photographs and a detailed physical description. Use these items to create Missing Dog posters with your contact information and the number of a person to call if you aren't there. Put these flyers everywhere: the veterinarian's office, the post office, community bulletin boards, the police station, on telephone poles, and drop off a couple at the animal shelters. Hand out smaller versions of your poster with your dog's name, picture, and your phone number on it to any kids you know playing in the area. But stick to kids you actually know so that you don't become that creepy guy who says he lost his puppy.

When you are out and about, take a flashlight with you so you can look under vehicles, porches, and in shrubbery. Your dog may be hiding.

And be sure you have these phone numbers handy because you'll be making a lot of calls:

- Call your local radio station and ask if you can place a lost pet notice. Most will do this service for free.
- Call the police station at least once every day. The officers won't know if your dog has been picked up by animal control, but they will likely know if the worst happened and he was hit by a car.

- Call animal control. But don't just call; go down in person and see what they have. Your dog may not have been properly identified, and it's best if you check yourself.

And most important of all: Don't give up! Your dog may have wandered into the next county, but he's probably still okay. Dogs have been found and returned to their homes months later. They'll just need a little rehabilitation to bring them back to normal.

## Get Linked

*You'll find a lot of solutions to common problem behaviors on my About.com site. These links cover topics that we discussed in this and previous chapters in greater detail.*

**OOPS! DO YOU REWARD BAD BEHAVIOR?**

This is what makes dog training so hard. Attention of any kind when a dog misbehaves is a signal to the dog: "Hey, this works. It's not quite what I want, but it's still attention." For him, even negative attention is better than none at all.

 http://about.com/dogs/badbehavior

**RESOURCE GUARDING**

This article explains why letting your dog get away with guarding his food and other valuables is a really bad idea and offers several ways to correct this dangerous behavior.

 http://about.com/dogs/resourceguarding

## Chapter 12

# Big Problems

### She Bit Somebody!

Dog bites are a media sensation—especially a bite from one of the nations' favorite breeds to hate. But small dogs bite, too, and despite having small teeth and small muzzles, they can do a lot of damage. Any dog bite is a serious problem, and you, the owner, are completely liable. It's very important not to get too cocky thinking that your dog is incapable of such an act. Any dog can bite.

**But what could cause an otherwise calm, well-trained dog to bite?**  Illness often plays a part in dog bites. A dog in pain will bite. A frightened dog will bite. A sick dog will bite. Most bites are provoked in some way, whether it's obvious or not. You may trust your dog and think "But she's so sweet! She couldn't hurt a fly!" But do you trust every single person that your dog comes into contact with? Even the sweetest dog in the world will bite given the right (or wrong) set of circumstances.

**WHAT'S HOT**

▶ An altered (spayed or neutered) state is in. According to the Humane Society of the United States, the most common dog bites are from dogs that are unaltered, unsocialized, and poorly trained. Don't let this be your dog. Make the decision to have your dog spayed or neutered as soon as he or she is old enough. For more information on spaying and neutering and their benefits, see Chapter 3.

**If your dog does bite somebody, you'll need to minimize the damage as much as possible.** Begin by removing your dog from the scene immediately and securing him somewhere safe. You don't want him to be where an angry person can do him harm in retribution, so put him in your car or house right away. If you are far from home and don't have a vehicle, tie him to something out of the way and put him in a down and stay.

Offer first aid if needed, call an ambulance, or drive the victim to the hospital, the police station, or home. This is going to hurt, especially if the victim chooses to go to the police, but do it anyway. It is the victim's right to file a report, and it's something that has to be done no matter how much it hurts you. By offering yourself as a means to reaching the destination of choice, you'll show that you are aware of your responsibility, are concerned about the victim, and are willing to cooperate.

Bite your tongue hard if you need to, but do not get defensive, even if the victim is a total louse who kicked your dog on the way by. You must not be seen as "the jerk who has a vicious dog" because public opinion always sides with the bite victim at first. Sometimes opinion can be swayed after the truth comes out, but don't count on that.

If the victim just wants to get away, take his name and address and the names and addresses of any people who were there at the time of the bite who might be potential witnesses. It's also time to start thinking about good lawyers. The sweetest person, one who's incredibly accommodating and swears that it was nothing, can turn around and try to sue you for everything you've got as soon as you are out of sight. Even the victim who says he won't report it might do just that. Do everything you can to prepare for trouble anyway.

Be wary of making remarks about the circumstances of the bite, or about the victim. I know it will be tempting to start mouthing off where you think nobody can hear you about how "So-and-so deserved it anyway" or "That's what you get for messing with my dog." Statements like these can be held against you, and it can turn a liability case into an assault if your victim has a crafty defense lawyer.

**You will probably need a few different documents to defend your dog.** You will need your dog's veterinary records, especially proof of a valid rabies vaccine. If you can't provide proof that your dog was vaccinated for rabies, he could be confiscated and placed in quarantine in a secure location.

Take a couple of hours to research the laws of your home state or province. You may be required by law to provide certain documentation above and beyond a rabies vaccine certificate. You may be required to have your dog's temperament tested in order to keep him. Or you may be required to quarantine him yourself.

Your dog's future will depend on how you handle this situation and on his past behavior. Once your dog bites somebody, he is instantly labeled "a vicious animal." It doesn't matter if it was provoked or not. It also doesn't matter if the bite victim reported it to the police or if it wasn't a damaging bite. Your dog will now have a reputation, and you cannot count on the victim to keep it to himself. Word will get around, and your dog will no longer be trusted. The fact is, your dog can no longer be trusted anyway, not by you or the people around you.

However, if he has a clean record until now and has a good reputation around town, you and he may come through this with little problems beyond the initial incident and outcome. His reputation will be tarnished, but you may be left in peace once the dust has settled and your dog has passed any evaluations that are required.

WHAT'S HOT

▶ Know your insurance policy! Some homeowner's insurance policies cover dog bites, even if they don't occur on the owner's property. Be warned, though, that your insurance provider may refuse you coverage after an incident for as long as you still own your dog. You may find it hard to get coverage elsewhere as well once you have placed a dog bite claim. Most insurance companies won't cover a dog that is considered "dangerous."

*Should I offer to pay for damages resulting from my dog's bite right away?*

▶ Yes, you should offer to pay for the damage your dog has done immediately, including all medical bills, even if the victim really is a jerk who kicked your dog (and thus was bit). Remember, if he was the type of person to kick a dog, he'll be the type of person to try to sue you for everything you have.

**Prevention is key.** The best way to prevent a dog bite before it happens is to be a responsible dog owner and socialize and train your dog. Breeding is only one part of a dog's makeup. Your dog will also become what you made of him, not only what his breed dictates, so follow these general guidelines:

- Never leave your dog unattended with children. Children are scary; they jump, run around, yell a lot, and can inadvertently hurt your dog.
- Muzzle your dog if you are unsure of how he will react in any given situation or if you do not trust him not to bite.
- Always keep your dog on a leash when he isn't in a secured and designated off-leash area.
- Desensitize your dog to strange places and people and loud noises (see Chapter 8).
- Do not allow people to torment your dog in any way.
- Do not allow your dog to become dominant over you or any member of your family.
- Don't wrestle or play-fight with your young dog. When your dog gets bigger, "play-fights" get painful and your dog won't know when to stop.
- Do not allow nipping to continue (see Chapter 11).

**Any children that come into your home must be taught to respect your dog.** Your children, your children's friends, and your friends' children must all be taught what not to do around dogs. They need to learn that pulling ears, tails, and fur is against your rules, and that jumping and screaming around the dog isn't allowed either.

Children are notorious for inadvertently causing injury to dogs. Dogproofing the child in your dog's life is one of the most important things you need to do when you bring a dog into your home. Children can, and must, be taught to play with your dog gently and safely. Most dog bite victims are children, and unfortunately, most of the bites are located on the face of a child, simply because a child's head is often on the same level as your dog's head, making it an easy target.

## Dominant Behavior

Always a problem, dominant behavior toward a human should never be tolerated from your dog. Dominance can be hard to recognize at first, so it's important to be aware of the early warning signs and catch this problem in its early stages. If your dog is allowed to believe he can dominate you or another member of your family, even for a short period of time, he can become pushy and aggressive and you will have a big problem on your hands before you know it. Small children are especially at risk from a dominant dog.

It starts subtly at first. Your dog may be reluctant to get off the sofa when you command him to, or he may just race you to the prime spot on the bed and resist your attempts to shove him over. From that point he may progress to growling at your attempts to move him out of your way. He may push your other family members to the side on his way through a doorway or down stairs. Your attempts to correct him may result in an outright challenge to your authority. You can see why it's important to catch this early and put your dog back in his place: far enough below all the humans so that even thinking about moving up is discouraged.

You are the alpha in your dog's pack. Behind you in rank comes every other member of your family: your spouse, your children, your grandmother, or your roommate. Behind all of these people in rank comes your dog. But between your dog should come the cat, the parakeets, the lizard, and the goldfish, because your dog should fall far enough down in rank that he won't even think about

*Will letting my dog sleep in my bed cause him to be more dominant?*

▶ If your dog is already showing signs that he's of a more dominant personality, then yes, it could exacerbate an already brewing problem, but it likely won't create one. I have always had my dogs in the bed and have only had minor issues with one of them, and they have all had rather dominant personalities.

moving up to your spot. The alpha position must be an obviously unattainable position.

If your dog has started showing signs that he's interested in your position or the rank of another family member, you can stop it before it gets out of hand. Start to reinforce your dog's original pack position (last) immediately, and get all the members of the family involved. Here are some pointers:

- **The first step is removing all of his placement privileges.** He should no longer be allowed in any of the most comfortable spots in the home, like your bed or the sofa. The floor, his bed if he has one, or his crate are his only resting places from now on. If he resists, physically haul him off the sofa and order him to his crate.
- **Make him work for every meal.** Before placing his full dish on the floor, make him sit, lay down, or speak first. Don't give him his dinner until he has done what you asked for.
- **Don't give him any loving until he's performed for you.** If he wants to snuggle up with you, make him sit and stay while you get up to get a cup of coffee or do something else, and then return to pet him after he's waited patiently for you.
- **Before your kids open the door to let him outside, have them make him sit first**, and only open the door once he's sitting properly.
- **Put your dog last in every way.** The dog that pushes past you to get outside is putting himself ahead of you in a very subtle way. Make him sit and wait until everybody else in the home has been fed or gone into or out of the door first. This will give your dog a very specific message: that he holds the bottom rank.

Everybody in your family needs to get in on this act. If you are the only person putting the dog in his place, he will learn not to take you seriously. Make sure each and every person in the house, including children, enforce your dog's status in the family.

## Thievery

Dogs are great opportunists, and they aren't very good at resisting temptation. Stealing things like food is its own reward, so it can be a really hard habit to break your dog of. It's really best if you can prevent it from ever becoming a problem, but I'm a realistic sort (and Raider wasn't named Raider because it was a cool name; he earned it early on his life), and I know that some dogs are just more prone to raiding counters and garbage cans than others.

**Counter surfing is the ultimate in self-rewarding habits for a dog.**   The food is there, and to your dog it's available and handy for him to snack on. For small-dog owners this really won't be much of a problem, but I had a huge problem with it, and I know other big-dog owners do as well. When your dog's nose is parallel to the counter and his front paws don't even have to leave the floor, everything is too easy for your dog to reach.

Preventing counter surfing is easy enough to do but not very practical in real life: You just don't leave food on the counter, ever. For me it meant not being able to thaw things out and not waiting any amount of time to put the dinner leftovers away. And I couldn't just leave bread on the counter, it had to have a place in the fridge or cupboard. I did this for a year with my first dog before I had enough and had to figure out how to get him to stop it altogether.

**ELSEWHERE ON THE WEB**

▶ The Dog Owner's Guide on the Web has a page listing the varieties of temperament in dogs and associated terms we use when discussing temperament. This page also tells you how to recognize each one in younger puppies. Check out www.canismajor .com/dog/behvterm.html and see what category your dog falls into. It may help you understand more about the behaviors you are seeing.

Pick your sacrificial meat and prepare to booby-trap your counter. Anything tempting will work for this exercise, but I prefer to use high-quality bait, such as a chunk of steak or sausages. Tie a long piece of fishing line, about ten feet, to your bait, and on the other end of that line tie as many aluminum cans as you have, at least six, to make a good racket. For good measure pour a few pennies in each can. You'll want this to be really effective, not something your dog will decide to risk if the food is tempting enough.

Leave your bait in plain sight with the cans pushed to the back of the counter. Now your trap is baited; just move to the other room and wait.

You'll know the trap has sprung when you hear the horrible clatter of the cans hitting the floor and following your dog out of the room. The noise will stop as soon as your dog drops the bait. It's possible that it will only take once for your dog to learn not to counter surf. It definitely won't take more than two or three times.

**Garbage raiding is the hardest habit to break in my opinion.** You can't reliably and safely booby-trap the garbage can, and 99 percent of the time you can't catch her in the act because she'll do it when you aren't around. The most effective way to put a stop to this is by putting the garbage out of reach of your dog's nose. A tight-fitting lid or putting it inside a cupboard is the way to go. Although if your dog is ridiculously smart, she may figure out how to open the cupboard doors to get the garbage anyway. Intelligence doesn't equal easy.

**Snatching food out of your hands is a dominance issue.** Your dog thinks he's high enough in the pack that he can literally take the food out of your mouth (or your child's), and he can't be

▶ Some people have great success just by making the surface of the counter uncomfortable for the dog. Double-sided sticky tape lining the edge of the counter might be enough to put off the casual counter surfer. Layering tinfoil on the countertop might also work to keep your dog from putting his front paws on the counter, preventing the theft of whatever is up there.

allowed to get away with it. It would be simple enough to crate your dog during mealtimes, but kids don't always follow a strict schedule when eating, and crating your dog for every snack and meal is just not a practical solution. Plus, this is a behavior you really want your dog to learn that is unacceptable, period.

I'm not a big fan of punishing dogs for behaviors that are natural to dogs, but this is one of those times where it is an appropriate response.

If your dog steals something from your hands, you should immediately grab his collar and retrieve whatever it is that he tried to make off with, while yelling "No" in your growliest voice. Try not to let him eat it (that's a reward), and once you have it back, haul him off into a room (not his crate) to be by himself for a little while. Don't talk to him, don't pet him, and don't apologize for shutting him away either. It will only take a few times for your dog to get the message loud and clear.

## Overcoming Fear

A fearful and nervous dog can be a ticking time bomb. More dogs bite out of fear than viciousness. Fear of strangers, fear of being hurt, or hurt more—fear covers a lot of ground, whether it's a reasonable fear or not. A dog with a nervous temperament will never be a trustworthy dog if you allow his fear to continue to take control. Once your dog is a fear biter, you have already lost control and you need professional, one-on-one help with a dog trainer.

Some dog trainers will refuse to work with a nervous dog and believe that a fearful dog can't be rehabilitated into a stable dog. I somewhat agree. I don't think a fearful dog can ever be completely trusted, but you can turn him into a suitable pet. I'm not saying it's going to be easy, but it is possible with a great degree of dedication and determination on your part.

**TOOLS YOU NEED**

▶ A head halter is a good training tool to keep on your dog when you are trying to break him of thieving. It not only gets his attention fast when you grab it, but the little tether that hangs under his nose is perfect for a fast grab. Because the Gentle Leader is made to allow your dog to pant, yawn, eat, and drink while wearing it, you can leave it on during the course of your day, enabling you to literally catch him in the act much easier.

**TOOLS YOU NEED**

▶ The booklet *Dominance: Fact or Fiction?* by Barry Eaton is a good read for owners of big, dominant dog breeds, like livestock guardians and working breeds. This book offers theories on why dogs try to dominate their humans, practical solutions to common dominance issues, and how to recognize problems in your own dogs before they get out of hand. You can buy this book online at www.dogwise.com.

**Never reward or punish your dog's fear.** Along with coddling your dog and offering comfort, another way of rewarding fear is to simply give in to it. Don't take your dog out with you; don't try to bring her out in public. Most owners hope this is just a stage that their dog will get over, and for some it is as long as the socialization continues at full speed. If you stop taking your dog out in public areas and places that seem to frighten her, you will only make her fear worse.

Likewise, any form of punishment, yelling, or worse, physical corrections will make your dog's fear worse. You are working with a dog that thinks everything is going to hurt her. Don't prove her right.

**Don't take your dog places that cause you anxiety.** For me, that was crowded public places. Once your dog feels your own fear, you've finished him for that particular place until you can conquer your own nervousness. Knowing that you are afraid will only intensify your dog's anxiety.

You can see why fear is such a hard thing to overcome. Any misstep over that invisible line, and you have either confirmed your dog's fear by showing he did have a reason to fear you (punishment) or you have reinforced his fear by agreeing with it (offering comfort or being afraid yourself).

**Give your dog a safety spot.** There should be places in your home that your dog can run to and be absolutely safe. If she has been crate trained, her crate will be one such place, but another might be your bedroom or underneath your desk. Dogs tend to pick their own safe havens outside of your home, and it's usually a familiar place like your vehicle or a spot in the yard.

**Practice desensitization for every step your dog takes.**
It's a very vague command, but it covers everything. You can't simply force your dog into new situations; you have to take it slowly. For every small achievement your dog makes, reward and praise him as much as possible. His whole life will be an exercise in desensitization. Every new thing may throw him back to the beginning.

There will be some times when we just can't take the time to let our fearful dogs get used to the situation, but if we keep those times to emergencies only, our dogs will come back faster and trust us more.

**Never force your dog into a corner.** This is what causes fear biting. Your dog is frightened, and now he can't run away to a safe place. Biting is the only way he can protect himself, and once he does it the first time he'll know it works. And now you'll have a dangerous dog on your hands.

Along with forcing your dog into a tight spot that he can't see a way out of goes leaving him in the care of a person he has never met before or is already afraid of. If you take your time socializing and desensitizing your dog to fearful situations and people, you will come out of it with a loving pet. But go in knowing that he may never be the dog you want him to be and you may never fully trust him with children (children are scary) or be able to leave him behind except with already trusted friends. You will need to look at your dog through open, objective eyes and evaluate him constantly.

## This Dog Has to Go!
It happens, and it doesn't make you a horrible dog owner. Sometimes the dog that was absolutely perfect for the first month has settled into a dog you can't stand. I hate to see it happen, but realistically speaking, it does happen and it's not necessarily your fault

**ASK YOUR GUIDE**

*Why is my dog so fearful?*

▶ This is a really hard question to answer. Some dogs are just very soft or are naturally of a more nervous and cautious temperament, and poor socialization has allowed their nervousness to get out of hand. Others will have been taught to fear through physical or verbal abuse and neglect. Through time and patience, your dog will learn to trust you.

▶ Are you moving? Even if you are moving into an apartment, it doesn't have to mean the end of your dog-owning days. Check out http://about.com/dogs/apartmentdog to help you find a pet-friendly apartment and how to make an apartment livable for your dog. Dogs can adapt to apartment life after living in a house with a yard.

unless you deliberately picked a breed that is way off your lifestyle groove (such as a Maltese when you really should have picked a dog with a more active personality). In truth, it is far better to find your dog another loving home than for him to stay in one where he's hated or neglected.

Sometimes life throws a curve at us as well, and circumstances change. An active individual may suffer an injury and is no longer able to give an active breed the exercise it deserves, or a work situation has changed and you can't spare any time to give your dog anymore and it's not going to change back for a long time. I do want to say, though, that temporary changes like the aforementioned are more common than you think, and your dog will weather them easily enough for a period of time. So please don't make any hasty decisions. Behavior issues can be addressed and corrected as well. If you can't handle the problems yourself, then a dog trainer should be your next step.

Rehoming your dog should be your last resort. This step should only be taken if you have exhausted every available option. If you aren't sure that your situation warrants such a drastic measure, consult a dog trainer or behavioralist for help.

Once you've exhausted all your options and you're left with no choice but to rehome your dog, sit down and write down everything you can think of about your dog. Write about his personality, his looks, temperament, and training. Try to be objective, and be completely honest. Don't gloss over his faults; it will only come back to haunt the dog later. People do adopt dogs with faults. Your deal breaker may not be somebody else's.

**Don't just drop your dog off at a shelter.** Call local shelters to see if they are able to advise you on finding your dog a new home. Most shelters are always full to capacity, so don't count on them taking your dog in. Remember that it's not the shelter's responsibility to find a new home for your dog—it's yours. Be absolutely honest with them and swallow your pride, because they may not be nice about it either. Shelter workers have to deal with a lot of crap from pet owners who should never have been allowed near animals to begin with, and their job is heartbreaking enough before having to deal with creeps.

Here's a very important point that I cannot stress enough: If you surrender your dog to a shelter, understand that he will likely be euthanized. Hundreds of dogs in shelters are euthanized every single day, and only a fraction of adoptable dogs are actually adopted. If the problem is that big, then you may want to consider euthanizing him yourself. That way at least he won't go through the fear and heartache of being caged in a shelter full of other terrified dogs before ending up under the needle anyway.

**Adopting him out yourself may give you more peace of mind in the end.** You'll know for sure that he has found a good home if you are the one to pick it out. Prepare your papers and questions ahead of time, and give yourself plenty of time to take care of these things.

- Ask for an adoption fee. If it's the right home, they will be willing to pay an adoption fee. If you feel they are the right family too, you can choose to waive the fee after a meeting. It's really there to discourage the unsavory types, who just want a cheap dog for any old reason, and impulse adopters.
- Have your dog's file ready for people to look through. If your file doesn't include it already, you should now put in notes on your dog's behavior around children, smaller pets, and other dogs. Include any other pertinent information regarding his personality: Is he a dominant dog or is he the

*If I give my dog away, what should I do with all his stuff?*

▶ When you find your dog a new home, make sure you have all his things handy and ready to go: his food and water bowls, information file, crate, toys, blanket, leash, and collars. Having his familiar items with him will make it much easier for him to settle into a new home. Also make sure you give his new owners any food that you have left over, in fact, it's a good idea to include at least a week's supply or more, and include dog treats, too.

more submissive type? Does he get along with female dogs but not males (or vice versa)? A new home will need to know all of these things.

- Put the word out that you are trying to find your dog a loving home with your friends, your veterinarian's office, and at animal shelters.
- Let any parties that are interested in adopting your dog know that you want to visit their home prior to letting your dog go with them. If your potential adopters refuse to allow you into their home, take that as a warning and scratch them off your list.
- Ask any interested parties to fill out an adoption application. Your application should ask information on their home, lifestyle, family members, and other pets.
- Ask your potential adopters for a veterinarian reference. This will give you a good indication of how responsible the potential home is in general. If their current or former pets (and why are they "former"?) are well taken care of with regular vet checks, then you know they'll take care of your dog too.
- Have any needed veterinary procedures, such as neutering or vaccinations, done prior to letting your dog go to his new home, and make sure any other health problems are addressed. Make sure you send your dog off with a full month (or more) of any medication he is on and a good supply of his usual dog food.

**Breed rescues may be able to help you if your dog is a purebred.** If they can't take your dog in, they may be able to help you find him a home. Sometimes, if they aren't swamped with dogs, they may have a list of interested homes that are looking for a dog like yours. Sometimes they may be able to help you with home and reference checks. If they are able to help you, it would be a good idea to consider making a sizable donation to the rescue after they aid you. It'll help cover their costs and allow them to help other dogs and families like yours.

## Get Linked

*Aggression, dominance, and biting are all big problems that are addressed on my About.com site, as well ways to train your dog out of them.*

**ABOUT THAT ALPHA ROLL**

Once hailed as the premier way to show your dog who's boss, it's time for the Alpha Roll to be rolled into the Closet of Outdated Techniques.
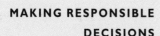 http://about.com/dogs/alpharoll

**MAKING RESPONSIBLE DECISIONS**

Responsible dog ownership is all about making the right decisions, even the really hard ones. Sometimes we have to choose the painful options.
http://about.com/dogs/toughchoices

## Chapter 13

# Traveling with Your Dog

## Travel Necessities

I am not a happy traveler. In fact, I'd rather never leave my home area at all, but there's usually no escaping it and I have to pack up and go somewhere. Luckily, my dogs do like to travel as long they are with me, and as long as I have them, traveling can be made more tolerable for me. And with these travel tips, I always make sure that my dogs are safe, happy, and welcome to travel with me wherever I may go.

**Make sure your dog always has identification.** Imagine what would happen or how you would feel if you were traveling along with your family in a foreign country. You don't speak the language, in fact, you cannot speak at all, but that's okay, your family does. All is fine until you are separated from your family. Now what do you do? Any attempts to communicate may be met by fear or hostility because the local people do not know you. You could be imprisoned if you continue to make overtures, and even if you try

ELSEWHERE ON THE WEB

▶ A really great Web site for planning a vacation with your dogs is www.dogfriendly.com. It has a large, comprehensive list of hotels, resorts, and campgrounds that allow dogs. It doesn't stop at places to sleep though. It also has a directory of major destinations and what pet-friendly shops, dog parks, dining, or other dog-oriented attractions are available at each one.

to avoid people, and without a way to make it known who you are or where you belong, you could never see your home again.

How much better would it be if you carried a neat card with you at all times that states who you are and where you are from? As long as you have that card, you will be fine, even if you become separated from your family. Anybody (or at least a vast majority) could read that card and return you to your family, hopefully no worse for the wear.

This is what a microchip is, and it saves dogs' lives.

As small as a grain of rice, the microchip is injected in the loose skin between your dog's shoulder blades. It carries an identifying number that links it to records of your dog's address and your emergency contact information. Most shelters, veterinarian offices, and rescues are equipped with universal scanners that can read the most common microchips available in the United States and Canada. If your dog is lost and picked up or taken to one of the above, the microchip can be scanned and your contact information retrieved from the chip company.

Collar tags are great for identifying where your dog came from, and from there, whom he belongs to, but only as long as they stay on the dog. Unfortunately, collars can come off, and tags can be pulled off even if the collar stays on a running dog.

Tattoos are rather hit or miss for identifying a dog. Only purebred dogs have their tattoos registered by the national kennel clubs (Canadian Kennel Club and American Kennel Club), and even then only if the dog is registered there to begin with. A few communities have established their own tattoo system, but it will only help if the dog is lost in its local area. You can see why I prefer the microchip over the other options for identification purposes.

**Always carry bags to pick up your dog's piles.**   Even when nobody's watching, always pick up after your dog poops. It prevents the spread of disease and parasites, and it just keeps the world a cleaner, more pleasant-smelling place. Some towns and cities also have penalties, such as fines, for not cleaning up after your dog.

**Water is something your dog will always need.**   An essential for survival, always carry at least one big bottle of water in your vehicle just in case you are out longer than you thought or it gets hotter outside than you anticipated. Rivers and lakes aren't always handy, and drinking out of puddles in towns can be a dangerous prospect when there are usually traces of gasoline, oil, or other toxins in the water.

**Keep a spare leash and collar in your vehicle.**   You never know when they'll come in handy. An extra leash can be used to give your dog a longer range if you need to secure him to something for a while, for tying a splint into place, or really, anything at all.

**A copy of your dog's vet records, particularly proof of a rabies vaccine, is a great thing to carry at all times.**   Keep a copy in your vehicle just in case your dog is accused of biting somebody, and always put the vet-issued rabies tags on your dog's collar. You may also need this proof if you take your dog into certain places, like dog parks, boarding kennels, and daycare facilities.

## Pet-Friendly Places to Stay

You may be surprised to learn that pet-friendly accommodations do exist. It's hard to believe that there are resorts, hotels, motels, hostels, and other places to stay out there that do allow pets—and they aren't as hard to find as you might think.

▶ Personalized dog collars are the perfect thing for traveling. Have your dog's name and phone number embroidered right on a nylon buckle collar as a secondary identification method. At Dog Owners World (www. dogownersworld.com) you can order embroidered collars, in a variety of colors, that have up to twenty-two characters. Tags for Pets.com (www.tagsforpets.com) has steel tags that allow more detailed information, and personalized leashes as well.

A simple phone call will tell you if the hotel you plan to stay at is pet friendly or not. Do not try to sneak your dog into a hotel that doesn't allow pets; try a different hotel instead. Some hotels require damage deposits when you book your room, and it's usually around twenty dollars. They may also want to keep all the allergens in one area, so you may end up having to stay in a "smoking" room. Follow these tips to help pet-friendly hotels stay pet friendly:

- Keep your dog clean. A dirty, scruffy-looking dog just isn't going to be as well received as a clean and well-groomed dog. Your dog's appearance is an advertisement of your dog ownership, and you want it obvious that your dog is well cared for.
- Keep your dog leashed at all times.
- Keep your dog quiet. If your dog is a barker, keep her crated or muzzled at all times. Before you leave, you might want to train her to stop barking on command, as outlined in Chapter 11.
- Never leave your dog in the room alone. If you need to go places that you can't take your dog, like shopping malls, or just want to get out for the day, take your dog to a daytime boarding facility. Some veterinarian hospitals offer afternoon boarding, or you can look for a doggy daycare to drop her off at for the day.
- Have your dog stay on her own things. Avoid the fur carpet that is often left behind on hotel furniture, and keep your dog in his crate or on his own blanket so the chambermaids don't have a huge pile of fur to clean up.
- Always clean up after your dog—even the piles of fur. If they are left behind, use a damp rag and try to clean up as much of it as possible. If your dog has an accident in the room,

clean it up. When you take your dog out to the potty area, make sure you pick up his piles.

**Not all campgrounds are dog friendly.** Due to the past poor behavior of some dog owners, many campgrounds are now going dog free. Don't assume that having your own camper is good enough to get your dog in; call ahead and find out for sure. It would a rotten thing to be turned away at the park entrance.

**Bed and breakfasts and resorts that cater to dog owners are a wonderful thing.** Look for them—they are heaven for dog owners. It's not all about the dog, but the dog is certainly part of the vacation when you find one of these unique places. They aren't cheap though, so watch your budget carefully, and plan in advance what you'll need for the trip.

## Flying

Flying is, without a doubt, the fastest way to get your dog farther. Short distances aren't worth the money or hassle of putting your dog on a plane, but when you are looking at a twelve-hour car trip as opposed to a four-hour flight, you can't beat the plane for getting your dog there quickly and safely. It's true that getting yourself on a plane is a whole lot easier than trying to get your dog on a plane, but if you plan ahead and get these important things done first, your trip should go smoothly.

**Use an airline-certified crate.** There are plastic kennels with air holes, and then there are airline-certified crates. Don't make the mistake of buying the wrong one. Look for crates that have a sticker or stamp on it that states it has been airline approved. Along with airline approval, there are a few other things you should make sure of before you buy one:

**TOOLS YOU NEED**

▶ Outward Hound (http://kyjen.com/pettravelgear/page_06.shtml) has a nifty selection of folding bowls and water carriers for whenever space is limited. Perfect for traveling, you can just fold up the bowl and stick it in your pocket when it's not in use. They come in a range of styles, from the standard travel Port-a-Bowl to Dis-pos-a-Bowl (a single-use container), and even a two-in-one food and water combination.

- **Size:** The crate needs to be big enough for your dog to turn around, stand up, and lay down comfortably. In this case, bigger is better. Airlines may refuse to ship a crate that is too small.
- **Door latch:** Does it close properly and securely? Are the holes small enough to prevent your dog from sticking his nose out?
- **Air circulation:** Does air flow freely through the crate? There should be enough holes around the top and sides that air can move easily in and out of the crate.

**Check for airline embargoes.**   Most airlines have embargoes that restrict pets from flying as cargo if the temperatures at the departure and arrival point exceed a certain degree or during the summer months. There are a few cargo holds that are climate controlled, and airlines are willing to ship pets on those days, but you may notice a big difference in price. If the airline allows some small dogs to travel as carry-on baggage, you can fly year-round.

**Check with the airline about dog restrictions.**   Every airline will have its own rules and regulations that must be met in order to fly your dog with them. Some even have breed restrictions; American Airlines in particular will not allow certain breeds on their flights. Most, if not all, have rules regarding aggression: if the dog shows any signs of aggression during loading, he will not be allowed on the plane.

**Have your dog checked by a vet.**   Before leaving, make sure your dog is healthy and up-to-date on his vaccines. Not all airlines will require a statement of health from your veterinarian, but some will ask to see one and having one will give you some peace of mind knowing he is in good shape.

**Don't overload him or his crate.**   Just give him a familiar blanket to lie on, and no food. Toys may get tossed around and scare him if there is turbulence (mind you, I've never flown in the cargo hold, so I can't say for certain that would happen), and food is just a bad idea. In fact, don't feed your dog before boarding at all. An empty stomach will help prevent your dog from vomiting from stress. Just give him a little bit of water before the flight and a good drink afterwards. Here are a few other things you should do to help keep your dog safe and comfortable on his journey:

**ASK YOUR GUIDE**

*How small does my dog have to be in order to be allowed as carry-on luggage on a plane?*

▶ His whole crate needs to be able to fit underneath the airplane seat, since he can't be stuffed into the overhead compartment. He can't come out of his carrier either, not even for five minutes while on the plane.

- Before you leave, print out an information sheet with your dog's photo, name, age, destination, and contact information. If the unthinkable happens and your dog gets loose from his crate, or if he ends up in a different destination that you do, then people will be able to notify you and send him along to where he is supposed to go.
- Remove your dog's collar and duct tape it in a baggie on to the top of your dog's crate. If it is left on your dog, it may present a strangulation danger if it gets caught on something.
- Do not tranquilize your dog unless your veterinarian has recommended it and given you a tranquilizer.
- Make sure your dog has completely emptied his bladder and bowels before loading him up in the crate. A few small sips of water after he is in the crate will not cause him any grief if he has an empty bladder.
- Try to fly directly to your destination with no stops or layovers in between. If you have to have connecting flights, the airline personnel may allow you to check on your dog

during transfers. Make sure that boarding personnel, flight attendants, and security guards all know that you are traveling with a dog.

**There are specialty services available for flying pets.** Pet travel agents exist to make your dog's journey as smooth as possible if she's flying solo. Pet Air (www.flypets.com) and Puppy Travel (www.puppytravel.com) are two specialty travel agents for pets. If you don't want your dog to fly in the cargo hold, there are other options. There are also now a large number of specialty travel companies that deal only in shipping animals and their people. They aren't cheap, but for your own peace of mind you may find that they are well worth it.

## Long-Distance Driving

For those who prefer driving, a long-distance road trip with a dog (or three) doesn't have to be the nightmare most people think it is. If you are somewhat organized (I'm not) and your dog is used to riding around in your vehicle, a long drive can go just as smoothly as a short jaunt. If your dog isn't used to driving around with you, start a good two or three weeks ahead of time and acclimatize him to it.

There are a few things you'll need to take care of before you leave. Make sure your dog is up-to-date on her vaccines and that she has a complete checkup to ensure her overall health. Check that she has identification that will stay with her at all times (a microchip and collar tags are a good pair to have), and that the information connected to whatever form of ID she uses is current.

Have a checklist handy of things to have in the car so you don't forget anything:

- ○ Full water bottles
- ○ Spare collar and leash

▶ We have a pet barrier in our truck. It's a metal grate that separates the front of the truck from the cargo area in the back. Our particular model is a Barrie-Aire from Kennel-Aire (www.kennel-aire.com). It won't put holes in your upholstery and it doesn't need to be bolted in place. It can also be used in more than one vehicle.

- Copy of your dog's rabies vaccination, receipt for proof of vaccination, or your dog's information file
- First-aid kit (see Chapter 9 for information about creating a first-aid kit)
- Poop bags
- Enough food for the duration of your trip, plus a couple of days worth of extra food in case of emergencies
- Pet hair lint brush to keep your clothes somewhat fur free
- Brush for your dog—dogs will shed a lot of fur from the stress of a trip
- Toys for your dog
- Any medications your dog is currently taking

Make sure your dog has gone to the bathroom before starting a long drive, and don't feed her until you have stopped for the night. Even then, only feed her a small amount to settle her stomach if you still have a lot of driving to do the next day. Dogs get carsick very easily if their stomachs are full, so a small amount each night before bed is best if you have a multiple-day drive. Give her enough to feel comfortable but not as much as a regular meal.

Take her for a run before loading her up in the car so she won't be quite as wound up. Make sure you budget enough time during your drive for stops every four hours to let your dog out of the car to run around a while (on leash) and do whatever she has to do.

When she is in the car, make sure she is secured in one place either with a crate, behind a pet barrier, or seatbelted into position on the backseat of your car. Dogs that are loose not only can cause accidents when they are moving about the car, but your little twenty-pound poodle could turn into a deadly projectile if you are in an accident.

▶ I really like a 3-in-1 dog harness from Hounds Around Town (http://hound saroundtown.com/travel/dog-seatbelt.html). It looks comfortable, comes in a selection of different colors, and the price isn't enough to make your wallet cringe. When your dog is out of the car it becomes a walking harness to stop leash pulling, and it functions as a protective vest for a dog's soft belly during wilderness romps.

Never leave your dog in the car. Not for a few minutes, or an hour, and especially not overnight. Even if you think you'll be out in time to let your dog out before the sun comes up, the car will still heat up. Dogs can die from heatstroke in a short period of time, and even just a few minutes may cause your dog irreparable harm. Plan your trip to accommodate her need to go with you everywhere, or have somebody wait in the car with her so you can leave it running (with the air conditioner on).

## International Travel

International travel is a daunting prospect for pet owners. A lot of countries simply aren't pet friendly, and the effort it takes to get to your destination can seem overwhelming. Traveling or moving overseas is one reason that dogs get dropped off at shelters. Don't take this route. There are ways to bring your pet with you.

One thing you may have heard about is a pet quarantine. Many countries will require pets coming from outside their borders to be quarantined (or detained for inspection) for a certain period of time. Thoroughly investigate any country you are planning to visit. Rabies-free countries, such as Australia and Finland, may have a mandatory quarantine period for any entering pets.

International travel plans involving your pet should not be left until the last minute. In order to cross any border, your dog must have two things:

- A valid rabies vaccine, given no less than thirty days prior to crossing the border, and
- A statement of good overall health from a veterinarian issued no more than ten days prior to crossing.

If you need to leave on short notice and don't have time to get these things taken care of, have a trusted friend send your dog after you.

If you still think taking your dog is an impossible task, don't give him up for good. Leave your dog behind to stay with trusted family members or friends. Long-term boarding may also be an option. And if you are an avid traveler or someone who frequently travels on business and are thinking of getting a dog, think twice. Will it really be fair to a dog to leave him behind for weeks at a time several times a year? Sometimes you just can't have your cake and eat it, too.

## Leaving Your Dog Behind

It's not an easy decision to make, but often we need to go places that our dogs just shouldn't go. It may be because we won't have time to care for them, or because it's not a safe situation for animals, but no matter the reason you will have thought it through carefully.

**Quality in-home pet care costs money.**  I'm not going to say that in every instance you will get what you pay for when it comes to pet sitting since a close friend will watch your dog for little money but give excellent care, but professional services should be worth the price you pay.

Larger professional pet sitters may be bonded and insured, but smaller organizations may not be. You will know at what level you are comfortable with, both security and wallet-wise. Every pet sitter should be able to supply you with three or four references from satisfied customers, and make sure you call them. To find pet sitters in your area, ask your veterinarian or other dog owners.

Professional pet sitters will care for your dog in the comfort of your own home, reducing the amount of stress your dog goes

ELSEWHERE ON THE WEB

▶ The Pet Travel Web site (www.pettravel.com/passportnew.cfm) has a listing of more than 100 different countries and their rules for importing pets. Use this Web site as a starting point for planning your international vacation well in advance. All countries require health certificates and proof of valid rabies vaccinations, but some have quarantines upon entry. Some countries also have countrywide breed bans in effect.

through. This is the best option if you have a dog with special needs that require medication or physical therapy.

You may decide to leave your dog with other family members or friends while you are gone. Don't assume; make sure that whoever you leave your dog with actually likes your dog as much as you think they do. Just because they are family doesn't mean they will take good care of your dog. Your dog should be excited and happy to see them, not nervous and shy.

Always have the pet sitter (whoever it may be) come in a couple of days before you leave and meet your dog first. Have your pet sitter take him out for a walk each day so your dog is used to going in and out of the house with him or her. Show the sitter where you keep the food and treats, and tell your sitter what time your dog usually eats and how much food to give him. Your sitter should also know how often your dog needs to go outside and how many times your dog needs to go for a walk (not just putting your dog out in the yard).

Keep your information file in a handy place so your pet sitter can refer to it whenever she needs to. Give detailed instructions about medications and other needs your dog may have, and have them written down as well as giving oral instruction.

If your dog does not like the pet sitter for any reason, find another one. Dogs have excellent instincts about people, and while it may just be a personality clash, it's not worth it to force your dog in the company of somebody he dislikes. And it's certainly not fair to expect a pet sitter to have to deal with a dog that doesn't want her to be there either.

**Boarding kennels are a good choice for long-term stays.**
All boarding kennels are different, so be sure to check each one over carefully and not just drop your dog off on the way out of

▶ Take your dog's file of information with you when you travel, or leave it with whoever is caring for your dog while you are away. In it should be a record of your dog's vaccinations, any medication he is currently taking, and emergency contact information. Also include a recent photo and notation of any unusual markings or features your dog has in case he goes missing.

town. Ask friends and even other travelers if there is one they recommend in the area. Visit each potential kennel in person before committing your dog to them. Ask questions and use your own observations to determine if it is the right place to bring your dog. Make a note of these things to compare with the other kennels.

- ○ Is each individual dog run clean?
- ○ Are the dog kennels indoors or out?
- ○ Is the kennel area climate controlled?
- ○ Do the dogs get individual playtime, or do you have to pay extra for it (yes, this may happen)?
- ○ Is the kennel area close to the operator's living quarters; close enough to get to in a hurry if there is a problem?
- ○ Do they insist that all dogs are vaccinated prior to boarding and want proof? If they don't, run away.
- ○ Do they allow multiple pets from one home to board together?

It will be up to you to decide which kennel is best for your dog. Just remember that one poor experience can sour your dog on vacations altogether.

The first time you leave your dog in a boarding facility, make sure you leave him with something he is familiar with, like his favorite blanket or a few stuffed toys to snuggle up with. Don't wash them for a few days beforehand so they smell like home and family. Make sure he has his own food and water bowls, as well as enough of his regular food to last the entire time he is at the boarders. As you are dropping him off, don't drag out the good-byes, and don't get emotional. Your dog will feed off of your emotions. If you get stressed out, so will he, and he won't be able to calm down as easily without you there.

You may want to consider having your dog vaccinated for canine bordatella (kennel cough) if he is staying in a boarding kennel. This vaccine should be given at least four weeks prior to boarding your dog in order for it to be effective.

## Moving Your Whole Household

Moving, at the best of times, is a really stressful event, and adding pets that pick up on your every emotion makes it even harder to stay calm. I know that when I am stressed out and edgy the dogs just seem to cling to my legs and follow me everywhere I go. Trying to pack a household up when you trip over a dog every time you turn around is enough to make you scream.

It doesn't have to be such a nightmare though. There are a few things you can do to make the move go smoother, keep your head firmly attached to your neck, and keep your dogs from driving you insane.

**Before you move, ask about animal bylaws and restrictions.** Actually, it's even better if you do this before you even settle on a location to move to. Some locations have established legislation that regulates the types of dogs that are allowed in the city limits. If your dog is one of the breeds or types banned, you may need to make arrangements ahead of time with local authorities in order to move in with your restricted dog. There may be certain rules that you have to follow, like muzzling your dog whenever it is off your property or paying for a special license. If you know these things ahead of time, you can prepare yourself or maybe even opt to move elsewhere.

**It's easier to pack if the dogs are not underfoot.** This is the understatement of the year. If you have teen-aged children, have them take the dogs out for a day at the park, beach, or wherever,

ELSEWHERE ON THE WEB

▶ The American Boarding Kennels Association has a wealth of information on choosing a boarding kennel and other pet-care facilities. If you want to learn more about starting your own boarding kennel or pet-sitting service, www.abka.com has information on getting started, getting licensed, and building a reputation. You can locate a service in your area using their member search feature or order special supplies online.

and make good use of your time while they are gone. Ask a friend if she can take them to her place for the day, or even look into a day or two of doggy daycare. It will be well worth it, just for your peace of mind, knowing that the dogs are looked after and you won't need to worry about them. Not to mention a worn-out dog at the end of the day will be much easier for the worn-out humans to handle.

**Planning ahead will take some of your stress away.** During the packing phase of your move, keep a box of your dog's things clearly labeled by the door. I'm actually using one of the crates for this instead of a box. It's easily identifiable, and I can quickly pick it out of a room stacked ceiling high if I need to. Throw his usual play items in the box along with some of his favorite things, like a bag of chewy treats or one of your (unwashed) sweaters. Keep it open so that on your last day in your old home you can toss in his pillow, blanket, dishes, and whatever toys he still had out to play with. Keep his leash hanging by the door or on top of the box so that you can take it with you on your way out.

On moving day make sure this box (or crate) is packed either in the car with you and the dog or last in the moving van (to be unloaded first). Once you are in the new home, the first things your dog sees will be his familiar and well-loved items.

Don't use up the rest of your dog food thinking that you won't need to pack it and you'll get more when you are there. I can't tell you how many times I have done just that and arrived to find that there's no place to get food at that time of night, my dog's regular brand isn't available, or I just couldn't locate a nearby pet store during the first day.

Even if you're already familiar with the layout of your new town, bring enough dog food for a good week's worth of meals. This way you not only will be prepared for any unexpected problems,

**WHAT'S HOT**

▶ A great way to get your dog out from underfoot while you pack is sending him to a doggy day spa. A trip to the groomer's to be washed, dried, clipped, and pedicured will keep him occupied and you somewhat sane. It will get rid of some his undercoat that is probably shedding like mad from the stress around him. Even better, you'll have plenty of time to get things done if your dog's spa experience lasts a few hours.

but you also won't need to worry about buying more for the first week. You'll be busy enough without adding a hungry dog to your plate. If you find that you need to switch your dog's food due to availability problems, a week's supply of his old food will be enough to wean him onto the new brand.

**Proceed to your new home in an orderly fashion.** Of course, at this stage of the move progress in any fashion is to be applauded. Put the dog in the backyard or his crate until the last vehicle is loaded. Make sure he has gone to the bathroom and had a good run before loading him up, too. Try to convince yourself that this is just another road trip, and try to stay calm. Your dog will pick up on your stress, and it may make him anxious and unsettled.

When you reach your new home, keep your dog crated until you have some of his familiar things unpacked. Do not let him outside unattended. He may try to return to the old home, and he may be frightened by the strange neighborhood, smells, and sounds. It will take him a while to settle in and realize that his family isn't going to leave and that this is the new home.

## Get Linked

*I can't guarantee that your travel with your furry friend will be stress free, but I hope that these articles on my About.com site help bring you closer to that goal.*

**BOARDING YOUR DOG FOR THE FIRST TIME**

A lot of dogs experience anxiety when they are boarded at a kennel, or even any place that's not home, for the first time. Their owners do too, and each feeds off the other's worry. These helpful hints will hopefully make this first time a little less nerve-racking and stressful.

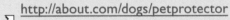
http://about.com/dogs/boarding

**THE PET PROTECTOR SYSTEM**

This is a service for lost or injured pets available in both Canada and the United States. You can read about this service here on my Web site.

http://about.com/dogs/petprotector

# Chapter 14

# Advanced Dog Ownership

## The Multidog Home

Nothing goes better with one dog than another dog. Once your dog reaches a certain age and settles down as a nice, loving pet, it's natural to want another—either another just like him (we have two hands, right?) or one full of puppy exuberance. It'll be just like picking out your first dog all over again only with one little change: You now have a new family member that has to approve of the new dog.

**Puppies are universal.** Every well-socialized dog will tolerate puppies, and some will adore them. But puppies grow up, so it's still important to be careful when selecting a puppy to go along with your older dog. A submissive puppy, one that hangs back when the others rush forward but not one that shies away, is going to be a good match in almost any household. If you want more of a challenge or if your dog is already the submissive type, go for a pup that comes up to you and makes overtures of friendship but isn't dominant enough to shove other puppies out of the way. Mind you, this is no guarantee that your dogs will be best friends when the pup grows up; individual personality will dictate the dogs' future relationship.

When you bring your puppy home, you shouldn't just throw him at your dog and expect them to get along, even though most dogs accept a puppy's presence easily.

Whatever you do, don't make the mistake of thinking two puppies are as easy to raise and train as one. Don't do it! I made this mistake and I'll never do it again. Both puppies bonded with each other, and they took three times as long to train. Puppies that sit and listen patiently while awaiting instruction only exist in fairy tales. Separate training sessions was the only way we could accomplish anything, and it was very time consuming.

**Make sure you have the time to devote to training your new dog.** Even with just one puppy, you still need to have one-on-one training sessions. Arrange for another family member to take your older dog out for a walk or play session—something fun so he isn't just crated while you train the new dog. You'll need several short sessions of about fifteen minutes each with the new dog, and also one or two remedial sessions with your older dog to reinforce what he knows and just to spend time with him so he isn't left out.

Your first dog will correct your puppy when he gets out of hand in your dog's eyes. A bit of snarling, maybe a nip here and there if puppy gets too rough, but there's nothing for you to be alarmed about. These things are necessary for your pup to learn (see Chapter 8 on doggy manners).

It seems only logical that the older dog would be ranked higher in the pack than the new dog. As long as the new dog stays a puppy, this is probably what will happen. It may stay true throughout

▶ A coupler is a device that allows you to walk two dogs on a single leash, as long as the dogs are of a fairly equal height. I must warn you, though, if your dogs are not trained to walk nicely on a leash, it could be a hairy operation. Use a Gentle Leader head halter on both dogs with the coupler attached to the halters of each dog. This will allow them a little more room, and they'll automatically correct themselves when they try to go off in another direction.

the new dog's life if he is of a submissive temperament. If he isn't a submissive dog, though, sooner or later pack order will ripple and shift. This is perfectly natural, and as long as both dogs continue to be ranked far below any humans in the pack it isn't a very big deal.

Fights between your two dogs will probably break out once your new dog reaches maturity or a bit younger, at about eighteen months of age. Most of these fights will be nothing more than jockeying for position in pack order and are not serious: a lot of noise and movement, little actual physical contact. Left alone, the dogs will likely sort this out on their own in a short time.

Make sure that members of your household are aware of the potential for dogfights. Children especially can be terrified by the noise and action, so if you see a scuffle brewing, put the kids in a safe location: in the house if outside, and in their bedrooms if in. It's best that they are out of harm's way, since dogs in the midst of showdown won't look where they are going.

If it looks like a fight is going to happen inside the house, do your best to distract them: loud noises, running the vacuum cleaner in the same room (often giving them a common enemy), or even spray them with water, and shove them out into the yard (fenced yard, that is). And then your best bet is to cover your ears and watch for blood. If a serious fight breaks out, you will need to separate the dogs before they hurt each other. For information on how to do this, see Chapter 8.

Once your dogs have settled into the order they will probably keep, you might notice things that reinforce their positions. The higher-ranking dog probably eats first, goes out the door first, has the comfiest sleeping spot, and gets the majority of the petting. As dog owners it's hard for us to not give both dogs equal treatment, but forcing equality on them will only cause confusion and more fighting. Dogs need to be sorted; it's in their nature. One

**TOOLS YOU NEED**

▶ Managing the multidog home can be really challenging, stressful, and frustrating. Feeling Outnumbered? *How to Manage and Enjoy Your Multi-Dog Household* by Karen London, Ph.D., and Patricia McConnell, Ph.D., is a book written just for the home with more dogs than masters and helps you deal with some of the more common and hair-pulling escapades that dogs can get into when there's more than one. Tackling issues like the contagious emotions, fights, and dominance between household members, this short but practical guide is a must have.

*How can I tell if the*
*fight between my dogs is*
*serious?*

▶ Most fights between dogs
that live together are loud
and boisterous affairs with
little bloodshed. However,
fights can turn ugly, and one
dog may actually be intent on
harming the other. If you see
blood, or if one dog refuses
to let the other go even after
the losing dog has submitted,
then the dogs need to be
separated.

dog will always come out ahead of the other; anything else causes
insecurity.

When you have more than one dog at home, things like parasites and illnesses affect all the dogs in the home. If you notice that
one dog has worms, you still need to treat both dogs, even if the
other dog shows no signs or symptoms.

**Dogs feed off of each other's emotions, and you as an
owner may find this incredibly irritating.** When you are
trying to accomplish something and one dog gets excited, the other
will, too, and before you know it you have to dodge a swarming
sea of bouncing dogs (because two dogs feel like six when they are
excited) and thumping tails, and what you were trying to do gets
forgotten. Unfortunately, it's not just excitement that does that
either. One fearful dog can make the other afraid, too. Or one
brave dog can loan the fearful dog a spine for a time or two. This
really depends on the dogs' relationship with each other.

**Your only hope to control the hive mind in your dogs is
to enforce very strict greeting rules.** By teaching both your
dogs the basic petiquette rules on greeting with decorum, you'll be
able to reward them for sitting nicely and ignore the madness of
overexuberance.

That sounds so nice and simple when I put it like that, doesn't
it? It's a simple concept, but it's almost impossible to enforce when
you have more than one dog that's bouncing circles around your
feet. This would be the number one reason I think that adopting
two puppies at once was sheer madness on my part. You really
can't do this alone. Or should I say, you really can't do this alone
when you have an armload of groceries and an infant in your other
arm with a seven-year-old clinging to your leg. If this is you, crate
your dogs. In fact, even if it's not you, crate your dogs anyway.

Your only means of controlling the excited swarm is to contain it entirely. Let your dogs get as excited as they want in a controlled environment. Start them in the crate. Completely ignore the excited yips, hellos, and bouncing crates, and don't greet them until they calm down. Eventually, and I say eventually because it will happen but it won't happen overnight, they will stop the yips, howls, and bouncing and wait patiently for you to let them out.

It is entirely possible that once they are let out of the crate they will resume the excited swarm, no matter how long it has been. After all, now they finally get to sniff you, touch you, feel your return. At this point, however, you have more control back as you'll have divested yourself of the infant, the groceries, and seven-year-old is no longer clinging, leaving your hands free.

Grab their collars and give a firm "Sit" command. As soon as both butts hit the floor praise them and give the attention they've been waiting for. This is going to be your new routine. Everything that comes before the sit must be ignored—actively ignored, too, not passively ignored. Don't just go about your business. Turn your backs on them as they lobby for your attention, and make a point of walking away as they bound around your feet. Pretend they aren't there as obviously as you possibly can until they stop and sit.

Then give them what they've been craving: your affectionate greeting. As soon as they start to bounce around again, walk away again. They will get the message.

## Breeding and Whelping

Dog breeding is something that most responsible dog owners just don't do. It's a messy, time-consuming, and frightfully expensive undertaking when it's done properly, and it opens you up to a lot of judgmental eyes from the dog community. And people are judgmental in the dog world. Nobody is immune when the welfare of our beloved canines is in question.

**Irresponsible breeding kills dogs.** Millions of dogs are euthanized in shelters across North America every single year. Mixed breeds and purebreds alike land in shelters every day, and most have come from irresponsible breeders, either directly as dumped animals they couldn't sell or indirectly from people who bought from irresponsible breeders.

If you want to breed your dog, then you are going to need a top-quality dog that is worthy of reproducing. Yes, that does sound snobbish, but in dog breeding, only the best should be bred. I firmly believe that it's the only way to work toward eliminating unwanted health issues. If every dog bred was certified with a good or excellent hip rating, canine hip dysplasia would become a rare occurrence rather than the widespread problem it is today. Other diseases are hereditary and can be controlled by selective breeding as well. Glaucoma, diabetes, and thyroid disease are just a few of them.

Temperament can also be controlled by selective breeding. If you breed a dog with a serious aggression problem, that dog's pups may have an aggression problem. And because you bred your aggressive dog, chances are very good that you won't be very careful about where those potentially aggressive pups end up. And if the homes those pups are in aren't responsible either, there could be more puppies later on with aggression issues.

Before you even get started, talk to breeders at dog shows, and let your dog's breeder know that you are thinking of breeding your dog later. Your breeder should be willing to mentor you through the process of determining if your dog is worthy of breeding, showing your dog, and selecting a mate that compliments your dog. If she knows ahead of time, before you even select a puppy, she can help you pick a pup with showing and breeding potential. Understand, though, that even if your pup shows a lot of potential early on in life, he may not live up to it.

**ELSEWHERE ON THE WEB**

▶ Read "Breeders' Ethics: Myth and Legends" at www.ibizan.freeservers.com/ethics.htm. This article tells you what you need to know about breeders' code of ethics, how it's not an ironclad guarantee of quality and what you need to watch out for. It's an eye-opening look at the claims breeders make to sell their dogs, like "free of hereditary defects," and what they really mean.

It may be determined later that he just isn't cut out for shows or sports or that he has developed problems that make him a poor choice for breeding (but an excellent pet). My dog Kari is a beautiful Beauceron, physically sound, and, in appearance only, a perfect specimen. But his temperament is one that I wouldn't want to pass on to future generations (shyness), so I had him neutered at an early age.

**Breedings between healthy, sound dogs produce healthy, sound dogs.**   Physical health is a huge part of breeding dogs. Any dog that is considered worthy of breeding should be in perfect health, with his hips and elbows certified by either OFA or PennHIP. These organizations grade a dog's hips and elbows and determine whether or not he is likely to develop or pass on a propensity for dysplasia. Eyes should be checked and certified by CERF to be free of inherited diseases and defects. Dogs should never be bred before two years of age.

Before your dog is bred, there a number of other health checks that need to be performed. Brucellosis is a serious sexually transmitted disease, and your dog needs to be tested for this disease right before breeding. Your dog's potential mate needs to be tested for all of these issues as well. Both dogs should be fully vaccinated.

**Proper prenatal care for the pregnant bitch will help prevent problems.**   Good food that gives her plenty of energy for developing puppies is essential. She will probably eat almost twice as much, too, so count on your food bill going up quite a bit for the next few months. Don't forget; she'll need those extra calories and nutrients during nursing, too.

Set aside a good chunk of money in case any emergencies come up and your dog needs emergency medical care. In small dogs it's not unusual for the bitch to need a cesarean section to

**TOOLS YOU NEED**

▶ If you find yourself in charge of a pregnant dog and you suspect she may be close to whelping, she's going to need a whelping box. A large crate covered with a blanket will work for small dogs, and a plastic kiddie pool will work for bigger dogs. It should be able to be easily cleaned and disinfected, and it should have enough room for momma dog to stretch out with all the pups and lay down in comfort.

▶ If you truly want to learn more about breeding dogs responsibly, these books will get you off to a good start. Before you even commit to becoming a dog breeder, *The Complete Book of Dog Breeding* by Dan Rice, D.V.M. should be in your hands. It's an excellent overview of the whole breeding process. And once you are ready for the heavier reading, I suggest *Genetics: An Introduction for Dog Breeders* by Jackie Isabell. This is the book for anybody who wants to learn more about how genetics affects a breeding and how to apply basic genetic principles to the act of selecting a mate for a dog.

deliver the pups. It's not even that unusual for bigger dogs to need help delivering puppies.

Your vet and your breeder-mentor are going to be your closest companions once she is pregnant. Your vet can tell you how far along she is, and what, if any, specialized treatment she needs. Your vet may have his own schedule of visits that he wants you to keep. Your mentor will be able to instruct you in what type of whelping box is best for your particular breed of dog and what should go in it.

At eight or nine week's gestation, your dog should be starting labor. If all goes well, she could take several hours to deliver her pups, one by one. There may be intervals as long as ninety minutes between puppies. If she has any complications, it could cost you either a small fortune at the veterinarian's office or your dog and all her puppies. Breeding is a risky business.

I know that I have barely scratched the surface of what's involved in dog breeding. There is so much more to it that there are entire books dedicated just to breeding your dog. I am not a dog breeder and cannot go into the details that you would get from a responsible breeder as a mentor. What little information I have given you will not help you become a dog breeder. I hope, however, that it helps you to not become a dog breeder.

**There's no such thing as an average litter size.**  Your dog can have one or twelve puppies, and every number in between. Born after approximately sixty-days gestation, a puppy's eyes and ears are sealed shut, and his strongest sense is touch. Warmth is essential since he cannot regulate his body temperature and his nervous system hasn't matured yet. All he knows right now is mom.

At about two weeks of age, possibly earlier, his eyes will open, although he still cannot see well and bright light hurts his eyes. Now he'll finally get to see what all the other warm and comforting bodies around him are. At this age, you should start to handle him more, getting him used to a human touch.

Once your puppy starts to become more alert, he'll begin exploring his surroundings more. He's still a weak and round little thing, so much of his wandering is done by rolling and crawling. He'll stumble over his littermates and bump into things.

At three weeks of age he should begin to wean off of his mother and start eating semisolid food. Use a high-quality, dry puppy food (the amount they actually eat will depend on the size of your puppies, but two cups of dry should be plenty), pour it into a flat dish (a cake pan works well), wet it down with a half of a cup of warm water, then let it set for a bit to soften it up before putting it down for the puppies. Never leave young pups unsupervised while feeding, as they can fall in and drown, even in thick dog food sludge.

**Puppies develop quickly and learn a lot from littermates.** The longer a pup stays with the litter, the more education she receives. At around four weeks of age the puppies should be playing and learning what is not acceptable to each other. Momma dog will guide the puppies in their interactions with each other and put a stop to any ill behavior that she is unwilling to tolerate.

This is also the age that human socialization with other people should start. Introduce people, young and old, to your puppies with careful supervision and the puppies will learn to accept handling by different people. Make sure that any visitors wash their hands carefully before handling the puppies and that they haven't come directly from a place with other animals that might possibly be sick (like an animal shelter or veterinarian's office).

At six weeks of age the puppies should receive their first series of vaccinations. See Chapter 3 for more information on what

**ASK YOUR GUIDE**

*How early can I send my pups to their new homes?*

▶ Puppies should not leave the litter until they are at least eight weeks of age. Any younger is against the law in some states. Twelve weeks is the ideal age. Puppies learn an awful lot from their littermates, like bite inhibition and dog manners.

ELSEWHERE ON THE WEB

▶ Dog Owner's Guide
writer, Ozzie Foreman,
writes of the testing his
Newfoundland, Spirit, under-
went for a Water Rescue
title at www.canismajor.
com/dog/watresc.html. He
describes each exercise and
individual test that his dog
had to go through and pass
and what constitutes a failure of each test. It's a great
descriptive page for this particular working dog title.

vaccines are given and when. Now you can start to socialize the puppies with other healthy and vaccinated dogs.

**At eight weeks of age you can start to find them homes.** You want them to go to good, responsible homes, so have a list of questions to ask potential adopters (see Chapter 12 for a list of things to ask), and ask for an adoption fee. Remember that you can choose to waive the fee if you feel like it later. The adoption fee will put off any unscrupulous people and give pause to impulse adopters who may regret their decision later.

## The Public Service Dog

Service dogs come in all shapes and sizes and fulfill a large number of roles, from private service to public servants. Any dog breed can be a service dog as long as he has the right disposition and temperament for it. However, not every owner can be part of a service team. It takes a lot of training for both human and dog to be in some service capacities, and both members of the team need to be in excellent physical health.

Public service dogs serve the community in many capacities. One of the most rewarding things for a dog and owner to do is become a working team in a rescue capacity. Search and rescue encompasses quite a few different areas. Dogs are trained to track people down in all types of geography and ground cover, even in water and under snow.

**Water search dogs locate drowning victims.** They follow the scent of human flesh over the water to its originating location. Water rescue dogs, typically Newfoundlands and Labrador retrievers, collect people out of the water if they are in trouble and tow them to shore.

**Avalanche dogs can locate people trapped under the snow after an avalanche.** They train using the Hide and Seek game, locating their handlers underneath snowdrifts and in crevasses.

**Wilderness search-and-rescue dogs find missing persons who are lost in the bush.** They are able to follow a human scent even amid the distractions of game trails and other humans.

**Urban search dogs play an advanced game of Hide and Seek when they are working.** Every find is a reward, and these dogs work hard to get their rewards by locating missing children, wandering seniors who may have forgotten where they are, and even criminals on the run. Urban search dogs are trained to track people over concrete and through heavily populated areas where the scent of hundreds of other people mingles with the scent of their reward person.

**Disaster dogs are highly trained dogs that are taught to locate victims buried in rubble from collapsed buildings and other disaster areas.** These dogs must be agile to navigate piles of concrete and rock and squeeze through narrow passages. Disaster dogs are trained to work independently of their handlers, going into sites that humans might not be able to navigate.

If you want to learn more about disaster dogs, the kind if work they do and how they are trained to do it, check out www.disaster-dog.org. There is a wealth of information on this Web site including course outlines, veterinary information, news articles, and more.

**Detection dogs are used to detect illegal substances all over the world.** Specially trained dogs are used at border stations to sniff out contraband and even people hidden in vehicles that try to cross the border.

**Cadaver dogs do the job that nobody else wants.**   Trained to detect even the faintest scent of decomposing human flesh, cadaver dogs can locate bodies almost anywhere, even underground.

Hounds are ideally suited to tracking and air scenting, two specialized skills that are high in demand in hunting and law enforcement. Tracking is following the scent of game over land using scent "imprints" on the ground. Most obedience clubs offer courses in tracking if you are wondering if your dog has what it takes.

## The Private Service Dog

Private service dogs serve their individual people rather than humanity as a whole. Trained to handle individualized tasks specific to the person they are servicing, these dogs can make it possible for people with some disabilities to live on their own independently.

**Any dog with the right temperament can become a therapy dog.**   Pet therapy animals and handlers have been welcomed into hospitals and long-term care facilities all across North America for a few years now. Health studies have shown how having a well-loved pet can lower a person's blood pressure and reduce the risk of heart disease. For people who can't have pets, animal-assisted therapy can make a big difference in their lives.

- The soft touch of an animal can bring joy to a person who has lost a beloved pet. People in long-term care facilities have often gone a long time without a gentle touch.

- Animals are nonjudgmental, forgiving of mistakes, and offer unconditional love where a human being may not.
- Animals offer entertainment, a willing ear, and tend to increase social interaction.
- A patient who is in pain or cannot speak will not feel pressured to interact with an animal.
- Animals accept the patient for what he or she is and will not stare or ask awkward questions regarding any disabilities.
- Having an animal present can often focus a patient on itself rather than the patient's current infirmity.
- Pets help people to relax, thus lowering blood pressure.

Animal-assisted therapy is a great way to become more active in your community as well as bring joy to dozens of other people.

**Guide dogs, or eye dogs, assist the blind in day-to-day living.** Guide dogs are raised by volunteer families until the pup is around one year of age. The foster family has the job of socializing the puppy in all types of situations. They will train him to sit quietly and patiently without begging in a restaurant or grocery store, how to walk in a proper heel, how to respond to verbal and nonverbal cues, and bring the dog to obedience classes put on by the guide-dog facility. If you want to be a foster family for guide dog puppies, check with these organizations to find out more about what is involved.

- Eye Dog Foundation for the Blind, Inc. (www.eyedogfoundation.org)
- The Seeing Eye, Inc. (www.seeingeye.org)
- Guide Dogs of America (www.guidedogsofamerica.org)
- Guide Dogs for the Blind (www.guidedogs.com)

**WHAT'S HOT**

▶ Most therapy dogs that are part of a larger organization need to have a Canine Good Citizen (CGC) title. This is a test that requires your dog to be on his best behavior when confronted by and left alone with strangers, among other things. If you want to learn more about titling your dog with a CGC, check out http://about.com/dogs/cgctest. Any dog can be a Canine Good Citizen.

**Hearing dogs alert their people to sounds they cannot hear.** Hearing dogs are usually adopted from shelters and rescues and trained to alert their hard-of-hearing handlers to specific sounds. Not all hearing dogs are formally trained; some are trained by their handlers at home to react to certain sounds in a specific way. For more information on hearing dogs, visit these organizations' Web sites:

- Dogs for the Deaf (www.dogsforthedeaf.org)
- Hearing Ear Dogs of Canada (www.dogguides.com/programs/programs03.htm)
- International Hearing Dog, Inc. (www.ihdi.org)

**Seizure-alert dogs can sense an impending seizure in their owners.** Something in the human body's chemistry changes during the preictal stage of a seizure that dogs can sense. There is a theory that all dogs feel or smell it but only a few will noticeably react to it, just as every dog does not react to a thunderstorm the same way. The dogs that do react in a noticeable manner are able to be trained as seizure-alert dogs. They are taught to nudge or otherwise alert their handler of the impending seizure so that she can find a safe, out-of-the way place where she won't be injured during a seizure. Other conditions that dogs can sense and alert to include asthma and low- or high-blood sugar. You can learn more about medical-alert dogs by visiting these Web sites:

- The Epilepsy Foundation (www.epilepsyfoundation.org/epilepsyusa/aboutseizuredogs.cfm)
- Heaven Scent Paws (www.heavenscentpaws.com)
- Great Plains Assistance Dogs Foundation (www.greatplainsdogs.com)

**Service dogs bring greater independence to many people.** Service dogs can be trained to take over a large number of daily tasks for the handicapped individual. These dogs can do everything from dialing 911 on the telephone to opening doors and pushing elevator buttons. For many disabled people, their service dog is not just their best friend, he is also their hands and feet. Assistance dogs for the physically disabled are trained to retrieve things by name, pick up items that have been dropped, carry items, and even help a person who has fallen get back up again.

## Getting Involved in Dog Welfare

Rescue, rehabilitation, and educational work are emotionally draining jobs. Any time you have to clean up what other people have ruined, you can expect to be frustrated, heartbroken, and angry all at once. Those feelings are magnified when you are dealing with dogs and dog owners who should never have been turned loose in public. Some of these jobs are volunteer positions only so there may be no actual paycheck involved, just the satisfaction of knowing you are doing something that needs to be done.

**Animal control officers usually have to deal with the dog owners directly.** They enforce a town's animal bylaws and confiscate animals that are being abused or used illegally. This is not a pleasant job to have, but it is a much needed one. People dislike you for the work you do, accuse you of hating animals, and sometimes get violent. You'll have to euthanize animals, even healthy ones, and you'll probably be bitten a few times. On the flip side, you get to rescue animals from abusive situations and help prosecute the people who abused them. You may even be authorized to make arrests.

▶ Offering your home up to foster dogs from your local rescue or shelter is one of the biggest commitments and gifts you can give. A foster home is a temporary placement for dogs in a rescue or shelter. The foster home will be responsible for basic housetraining, socialization, health care, and temperament assessment of a placed dog. Foster homes are a much needed resource and always welcome. If you want to help save the lives of dogs, becoming a foster home is just one way to help.

**Being a shelter worker is a heartbreaking occupation.** It takes a heart of gold, and steel, to last in this job and keep your compassion. Shelter workers have to deal with irresponsible owners every day who "just can't keep Bucky" for one reason or another, and rarely are any of the excuses more than just an excuse. Having to euthanize healthy and adoptable animals is the worst aspect of working in a shelter. But you also get to help animals on their way to their new forever homes, by training and evaluating the animals and coaching families in their quest for a pet.

**Rescue coordinator is also a very frustrating job with little thanks.** Like the shelter worker, you'll have to deal with people who just want to dump their dog off and are rarely honest about why. But there are happy parts to this job. You'll be able help send dogs to their new homes and pull them from shelters before their time is up. You will also educate people about the realities of breeding recklessly and how to care and train the dogs they have already.

**Becoming a foster home is one of the most rewarding dog experiences you will have.** Foster homes take in dogs from shelters, evaluate them on whether they are suitable for homes with other dogs, cats, or children, and basically continue to raise the dog until a forever home is found. The foster family takes a dog out of an environment where he is not doing well (the shelter) and gives the dog a chance to shine in a home environment. Foster homes are desperately needed by many rescue organizations and animal shelters.

## Get Linked

*There is a lot more information on showing and working with dogs on my About.com site. Here are three links to get you started.*

**JOBS FOR STUDENTS**

Dog lovers come in all ages, and while attending school there are ways to still be able to work with the animals you love so much. Here are three things you can do to help you get experience working in the dog world.

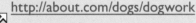 http://about.com/dogs/dogwork

**ANIMAL-ASSISTED THERAPY**

More information on how to get started in animal-assisted therapy and what is required of you and your dog.

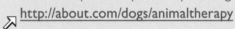 http://about.com/dogs/animaltherapy

**CONFORMATION DOG SHOWS**

Conformation shows are the beauty pageants of the dog world. Dogs are brought in from all corners of the country and judged against their breed standard. The perfect breed representative must match the official breed standard in looks, temperament, and movement.

http://about.com/dogs/conformation

## Chapter 15

# Your Senior Dog

### The Signs of Aging

It will happen to all of us. One day we will turn around and suddenly realize that our black dog has gone gray around his nose, or that he just isn't as quick to rise and run after the kids when they yell for him. I know that it surprised me to hear Kari referred to as a "senior dog." But, at eight years old, he is. According to veterinarians, and his health insurance, he's an old dog! Dogs are officially "seniors" at seven years of age.

Now, dog owners know that the number means nothing. A healthy, active dog will likely still be a healthy and active dog well past the age of seven. In general, small dogs live longer than big dogs, and the larger a dog is the shorter his expected life span. This doesn't mean that you should immediately switch to a senior dog food and break out the pet ramps as soon as your dog turns seven years old. Every dog will start to show his age whenever he starts to feel his age. If your dog is not physically sound to begin with, he'll likely start to slow down at a younger age.

## About.

*What is a dog's average life span?*

▶ Not long enough, unfortunately. The larger the dog, the shorter his life span is going to be. Giant-breed dogs like mastiffs have an average life span of only seven to ten years, but small breeds like Chihuahuas and Shih Tzus can live fifteen years or more if they are healthy and well cared for. Don't let this discourage you though; dogs pack a lot of living into a short life, and even having a dog for only ten years is worth every second of heartache at the end.

**The first and usually the most noticeable sign that your dog is entering his golden years is the gray hairs.** These will start to show up around the fringes of his ears and around his muzzle. Usually he'll look like he's sporting a goatee if he's a dark dog, while light-haired dogs may not have noticeable gray at all. Don't worry—the gray hairs don't bother him.

**His eyes may also take on a milky appearance, but this doesn't mean that your dog is going blind.** It's caused by the lens of the eye hardening and losing some of its flexibility, and it probably won't even be noticed by your dog for a long time yet.

**Like humans, aging dogs need to empty their bladders more often.** When your young dog may have been happy with four trips to the potty area each day, your aging dog may need six or more. This could be problematic for owners who are seniors themselves or who live in a high-rise apartment building. If you are one of those owners who may have difficulty bringing your dog outside every few hours, there are a few things you can do:

- Use an indoor dog litter box. Small dogs can be litter trained (like cats). There are special litter boxes and litter available that are made to absorb the heavier amounts of urine a dog can put out.
- Limit the amount of water he drinks in the evening and avoid the four-in-the-morning potty prance—you know, that dance that your dog does on the bed when he needs to go outside? Or you may have the really mean dog that pulls all the covers off of you and then sticks his cold nose on the bottom of your feet. Giving your dog only a little bit of water after dinnertime may help you avoid those hazards.

- Doggy diapers may be your sleep saver if your dog has less control over his bladder than he used to. Spayed female dogs often experience incontinence after their surgery, and these will help you keep your sanity. Since special dog diapers can be pretty pricey. You may find it more cost efficient to remodel adult human diapers, like Depends, or large toddler diapers to fit your dog.

**As your dog ages, she may decide that it's not worth it to get up from a comfortable spot every time one of the kids runs by.** Especially if she's already been out running around with them earlier. It can be as subtle as that: just not joining in the fun when it presents itself every time. Older dogs don't have the stamina for play like they used to, although most give it their best shot.

**At around seven years of age your dog's bones start to lose density.** This makes it harder for her to heal from fractures. Because she is exercising less, her muscles also lose mass, and the cartilage in her joints wears thin. This is the age where arthritis usually starts to become noticeable.

**Your dog may be irritated a lot easier than he used to be.** Patience tends to wear thin faster in older dogs. He may not tolerate a lot of activity like kids jumping, running, and yelling around him. It's important that he has a quiet spot to retreat to whenever he feels the need, and that your kids know not to bother him when he's in that spot. He may not be so patient when it's time to eat either, wanting his food immediately.

**Older dogs pack on the pounds a little more easily than younger dogs as their metabolism slows down.** For this reason it's important to keep up with your dog's usual exercise

**TOOLS YOU NEED**

▶ *Complete Care for Your Aging Dog*, by Amy D. Shojai, is the bible for elderly dogs. It covers everything about the aging process and goes into detail about the small stuff that affects your dog's day-to-day activities as he ages. From nutritional needs to advanced veterinary care and grief support, this book should be on every dog owner's shelf.

routine. Just watch for signs that he can't take some activities any longer. If he is limping after a three-mile run, switch that to a three-mile walk instead. Or cut a mile off the end and go at a moderate pace. Instead of a half hour of jumping over hurdles, swimming for an hour might be a better choice.

**As he ages, your dog's teeth may start to break down, too.** It may get harder for him to chew regular dry dog food, so you should add warm water to his bowl and let it soften a bit before giving it to him. Have his teeth checked at every veterinarian's appointment for periodontal disease. Plaque and tartar buildup over the years may have taken its toll and your dog may lose some teeth to gum disease. Switching to a canned dog food might be an option you need to look at as well.

**Dogs that have lost their eyesight will learn to get along fine, and so will you.** He will quickly pick up on any verbal cues you give out, such as warnings about obstacles and hazards. If you keep your dog's surroundings the same and don't move the furniture around a lot, he'll be able to get around the house fairly easily.

**Deafness is another age-related hurdle that you and your dog may have to face.** Hand signals and other nonverbal cues will take the place of spoken commands, and your children may have to learn not to sneak up on the dog but stomp their feet as they come up behind him. Most deaf dogs do very well in households.

**As sad as it is to consider, your dog's mind will also show signs of aging.** Cognitive dysfunction is a common occurrence in aging dogs. Your dog may forget where he is at times and fail to

**ELSEWHERE ON THE WEB**

▶ This is a neat idea. This is a Web site designed to help owners of deaf dogs find other deaf dog owners for training help, support, and encouragement. I love this concept! Check it out for yourself at www.deafdogs atlas.com. I found more than a dozen dogs and owners in my area alone. What a terrific tool for the dog community.

recognize people he has known his whole life. His formerly house-trained self may suddenly start having accidents in the house as if he has forgotten all his earlier training.

And he has.

## Keeping Your Older Dog Happy and Healthy

As your dog ages you will notice both physical and behavioral changes in her. An older dog will begin to slow down—you'll notice she keeps a slower pace during walks, isn't as rambunctious when playing with the kids, and isn't as eager to join you for a car ride. These changes are not necessarily things to get depressed about; it's just the way it goes. Your responsibility as your dog's owner is to make sure she is comfortable and all her needs are taken care of.

**Keep your vet in the loop about your dog's advancing age.** Once you start to notice that your dog is showing the signs of aging, you should really have her examined by a veterinarian at least twice a year instead of the once a year exams. Problems can develop quickly in a body that is stressed by age, and catching them early on will help your dog retain quality of life for longer.

Your vet will want urine samples and possibly blood tests for the first visit so that he can determine what "normal" is for your dog. What's normal for one dog may be an extreme measurement in another. At each visit, after he should ask you how your dog behaves, if you notice any changes in personality or behavior, and if you have any concerns about how your dog is eating or acting. Your vet will also examine your dog's internal organs for signs of disease. As your dog ages her organs may start to fail, and if it's caught early enough there may be something that can be done to stop or slow the deterioration.

**Stiffening joints and arthritis are two of the most common conditions associated with your dog's advancing age.** Pain will make it hard for your formerly boisterous dog to hop up and join in a jog, and it may make him reluctant to move at all. Cold and damp weather only make these conditions worse. On those kinds of days, your dog probably doesn't want to move at all.

Old dogs are often arthritic dogs. We can't fix this, but we can help with some kind of pain management. Your vet may prescribe an anti-inflammatory for the really bad days when it's cold and damp outside. To help your dog stay limber, there are several things you can do aside from medication.

Sleeping on hard surfaces can make your dog feel stiff and uncomfortable. Even if he did sleep on the floor from puppyhood, it should come as no surprise if he can no longer tolerate it. A soft bed, but not so soft that he sinks in it like an old sofa cushion, will make a big improvement in the mornings. Moving the bed closer to a heater will also make a big difference. If you don't have a heater handy, a heating pad will do the trick. For the really bad days, ask your veterinarian for an anti-inflammatory.

Ramps will make your dog's life easier. Jumping in and out of vehicles becomes an exercise in pain at some point in your dog's life. Having a ramp or small set of stairs available will help your dog manage these necessary tasks.

Nothing keeps joints limber and a body feeling good better than heat does. Warm blankets, heating pads, and even just placing your dog's bed next to the radiator (but not too close) will make a big difference for him. On cold days, turning the heat up or wrapping up a hot water bottle in a towel and placing it on your dog's sore joints will make him a lot more comfortable while he waits for the pain medication to work. Hot baths will help soothe his sore joints too. Don't make him jump into the bathtub though; lift him in, or have a ramp for him to use.

Acupuncture might also be something to look into. There are no negative side effects, and if it works, it works very well, giving some dogs months of pain-free comfort.

You might notice stairs may start to be a problem as he ages. If you find he's having trouble getting up and down stairs, you may need to re-evaluate your dog's living arrangements. If his bed is upstairs, move it downstairs to a warm location. If a staircase is something that can't be avoided, carry him up or give him a helping hand. Using a towel, wrap it underneath his hips and hold the ends so you have a sling with your dog's back end supported. You can hoist his rear up the stairs behind him, one stair at a time.

It is very important that your older dog still gets the exercise he needs, even if it's three turns around the block at a snail's pace or a slow game of soccer. Dogs need the exercise not just for their body but to keep their mind healthy, too. Play games with your dog still, and make him think. If he starts to feel like he's a useless lump, he'll become depressed and his quality of life will go downhill really fast.

**Adding a new pup to your home may bring back the spark in your old dog.**  Many owners find that once their dog has started to slow down, bringing in a new puppy seems to perk him back up again. There's just something about having another furry playmate that makes old dogs feel younger again.

Of course, this doesn't work with every dog. Some old dogs find themselves irritated and annoyed by puppies. If your dog is one of the irritable ones, make sure he has a safe and quiet place to retreat to that the new puppy isn't allowed to invade. If he's given his time alone, he may be more tolerant of youthful exuberance.

## Age-Related Illnesses

As dogs age their bodies can't fight off illnesses the way they used to. Infections take a bigger toll on their bodies, and age-related

**TOOLS YOU NEED**

▶ Ramps will make any trip in the truck a lot easier on your old dog. In fact, they'll make getting into and up onto things besides trucks a whole lot easier, too. Use a ramp to help your dog into the bathtub, especially if you have an old claw-footed tub like mine, and down the icy stairs in the winter to go outside.

diseases and organ failure may show up. Not all of these conditions automatically spell doom for your dog. Through medication, physiotherapy, and possibly surgery, your dog can actually live through a lot while still retaining quality of life.

**Canine hip dysplasia affects millions of dogs.** A degenerative malformation of the hip joint, in hip dysplasia, the ball of the femoral head and the hip socket do not fit snugly together, causing inflammation, pain, and lameness. If your dog has hip dysplasia, there are a number of treatment options available.

There are two common surgeries available for older dogs. Femoral head excision, or ostectomy, will remove the ball of the femur head, leaving a floating, false joint of connective tissue and ligaments. Most dogs do very well with this surgery, as long as they follow a strict exercise regimen and postoperative physical therapy to keep the joint limber and help build up the tissue between the two bones.

Total hip replacement is the more expensive of the surgical procedures, but it is also the most effective. The entire hip joint is removed and replaced with a prosthetic joint. Your dog will be free of problems from that hip for the rest of her life.

Any size of dog can develop hip dysplasia, but it is more common in large breeds, especially German shepherds and mastiffs.

**Diabetes affects a large percentage of the senior dog population.** Diabetes is usually diagnosed when routine urinalysis and blood glucose testing are done during your dog's regular vet visits. This is why it's important to start going for a routine health exam every six months after your dog starts to show signs of aging. Dachshunds, keeshonds, and schnauzers are a few of the breeds that are more prone to diabetes, so keep an eye out for early signs of trouble, like continued weight loss, excessive urination, drinking

▶ Senior dogs are a wonderful addition to most dog homes. Check out http://about.com/dogs/adoptasenior for a list of reasons why senior dogs make fantastic pets. Remember, senior doesn't have to mean elderly or infirm. Most of the so-called seniors available for adoption still have quite a few years of quality time left. Don't let them be wasted in a shelter cage.

large and unusual amounts of water, and an increased hunger. While it does require a firm commitment from the owner, diabetes can be managed with help from your veterinarian. Dietary changes and medication therapy will make a rapid improvement in your dog's health once he is diagnosed.

**Very common in aging dogs, cancer can be managed for quite a while.**   Tumors can be removed from most locations by conventional or laser surgery, and chemotherapy is an option to consider as well. It can be difficult to weigh the amount of quality time these procedures could add to your dog's life against the cost of the procedures themselves and the followup care that is usually needed. Discuss your options carefully with your veterinarian and take the time to decide which route will best fit you and your dog.

**Something that seems like a regular old-age issue could be something that can be treated and corrected.**   It's easy to write off some things that seem they are just part of the aging process, but you could be doing your dog a disservice by doing so. A trip to your veterinarian could put an end to your dog's reluctance to climb stairs or unwillingness to go for a jog with you. Even incontinence can be managed to some extent with doggy diapers and medication.

Some changes in behavior, especially changes that occur quickly, should be looked at by your vet right away. Despite what I've said about not noticing the passage of time, age doesn't really happen overnight. Your dog won't wake up one day, grouchy and listless after a lifetime of happiness and energetic play. If she does, you need to get her to a vet pronto.

Other signs to watch for in your older dog that might seem like regular aging are confusion, difficulty walking, rapid weight gain,

**ELSEWHERE ON THE WEB**

▶ The Senior Dogs' Project is a wonderful Web site dedicated to the old dogs in our lives. This site offers senior health tips, help for finding your senior dog a new home if you need to, or finding a new senior dog for your home if you have the room and heart. This is one of my favorite Web sites to just read for no reason at all. Pull up a stump and browse for a while at www.srdogs.com.

**ASK YOUR GUIDE**

### What is euthanasia?

▶ Euthanasia translates as "gentle death." Euthanasia is given as a merciful, peaceful rest after you, the responsible human, have decided it is time to let go. It is usually administered by an overdose of barbiturates through an intravenous catheter or by standard injection (like a vaccine), causing the heart to stop. There is no pain. This is the most humane gift you can give your pet when her time has come.

and straining to urinate. These aren't normal problems that come up suddenly; they are signs of bigger trouble that need to be taken care of right away.

Many things can bring on confusion, including poor circulation, lack of oxygen, and sleeping troubles. Confusion might be one of the early signs of cognitive dysfunction, or it could be a symptom of a brain tumor or stroke. Only a vet's visit will be able to rule out any other conditions before labeling it as a sign of age.

If your dog wakes up one day and simply cannot rise, you need to get her to an emergency vet. While it may be something as simple as a pinched nerve, it could also be something serious that could require immediate treatment. Remember that arthritis, while a naturally occurring condition in older dogs, does not happen overnight. Your dog will have shown signs of discomfort long before she reaches the above stage.

## When to Let Go

There comes a point in every dog's life when his owner needs to consider letting him go. Whether it's pain, illness, or age, it will be the hardest decision an owner ever has to make, but it will also be the greatest gift one can give. How do you as a responsible owner know when that time has come?

If you are struggling with these questions now, it is time to take a step back, look at things from a neutral point of view, and ask yourself some very hard questions.

Is he still here because he wants to be here or because you want him to be? If you are the only thing holding your dog to life, you need to let go. At this point in our dog's lives they have given us everything. We shouldn't be asking for more, but rather we should be giving to them. Even if that means giving him eternal rest.

Are extended treatments adding length to his life without adding quality? It makes no sense to add weeks or even months to your dog's life if he won't enjoy them.

Do his good days outnumber his bad ones? This is really the most important question. If he can no longer do the things he enjoyed doing, and all he does is lie in one spot watching the world go by, I would say it's time to re-evaluate your decision to keep him alive.

When you make an appointment to have your pet euthanized, you have the option of just bringing your dog in and leaving him there or you may choose to be present with your dog to the end. Choosing to stay with your dog may significantly raise the cost as an appointment will need to be made and an amount of time will be set aside for you and your dog.

When you arrive at the clinic, the veterinary technician may request to take your dog in without you. Don't panic; he will be returned to you. This part is just to insert the intravenous catheter if they use one, and possibly administer a mild sedative to calm him. You will then be shown to a private room for a short while. Take this time to say your good-byes, snuggle one last time, and prepare yourself.

When you are ready, a veterinarian will enter and inject the euthanasia drug. Your dog's body will relax; you may feel the last bit of air leaving his lungs, and possibly his reflexes will jump one more time. Your dog's eyes will not close.

Remember that this is your gift to him: peaceful and pain-free rest.

## Coping with Your Loss

Feelings of loss and grief are normal, no matter what other people say. You have loved a living, breathing, thinking being, and now that being is gone and he has taken a piece of your heart with him. It is

**TOOLS YOU NEED**

▸ *Jasper's Day* by Marjorie Blain Parker is a sweet book for anyone, not just children. A pet's passing is often a child's first experience with death, and this book will help to explain why we help dogs die when they are old and ill. *For Every Dog an Angel* by Christine Davis is another great book for any family recovering after the loss of a beloved dog.

right to feel pain at this loss. It's also absolutely normal to question yourself: Did you do the right thing? The answer is yes. Your dog is now free from pain and in a happy place. Don't try to ignore your feelings or tell yourself that there is no need to feel this way.

**Give yourself time to grieve.** Take time off work if you feel you need it. If you are the type to grieve in solitude, unplug your phone for a few days, too. If you need to talk to somebody, don't hesitate to call a pet loss help line. The Companion Animal Related Emotions Pet Loss Helpline's (CARE) toll-free number is (877) 394-CARE (2273), and it's just one of many help lines available.

**Kids need help coping, too.** Don't lie to them; they need to know that the dog isn't coming back. If they are young they may need help understanding that their dog has gone to a place with no pain. Try to put it in terms that your child will understand, like "Duke has gone to heaven to play with God." Be prepared to answer a lot of questions about death; it's natural that children want to understand. Don't be alarmed if your child starts to wonder when he will die, or when you will die. Dogs do go to heaven, and if you are a religious family, assure your child that he will see the dog again when it is time for him to go to heaven, too.

Try not to refer to your dog's euthanization as "putting him to sleep." Children can't tell the difference between that version of "sleep" and any other one that may later occur (like surgeries and dental work that require anesthetic). If you feel that you can't answer your child's questions, then have a friend or family member do it for you, but remember that your child is grieving and needs comfort from you too.

**Set up a memorial.** This can be a place in your garden, a tree that you have planted, or even a spot on your bookshelf. It may help

**TOOLS YOU NEED**

▶ Full of compassionate advice from an author who was facing the impending death of his own beloved dog, *Goodbye, Friend: Healing Wisdom for Anyone Who Has Ever Lost a Pet*, by Gary Kowalski, is a wonderful gift for the hurting dog owner. Assuring you that you are normal for grieving, this book will help you deal with the emotions that are left after we bury our best friends.

you and your family to build a scrapbook of photographs and other memorabilia of your dog. It will help you keep his memory alive. I keep my old dog's collar tags in my wallet and carry them with me as a kind of talisman. They bring me comfort in times of stress.

**Avoid stress.**   In every hurting dog owner's life there are those types of people who feel compelled to tell you to get over it because "it's just a dog." I really recommend avoiding these people at all costs. There's no need for you to let them torment you, and they wouldn't understand your reasons, so trying to explain why you are hurting is just an effort in futility.

Everybody handles grief differently, and I can only give you suggestions for when you find it hard to cope. You may find it comforting to walk the path you usually walked with your dog or to just sit and contemplate nature at your dog's favorite swimming hole. I found that sitting by the river where Loki used to play brought me peace when I was hurting.

Don't feel guilty if you find that you can only handle the grief by not handling it. If it helps you to avoid all thoughts of your dog by not visiting the places you used to go with him then that is what you need to do. Don't let somebody else dictate how you should feel or what should make you feel better.

## Beginning Again

Some people feel the need to open their homes to another dog shortly after the loss of their companion. If you decide to do this, it doesn't mean you aren't grieving for your old dog; it just means that you cherish the companionship a dog brings and want to keep that in your life. I know that I have never been able to go for very long without two dogs in my life. I crave the chaos and company that dogs bring, and I know that I will seek out another when Kari leaves my side.

ELSEWHERE ON THE WEB

▶ Pet Loss Grief Support (www.petloss.com) is a Web site for grieving families. Write your dog a tribute to his memory and read other people's tributes to their pets. The Rainbow Bridge poem brings comfort to a lot of people who have lost pets. There are a lot of suggestions to help you with your grief on this Web site.

It's important that you understand that you cannot find a dog that will replace your old dog. Many people make the mistake of searching out a dog that is similar in appearance to the dog they just lost. Once the new dog's personality comes through, they often find it is not the same as their old dog's and resent the new dog, or they continue to compare the two, usually with the new dog coming up short.

If you decide to open your heart and home again, just remember that this is a different dog and will be a different companion to you, and you will love him—just in a different way.

**ELSEWHERE ON THE WEB**

▶ The Rainbow Bridge poem has brought thousands of dog owners comfort when their beloved dogs have passed on. You can read the poem at http://rainbowsbridge.com/poem.htm, on Rainbow's Bridge, a pet-loss support Web site. I hope it brings you a measure of peace as well. You can submit your dog's memorial for publication as a "Rainbow Resident" on this site, and they have a one-on-one grief counseling service as well as support forums.

*Watching your dog age—and eventually coping with the loss of your dog—is the worst experience that a dog owner has to face. I hope my About.com site can help you deal with the aftermath of your dog's death so that you have time to grieve and eventually move on.*

**COPING WITH CANINE HIP DYSPLASIA**

This three-page set of articles discusses the various options available for CHD: medication, surgery, and equipment to help your dog get around.
http://about.com/dogs/hipdysplasia

**DEALING WITH SUDDEN DEATH**

Not every dog dies at the vet's office. When a dog dies at home, often the owner doesn't know what to do or how to deal with his dog's body. These are the answers you need if you are struggling to deal with this.
http://about.com/dogs/suddendeath

**AFTERCARE OPTIONS**

What you can do to help preserve your dog's memory after his death.
http://about.com/dogs/aftercare

# Appendix A

# Glossary

**AAFCO**
Association of American Feed Control Officials, the governing body of the pet food industry.

**aggression**
Seemingly unwarranted hostility toward people, other dogs, or even inanimate objects.

**CERF**
The Canine Eye Registration Foundation; eyes that have been certified by CERF are free of heritable eye diseases.

**chronic**
A recurring condition that lasts over a long period of time.

**conformation**
Adherence to the breed standard in looks, temperament, gait, and bearing.

**coprophagia**
The act of eating feces, either your dog's own or another animal's.

**dander**
What we are allergic to; the microscopic sheddings from a dog's coat and skin.

**desensitize**
This is the act of exposing your dog to something he fears a little bit at a time until he gradually becomes used to it.

**dominance**
The desire a dog has to put himself above others in the pack order.

**euthanasia**
The act or practice of ending the life of a domestic animal in a painless and merciful manner. This is usually done through intravenous injection.

**hip dysplasia**
A disease where the hip joint is malformed, causing pain.

**hot spot**
A section of irritated skin inflamed by constant licking or rubbing.

**hybrid vigor**
The idea that mixed-breed dogs are naturally healthier than purebreds.

**hypoallergenic**
Hypoallergenic doesn't mean nonallergic, but rather that it produces less of an allergic reaction in some individuals.

**incontinence**
The inability of a dog to hold its urine or control its bladder.

**inherited**
Passed down through the parents.

**inoculation**

Preventing certain diseases by way of injecting minute amounts of that disease either in live or killed form to boost the immune system.

**neuter**

To remove a male dog's reproductive organs.

**OFA**

Orthopedic Foundation for Animals; provides dog (and cat) orthopedic and genetic disease information, and maintains genetic database and reports on individual breeds.

**pedigree**

A list of your dog's ancestors, usually three or four generations back.

**posturing**

Posing and trying to make it seem as though he is a bigger dog who could handle the other.

**prey drive**

All dogs have some sort of prey drive; it's the desire to catch (and eat) what is running away from them.

**separation anxiety**

An anxiety and fear that some dogs feel when they are left alone.

**spay**

To remove the uterus and ovaries from a female dog.

**socialize**

This is the lifelong process of exposing your dog to new sights, smells, sounds, and people.

**temperament**

Your dog's personality base. Temperament determines most of how he will react to certain situations.

**vaccinate**

Pretreating your dog with a serum designed to prevent certain diseases.

**viral**

An illness caused by a virus.

**von Willebrand's disease**

This is the most common inherited bleeding disorder in dogs.

**whelp**

To give birth to a litter of puppies.

# Appendix B

# Other Sites

### About.com's Veterinary Medicine Site

Written by a veterinarian, the Vet Medicine site on About.com covers everything health related for dogs and other pets as well.

http://vetmedicine.about.com

### The American Kennel Club

The registry for purebred dogs in the United States. The AKC is the largest sponsor of dog shows and sporting events.

www.akc.org

### Canine Epilepsy Resource Center

The Canine Epilepsy Resource Center is the first place every owner of an epileptic dog should go. Featuring up-to-date medical information and holistic medicine, and support groups, it's the best place to meet others going through the same ordeal.

www.canine-epilepsy.com

### Dogs in Canada

The magazine for dog fanciers in Canada, *Dogs in Canada* has a plethora of dog information.

www.dogsincanada.com

### The Dog Owner's Guide Online

A complete dog resource at your fingertips, this site has everything from selecting a dog to breeding and whelping.

www.canismajor.com

### The Dog Show Game

It's not real, but it's a fun, virtual experience for those who want to get a taste of the dog show experience. Buy a show prospect puppy, show him to his championship, and breed him for more champions. For those of us who will get to do the real thing, this is a fun, new twist on virtual dog owning.

www.showdog.com

### Dogster

This is just a feel-good Web site. Go and look at the adorable doggy faces and upload your own, dog that is, not your own face. It has a large photo gallery to browse through and stories to read, as well as training articles and news feeds.

http://dogster.com

### Petfinder

It's the premiere place to go when you want to adopt a dog. Petfinder has almost all the shelters and rescues in its database with all of their adoptable dogs. Searchable by region, zip code, breed, age, and color, you'll find your new friend in no time.

www.petfinder.org

### Pet Friendly

Pet Friendly is a really great Web site for planning a vacation with your dogs. It has a large, comprehensive list of hotels, resorts, and campgrounds that allow dogs. It doesn't stop at places to sleep, though. It also has a directory of major destinations and what pet-friendly shops, dog parks, dining, or other dog-oriented attractions are available at each one.

www.dogfriendly.com

### Pet Education

Written by Drs. Foster and Smith, this Web site is a complete pet resource for everything you need, including dog supplies.

www.peteducation.com

### The Senior Dog Project

This site is dedicated to educating people about senior dogs and helping place rescue dogs that are in their golden years. This site has information about specialized nutrition and the aging process.

www.srdogs.com

### Working Dogs

For working-breed enthusiasts, the Working Dog Web is the place to go for nutrition information, rescue, a breeder's directory, sports information, and anything else you want to know.

www.workingdogweb.com

### Dog Play

Dog Play.com is a large Web site dedicated to the care and safe recreational activities for dogs. They have information on finding parks in your area, recognizing aggression problems in the people around you, how to start a dog park in your community, and other types of off-leash play.

http://dog-play.com

# Appendix C

# Further Reading

*Bones Would Rain from the Sky* by Suzanne Clothier

This is a wonderful look at the world of dogs that examines our relationship with our dogs and focuses on making that bond stronger.

*Culture Clash* by Jean Donaldson

This is a unique book that hasn't been duplicated yet. She gets right down to the nitty-gritty of the dog's personality. A lot of people are put off by her writing style, but while I find it blunt and to-the-point, I can't deny that she knows what she's writing about.

*The Dog Bible* edited by Kristin Mehus-Roe

This is the big book of dog information that should be on everybody's shelves.

*Don't Shoot the Dog! The New Art of Teaching and Training* by Karen Pryor

It is all about ending bad behavior, using behavior modification, and clicker training. Karen Pryor teaches us how to use the clicker and positive reinforcement to get the results we want.

*The Dog's Mind: Understanding Your Dog's Behavior* by Bruce Fogle

This book has great insight to your dog's thought process. Bruce Fogle is a favorite of mine. I have five of his books and plan to buy more. He has a nice, easy-to-understand style of writing.

*How to Speak Dog: Mastering the Art of Dog-Human Communication* by Stanley Coren

This book is exactly what it sounds like. The book deciphers dog language, from body language to vocalizations.

*Mine!* By Jean Donaldson

Another great book by Jean Donaldson, *Mine!* is a book all about one of the biggest reasons dogs bite: resource guarding.

*Dr. Pitcairn's Complete Guide to Natural Health for Dogs and Cats*, by Richard H. Pitcairn, D.V.M., Ph.D., and Susan Hubble Pitcairn

I recommend this for anybody considering a raw diet for their dog and thinking of making it themselves. It goes into great detail about the benefits of feeding a natural diet and has recipes that are properly balanced and meet your dog's nutritional requirements.

### Little Dogs: Training Your Pint-Sized Companion by Deborah Wood

Deborah Wood goes into how training the small dog is different from training big dogs. I agree and I'm really happy to see a book address these issues.

### The Other End of the Leash by Patricia McConnell

This is a great book that dives into how we communicate with dogs using our body language. Dogs pick up nonverbal cues far more than we humans do.

### The Dogs Who Found Me: What I've Learned from Pets Who Were Left Behind by Ken Foster

Ken Foster tells the stories of his dogs, strays, and shelter rescues, about how they saved his life and made it worthwhile. It's a good read, but it doesn't hold back from the unreal amount of stray dogs and their plight.

### When Only the Love Remains: The Pain of Pet Loss by Emily Margaret Stuparyk

This is a book of poems that are written while the author grieves the loss of her pet. You may find that it comforts you in your time of sorrow.

# Index

Experience, 2–3
Eye discharge, 161–62
Eyes, 49

## F

Family needs, 7–8
Fats, 58–59
Fearful dogs, 116–17, 118, 203–205
Fears, 131–36
Feces eating, 152, 153
Feeding schedules, 69–72
Fiber, 59
First aid, 154–56
Fleas, 42, 162–63
Flyball, 87
Flying, 215–18
Food guarding, 184–86
Food snatching, 202–203
Foster programs, 2, 244
Freestyle, 88

## G

Games, 83–86
Garbage raiding, 202
Gas, 167–68
Grass, 151–52
Grieving, 257–59
Grooming needs, 8–9, 41
Growling, 119, 126

Guarding behavior, 184–87
Guide dogs, 241

## H

Hand signals, 96
Health, and diet, 62–63
Health problems
    emergency signs, 147–51
    ingestion of poisons, 144–47
    signs of, 139–43
Hearing dogs, 242
Hearts, 50
Heartworm, 42–44, 49
Herding breeds, 5, 7
Hiking, 80–82
Hip dysplasia, 10, 254
Holistic medicine, 48
Home behavior, 123–24
Hound group, 6
House, puppyproofing, 26
Housetraining, 109–15
Hygiene, 39–42
Hypoallergenic dogs, 8

## I

Identification, 211–12
Illnesses, age-related, 253–56
Indefinite Listing Privilege (ILP), 89–90
In-home pet care, 221–22

# ▶ IT'S **About.** *INFORMATION DELIVERED IN A REVOLUTIONARY NEW WAY.*